One Thousand Names of Soma

Elements of Religious and Divine Ecstasy

The Secret History of the Vedas, Volume II

James Kalomiris

BALBOA.PRESS

A DIVISION OF HAY HOUSE

Balboa Press books may be ordered through booksellers or by contacting:

Balboa Press
A Division of Hay House
1663 Liberty Drive
Bloomington, IN 47403
www.balboapress.com
844-682-1282

Print information available on the last page.

ISBN: 978-1-9822-2639-8 (sc)
ISBN: 978-1-9822-2640-4 (e)

Balboa Press rev. date: 10/22/2020

DEDICATION

To all those who provided their love and support over the years, but especially to my children, Kelley and Alex, and to Niki, my Bright, Shining Star"

CONTENTS

INTRODUCTION

Epithet: "a characterizing word or phrase accompanying or
occurring in place of the name of a person or thing"

Merriam-Webster Dictionary

This is a book about Soma. It is about Soma's place in the Vedic dharma. This is a book about and Soma's place in the life of the worshiper. It is about the constituent parts that make up Soma. If Soma were a Lego model, this book describes the different pieces which result in the finished product. In the process, this book describes how religious and spiritual ecstasy is viewed by the Vedas. That religious and spiritual ecstasy are described in the best manner imaginable --- through the samans (mantras) in the Ninth Mandala of the Rg Veda.

Soma is many things. It is a deity; it is a divine force; it is a religious ceremony; it is an astronomical body; it is a plant; it is a mental state; it is an experience of religious being; it is a substance obtained, brewed, and consumed like beer. It is indeed all these. Or, Soma may be nothing at all. It may simply be a mental construct, an edifice imagined by the Rishiis and later by worshipers, erected for the purpose of directing their visions and prayers. It may be a presence as ephemeral as the Holy Spirit in Christianity, elusive yet all-pervasive. It is most likely all these things. Its very pervasiveness presupposes an actual substance called "Soma" known to people and worshipers. ... Or, it may have been a contemporary fiction, forever talked about but in reality not existing, an archetype or boogieman or specter, similar to, for example, ... "Voter Fraud."

What is certain, however, is that apparently there existed a cult around the presentation, preparation, distillation, and consumption of a plant called "Soma." By all accounts the distilled liquid had psychoactive, euphoric, entheogenic powers, producing feelings of intense spirituality and religiosity. The nearest modern correlate is peyote used among indigenous peoples in the American Southwest. An entire mythology, philosophy, and spiritual practice of religious piety was posited around this plant.

The plasticity and ubiquity of Soma is reflected in how it is used modernly. Its very name is invoked in modern times to reflect the names of consumer items consistent with the understanding the modern world attributes to Soma.

- Of course, first of all, Soma is the name of the mind-altering drug in Aldous Huxley's dystopia, Brave New World.
- It is the name of a message institute in Chicago, Illinois.
- This meaning was carried over for the generic name for Carisoprodol, an opioid pain and muscle relaxer.
- As with the Soma we will examine in this book, Food is a major category. Thus, modernly, Soma is the name of a restaurant chain in San Francisco, California; a Sushi restaurant in Houston, Texas; and an expresso bar in Queensland, Australia
- The principal quality of Soma is its divinity. Therefore, Soma is a self-described "family of churches."
- The modern derivations of Soma are used to convey exhilaration, pleasure. Therefore, Soma is the name of a well-known line of women's lingerie and clothing.
- In the other edge of the spectrum, Soma is a concert venue for punk and hardcore music in San Diego, California. Soma is the name of a luxury apartment complex in San Francisco, California.
- The essence of Soma is reduced to a liquid form, to be ingested at the Soma Sacrifice. This meaning is applied modernly to a company specializing in water products, bottled water, and glassware and other containers to carry water.
- Soma is the name of a video game.

- Soma is the name of a mushroom-based anti-booster, immune booster.
- In keeping with its Vedic character, Soma is the name of a yoga studio in Connecticut. Soma is also the name of a character in Anime.
- Interestingly, "soma" (σωμα) is the Ancient and Modern Greek word for "Body."

If there is a common denominator to all these consumer products and services, it is that Soma is associated with altered states of mental consciousness, excellence, religious zealotry, enjoyment, bliss, and ecstasy. We know for a fact that at one time in history there existed a plant which was used in sacrificial rituals. There are, of course, ubiquitous references of Soma in the Vedas, but also in other Vedic scriptures, such as the Brahmanas; Srauta Sutras, manuals for conducting sacrificial rituals; Aranyakas; and other Samhitas. By the time of the Upanishads, however, mention of Soma seems to have drop off precipitously. Indeed, the historical record indicates that at one point the Soma plant simply disappeared. Whether through over-use, environmental catastrophe, or another historically unknown reason, we know that at some point in history the plant from which the Soma elixir was produced became extinct and simply vanished. To this day, we cannot identify the plant the Ninth Mandala so eloquently and passionately lauds, and all we can do today is simply guess as to which plant was held in such esteem.

Soma is the dynamic Vedic force of religious ecstasy. We should be clear exactly what is meant by "religious ecstasy." The nearest modern equivalent to religious ecstasy obtained from the Soma experience is what goes on in Evangelistic religious churches. At such gatherings, the congregates flail their arms, shout, screech, run along the aisles, speak in tongues, and gesticulate as the Holy Spirit enters their bodies and captures their souls. In extreme cases, worshipers infused with the Holy Spirit speak in tongues and charm dangerous, poisonous snakes, all signifying that when possessed of the Spirit the physical laws of earth are defied or surpassed. Religious ecstasy in the Vedic dharma is a much more low-keyed, if not equally potent, affair. Religious ecstasy in the Vedic dharma is a direct line of communication to the divine. It is accomplished through the consumption of Soma. Just as in Hatha Yoga, where the purpose of the postures, poses, and mudras are to allow the kundalini to travel upwards through the susumna to the uppermost chakra to deliver a direct line to the divine, consumption of the Soma juice produces the religious euphoria and ecstacy to deliver the worshiper to the divine. Just as Holy Roller worshipers demonstrate independence from the laws of time and space by tempting the snake which could attack at any time, the accomplished yogi will break free, if not infrequently, from these same laws by attaining such extraordinary powers --- the siddhis --- which include weightlessness, travel between past, present and future, and others. Religious ecstasy is experienced with a detachment worthy of a Vedic, accomplished, yogi, but the experience of that ecstasy is no less genuine. The categories discussed in this book analyze the Element, the elements, of that ecstasy.

An entire Mandala of the Rg Veda, the Ninth Mandala, is devoted entirely to Soma and the Soma Sacrifice. The Ninth Mandala provides the raw material of what we know about the spiritual aspect of Soma. It is by no means the only recourse for Soma. Whatever or whoever it was, the mention of Soma is found in every type of Vedic scripture. It is spoken in the Vedas, and it is found in the Upanishads, the Brahmanas, the Aranyakas.

Soma's ubiquity confirms its importance to the message of the Vedas. Unlike in our present age, the Kali Yuga, where the main concern is materialism and consumption, the earliest ages wherein the Vedas were promulgated were concerned with discovering the inner workings of the dynamic cosmic order which pervades and runs this material world and how to live in harmony with that order. This concern was the preoccupation of the early philosophers and seers. These thinkers included the Rishiis who revealed the Vedas. The main concern of the Rg Veda is this dynamic cosmic order, which the Rishis revealed to be *Rta*, the Vedic dharma. The common thread of the Vedic dharma is the primordial essence or fundamental nature in the universe. The worshiper's mission is to live in accordance with that primordial essence, to be inspired and informed by that essence, thereby molding and providing accordingly the patterns to the worshiper's life. The Vedic dharma, *Rta*, is a vast concept. The vastness of this doctrine, if it could be limited to one deity in the Vedas, is personified by Soma, the heart and soul of the Vedas.

Soma's home is the entire Ninth Mandala of the Rg Veda. The Ninth Mandala is an important learning resource for the wisdom concerning Soma. The only presiding deity in the Ninth Mandala is Soma or Soma Pavamana, and contains pithy, concise statements about Soma. The Ninth Mandala is a gift of the Vedic Rishiis, and it is a veritable textbook about Soma, its properties, its characteristics, and its nature. This is the beauty of the Ninth Mandala. I culled rcs from other Mandalas in the Rg Veda. The Ninth Mandala has much to say about Soma and Soma Pavamana, but also much to say about their participation in the Vedic dharma, its main elements and how it originated. These "elements" are sometimes called "building blocks, and Soma's participation in building the Vedic dharma is vast and comprehensive."

A little something about what this book is about. This book is foremost about Soma, the Vedic force, the religious experience. Soma is a pervasive entity in the Vedic universe. This book is also about a ubiquitous concept, *Rta*, which is mentioned throughout the entire Rg Veda and other Vedas. *Rta*, the natural order, is the operative concept which operates the entire universe, the Vedic dharma.

The number one thousand was not picked out of the air. In the Vedic world there is a special significance to the number one thousand. Other Vedic and Hindu scripture speak of the "One Thousand Names of Vishnu," and so on. So, it is for Soma. Soma, in a purified form, is Pavamana. Pavamana purifies the worshiper in "one thousand streams." (T.B. 1.4.8.15.) It is only fitting that there be one thousand epithets to Soma.

These epithets accomplish three different functions. One, it provides the best way in understanding Soma. There is no better way to discover and understand Soma, so varied and diverse is its nature. This is demonstrated most clearly in the following epithet of Soma, "Vanaspati," "Lord of the plants." Kashyap notes that "vana" means both "plant" and "delight." He notes that "vana" connotes "delight" in the Upanishads. The double meaning is an appropriate use of wordplay which is so often found in the Veda. This epithet emphasizes how Soma is spoken of a deity and of the plant from which the juice is extracted.

Two, it also provides a good example of the meaning of Vedic divinity. The divine differs from the "religious." One can be religious simply by going to church every Sunday, meeting the weekly obligations, following whatever penance is obligated, and for the remainder of the week doing whatever suits a person's fancy regardless of the consequences. To be in touch with the divine is something else. Being touched with the divine is a feeling, and if that feeling is genuine, a very deep feeling. This is the function of Soma. The worshiper sought direct access to the divine through consumption of the Soma juice prepared at the Soma Sacrifice. If the samans (mantras) in the Ninth Mandala are to be believed, Soma served the same purpose that more modernly appeared with consumption of Peyote and Ayahuasca in Native Shamanistic rituals. This is where comes in the one portion of the subtitle, "Elements of Religious and Divine Ecstasy." Soma is academically classified as an "Entheogen," (*https://www.zamnesia.com/blog-soma-the-ancient-entheogen-n1178.*), a substance which induces a god-like trance. This aspect of Soma is covered in the Ninth Mandala, and details concerning the Soma Sacrifice are spelled out in the Brahmanas. The Soma Sacrifice deserves a separate treatment in its own book. God willing, that book will follow. This present book will provide a broad overview of Soma in all its aspects.

Three, the epithets of Soma provide the Elements for the spiritual aspect of the Natural Order. Anyone who has read the Ninth Mandala of the Rg Veda will notice, almost immediately, that the samans (mantras) appear to repeat certain phrases, use the same words, employ the same imagery, throughout the Mandala. Are the Rishiis simply being poetic, using an artistic device, or are they providing the constituent parts of the Natural Order, *Rta*, or at least one aspect of *Rta*? Given the antiquity of the Vedas and the purposes for which its secrets were revealed, it is much likely the latter alternative. The different categories which follow thus describe the Elements for *Rta*.

These epithets have not picked arbitrarily. The samans (mantras) in this work have been chosen to show and dig deeper to reveal the hidden meaning of Soma. The discussion of Soma is made with eye to describe and explain the Vedic dharma, that great, vast network we call the Universe and "*Rta*," the subtle basis for the Natural Order of the universe. To better illustrate Soma's role in the Natural Order, some of the basics should be explained.

The Natural Order

You will see three recurring, inter-linking, terms in this book. They are "natural order," or derivations therefrom, the word used many, many times in the Veda to signify the natural order, *Rta*, and the Vedic dharma. These words refer to concepts, all of which are in essence the functional equivalent to the Vedic dharma. "Dharma" is, of course, the series of moral and ethical laws regulating the daily life of the worshiper. The word itself, "dharma," however, is infrequently found in the Rg Veda. In its place, the Rg Veda spoke of *Rta*, the dynamic cosmic natural order. References to *Rta* in the Vedas are legion. *Rta*, or derivatives of *Rta*, occur well over two hundred times in the Veda. Dharma also has a wider meaning. These concepts influence the objects present in the Vedic dharma. In the Vedas, dharma is the totality of the natural order (VS, 1.1.1), tangible and intangible. In other words, it is everything, both great and small. Those objects include the Sun, Moon and the Stars; the three existential levels of Earth, Mid-World, and Heaven. It includes the material world, we all live in. All those objects we see, feel, touch, and smell. It ranges from the outermost edges of the cosmos, to the most minutest sub-atomic particle. It is not only the material world, but it includes the subtle, intangible world which serves as its foundation. It is, quite simply, Everything. Not only everything, but the theory of everything.

In the Vedic Dharma the anchor of the natural order is *Rta* itself as reflected in the Vedic deities, themselves the dynamic forces of that natural order which are incorporated into the lives of worshipers. The aim is that we all learn from the dharma (*Rta*). It was assumed that the human population is not only composed of the same ingredients of the universe but is also ruled by the same universal principles. The purpose of individuals and not simply the worshiper is to discover the relation of the cosmos to the natural order of things (*Rta*) and relate that natural order to the material world and to the people who inhabit it who incorporate those precepts into their lives. This quest is essentially the purpose of the worshiper's spiritual journey. Dharma is that enlightenment and understanding obtained from the natural order (*Rta*). (VS, 1.1.2.)

The Natural Order is a concept which seemingly has no place in this confusing, contradictory, rough and tumble material world. But even in this turbulent world in which we live, amazingly, there is a fundamental order underpinning the chaos. In ages past, the focus was not to accept the surface image of what we call the "real world," but to delve beyond the imagery and discover the true reality beneath. The goal was to understand the underlying basis beneath the surface noise and live in accordance thereto. The clock was not taken at face value but an understanding of the mechanism running the clock was sought. This underlying, fundamental basis of the material world goes by different names in this and the other books in this series. Generally, it is known as the Vedic dharma. Specifically, it is known as a word-concept which is repeated hundreds of times in the Rg Veda --- *Rta*.

It comes as no surprise that this foregoing language seems strange to a modern reader. The modern attitude is to simply live with the chaos. The reliance however to the Post-Enlightenment reason is eroding. Yet, the contemporary ethnos does not well tolerate abstractions.

Rta, the Natural Order, however, is an abstraction, perhaps the most abstract of all abstractions. This abstraction becomes more concrete, more manifested, in different levels. The first step in concreteness is found in the Vedic Field. The Vedic Field was not unknown to the Vedic ancients. Krishna later spoke of the Field in Book XIII of the Bhagavad Gita. There, the field was taken to be prakriti, the subtle basis of physical matter. The Vedic Field is one step beyond the subtle beginnings of creation itself.

A full discussion of the Natural Order would require several volumes. This book attempts to provide a remedy in focusing on one Vedic force, Soma. Soma has a unique participation in that order in that it touches many issues in that order. There are basic concepts pertaining specifically to the Natural Order, *Rta*. Soma provides the Elements to this Natural Order. The Rishiis sought to isolate the natural order to its most fundamental essence. They also sought to find a common denominator to the essence of the Vedic dharma. The Rishiis linked Soma with this discreet essence and concluded that Soma was one such common denominator. To describe

Soma's link to the Natural Order they resorted to symbolism. Knowing that the Mahabharata identified Varuna as the Vedic force generally for the Vedic dharma (*Rta*, the natural order) itself and specifically the Vedic force responsible for water, the Rishiis concluded that water is the essence which links Soma to this greater Natural Order. Water, indeed, is the basic source of all created beings and objects. (GB, 1.1.29.) Sacrificially, this concept is represented by the liquid basis for the Soma Juice. Through the Soma Sacrifice the fundamental essence of the Vedic dharma is symbolically conveyed in the Soma juice and channeled into the worshiper's psyche by the feeling of religious ecstacy. Does this mean that everything is "all wet"? Obviously not. What it means is that the fluidity and flexibility of water forms the basis of processes at work in the Natural Order.

In a very deep sense Soma is representative of the Vedic dharma in ways that are more essential than other Vedic forces and energies. This comes down to the simple fact of the outward appearance of Soma. Soma is known as the sacramental elixir which is prepared and consumed at the Soma Sacrifice. The liquid consistency of the Soma juice, in addition to assisting the worshiper to experience divine life, is representative of the most fundamental basis of the Vedic dharma --- water. While this is the general characteristic of this fundamental basis, Water possesses a few specific characteristics in forming the basis of the Vedic dharma and consists of the very basis of essential functions found in the Vedic dharma.

Water is the Agent for Creation or Generation

Water is material cause of the universe. Water is the root (i.e., the cause) of an evolutionary process from where the shoot sprouted (the result) therefrom. (AA, 8.1.) Water is the agent for creation and generation. (SPB 3.7.4.4.) Water is also the inner essence of the Vedic dharma (*Rta*).

Creation is ritualistically represented through sprinkling. The creative powers of water are testified in the various stages of Vedic creation. Water is everywhere, not only as a physical presence but as the subtle basis of matter. The character of the indeterminate, unmanifested mass of neither existence nor non-existence, before the very creation of the Natural Order, *Rta*, was fluid, indeed it was, water. (RV 10.129.1.)

Water is fluid and is instrumental in the creation of the Soma juice obtained during the Soma Sacrifice. Soma is possessed of the creational powers of the Vedic dharma via the physical and subtle, symbolic, properties of Water. The subtle, representational properties of Water are conveyed to Soma which further conveys these properties to the Vedic dharma. Soma is thereby responsible for the creation of all things, seen and unseen. Purification and Theosis, which is Soma personified, is the sustainer of all things:

- It is *dharNasiH*, the sustainer of all. (RV 9.37.2; also, 92.2. and 9.38.6.)
- It is the maker of many, *dharNasim bhuuridhaayasam*, (RV 9.26.3) which is seen as the cause of multiplicity in the manifest universe.
- He is krtvyo, the maker of everything. (RV 9.77.5.)
- Soma is the maker, the creator of all. (RV 9.77.5.)
- Soma is the generator of all. (RV 9.86.5.)
- Soma is the simulator of all. (RV 9.97.48.) In this mantra, this quality of Soma is entitling it to be brought in the "halls of the sacrifice," *rtavaa*, where it will be the object of praise, *Satyam*anmaa. Soma in this capacity is the grand architect of all physical creation.

Creation is a holy act, and in this capacity, Soma plays a crucial role:

- Purified Soma, pavamana, gave birth to heaven and earth. (RV 9.96.5.)
- Soma created the heaven and earth. (RV 9.96.5; 9.86.21.)
- Soma is the creator of the three worlds. (RV 9.73.1. Again, this power entitles to have Soma brought to the sacrifice, asvarann Rtasya.)

The mantra above, RV 9.96.5, is illustrative of the wide powers of janiita. Janiita is Soma's abilities to create, to give birth (RV 9.87.1, 2):

- Soma gives birth to our thoughts (maatiina);
- Soma gives birth Agni, Surya, Indra, Vishnu.
- Soma is the creator of all the gods.

This is not to say that Soma gives birth like a parent giving birth to its child; Soma is the very source of power for all the gods. This speaks of the divine nature of all physical and subtle things in the world. Soma not only permeates all creation, it permeates *Rta* itself. Purification and deification is this pervasion personified in Soma in its aspect as *rtavan*, born or possessed of *Rta*. (RV 9.96.12; 9.97.48.)

This is no mean characteristic, as the only other divinity possessed of *Rta* is Agni, the personification of the element of Change. (RV 1.72.1, 2, 5; 2.35.8; 3.13.2; 3.20. 4; 4.2.1; 4.6.5; 4.2.1; 4.7.7; 5.1.6; 5.25.1; 6.12.1; 6.15.1; 6.15.13; 7.3.1; 7.7.4; 5.28.2; 10.2.2;10.6.2; 10.7.4. Agni is also rtajata: 1.36.19; 1.144.7; 1.189.6; 3.6.10; 6.13.3.) One characteristic assigned to Soma is vishvaa, or "pervasion," its ability to pervade and permeate very nook and cranny of the Vedic dharma. This would include Soma permeating ---

- The cosmos, the sacrificial hall and the world. (RV 9.1.10; 9.3,4; 9.4.2; 9.8.7; 9.14.8; 9.16.6; 9.18.6; 9.20.1, 3; 9.21.4; 9.23.1; 9.25.4; 9.28.2, 5; 9.29.4;9.36.5; 9.40.1, 4; 9.42.5; 9.43.2; 9.9.54.3; 9.55.1; 9.57.2, 4; 9.59.3, 4; 9.61.19, 24, 25, 28, 30; 9.64.6, 8, 18; 9.65.2, 9, 10; 9.66.1; 9.73.8; 9.80.3, 4; 9.84.2; 9.85.11;. 86.6, 15, 24, 26, 30, 41, 48; 9.87.6; 9.88.2; 9.89.6; 9.90.1, 6; 9.94.3, 5; 9.97.51; 9.98.7; 9.100.2; 9.102.1; 9.107.23; 9.108.11; 9.109.4, 8, 9, 14; 9.9.110.9; 9.111.5.)
- The universe, the vast expanse of the material cosmos. (RV 9.17.1; 9.22.3; 9.25.4; 9.61.18; 9.66.24; 9.86.1, 2, 5, 27, 41;9.92.3; 9.111.1.)
- Soma is "all pervading," vishvacakSa. (RV 9.85.5.) Soma abides in all four regions or quadrants of the heavens. (RV 9.22.51; 9.63.10; 9.48.1; 9.54.3; 9.63.9; 9.72.8; 9.86.29; 9.894.3; 9.113.2.)

Soma permeates the "jagat," or all manifest creation, all manifestation, all movable things, a concept of the universe later developed more fully in the Upanishads. In the approximate fifty references of jaga and its derivatives, Soma does not figure in this word-concept. This is oddly appropriate. Jaga pertains to visible creation. In addition to this, Soma's treatment in the Rg Veda on the other hand is inherently and primarily internal and concerned with inner transformation.

Water Symbolic of the Process of Evolution and Dissolution

Water is symbolic of the process of evolution. Water is the source of all created beings. (GB, 1.29.) The waters represent the beginning of the world. (RV 2.1.1; 2.20.7; 2.30.) The waters are symbolic to the process of dissolution. (RV 1.143.3; 1.164.42; 1.168.2; 2.1.1; 2.38.2; 3.1.5; 3.5.3, 8; 3.9.1, 2; 10.121.7.) The fact that water is featured in the first mantra underscores the importance water plays in the creation process. Apsu (RV 1.23.19, 20; 1.59.3; 1.65.9; 1.91.4; 1.95.3; 1.108.11; 1.109.4; 1.117.4; 1.151.1; 1.163.4; 1.184.3; 2.35.4, 5; 2.38.7; 2.38.7; 3.39.6; 5.45.22; 6.19.13; 6.25.4; 6.31.1; 6.46.14; 6.66.8; 7.70.4; 7.103.5; 8.9.5; 8.82.8; 9.2.5; 9.16.3; 9.20.6; 9.24.1; 9.30.5; 9.42.1;9.62.26; 9.71.3; 9.80.5; 9.85.10; 9.96.10; 9.97.47, 48; 10.9.6; 10.32.6; 10.45.1, 5; 10.50.3; 10.65.9; 10.104.2; 10.148.2) is an epithet of Soma and soma juices, is a derivative of water, aa, the root of both apsu and ambhah. Soma has a specific role to play in this process of evolution and dissolution. Several mantras point to the monistic nature of Soma. Effused by the fingers, Soma both gladdens the seven rivers, who have made Soma "the One" (RV 9.9.60 and hastens to the One (RV 9.97.55), another element of the process of creation found in 10.129.3.

The association in the Rg Veda of the waters to the process of evolution and dissolution of the world are replete. (RV 1.143.3; 1.64.42; 1.168.2; 2.1.1; 2.20.7; 2.38.7; 2.38.2; 2.30; 3.1.12, 13; 3.5.3; 3.5.8; 3.9.1, 2; 3.56.5; 10.121.7; 10.82.5, 6; 10.82.6 (the Waters establish the One); 10.51.8; 10.106.6; 10.129.6; 6.34.4; 6.49.5; 6.50.7 (the Waters are the mother of the universe); 6.62.2; 7.34.2.) The eternal process of evolution, that process of growth and dissolution, the reverse process by which the individual, organism or the world is brought back to the source, is central to Vedic thought and Hindu philosophy. As demonstrated so amply in a recent book, this process of evolution and dissolution is central to the Yoga Sutras. In Vedanta, dissolution, usually indicated by the concept of absorption, is the process by which the individual arrives at the inner I-ness, the atman, and realizes Brahman.

In the Rg Veda, this process is symbolized by the waters. (RV 1.143.3; 1.164.42; 1.168.2; 2.1.1; 2.38.2; 3.1.5; 3.5.3, 8; 3.9.1, 2; 10.121.7.) This concept was indicated in the first meaning of waters in RV 7.49.2 which divided three tiers of waters, the celestial, physical water, and terrestrial waters. RV 3.5.8 carries this concept one step farther. This mantra speaks of Agni, who "as soon as generated he is borne aloft by the plants, which grow flourishing by moisture, as the beautifying waters descend; ..." The process of generation and evolution, holds the process of Change (Agni) aloft, upwards, towards the heavens where the celestial waters reside; then, once he flourishes, like a plant nourished by moisture, he descends downward in the path of dissolution.

Water Representative of the First Cause of the Universe

These issues — the eternity of the world, the process of dissolution and evolution of the universe, the very recurrence of many universes in this process, plus, the need to designate a first cause or eternal law — are ingrained in Vedic belief. (YV 3.5 (first cause or eternal law); 4.3 (eternity of the world); 4.47 (recurrence of numerous worlds).) The culmination of these principles is that symbol of the first case or principle of the universe, that foundation of everything.

The first principle of the Vedic dharma is Water. (SPB 6.7.1.17; 11.1.6.16; 1.1.1.4;11.1.2.3; TS 5.1.3.1; AA, 8.1.8.1.) As before, the subtle, representational properties of Water are conveyed to Soma which further conveys these properties to the Vedic dharma.

The re-generation responsibilities are assumed by the Principle of Change (Agni) and Conjunction and unity (Indra) and Divine Ecstasy (Soma):

- The Principle of Change (Agni) is the generator, creates the subtle and material basis, of the world. (RV 1.7.3.)
- The Principle of Change (Agni) is also the embryo of the waters. (RV 3.1.2, 6, 12, 13; 3.3.5; 3.5.3.)
- Conjunction and unity (Indra) renders form to all things and make them sensible and charges the clouds with water. (RV 1.7.3.)
- Soma, divine revelation and ecstasy, is the child of the ocean. (RV 9.61.7.)

Beginning with the subtlest level, Water, the Rishiis proceeded onwards to ever more and more concrete levels. The Vedic dharma, the Natural

Order, *Rta*, is still at a high level of abstraction. The journey towards everyday material life is calibrated in gradations. We are still in Subtle Land for the moment. In the journey towards physical appearance we are inching, ever so slowly, to a form and matter more material and concrete.

Vedic Multiple Universes

As are all things Vedic, numbers play a very significant role in the Vedic dharma. The universe is interpreted through number. The worshiper's spiritual development and very existence is measured by number. Indeed, in the Vedic dharma, everything is measured by and through number. While number is potentially infinite, there exists cardinal numbers, with which that potential infinity is reduced.

The universe is a complex organism, and numbers play a significant role in the composition and interpretation of the universe. The Vedic multi-universe is premised on the physical complexity of matter itself. To everyday eyes, physical matter is solid and while malleable, seemingly impenetrable. As modern physics demonstrates, however, the deeper one delves into the essence of physical matter, the less and less solid is it found to be. The seeming solidity is found to be far more rarified and subtle; the surface solidity pocked with abscesses and canyons, the surface placidly charged with electrical sparks. Modern physics has found that the deepest recesses of solid matter are not solid at all, but rarified, ethereal spaces. This is the basis of the Vedic universe, and it informs the Vedic dharma. It guides the worshiper to liberation from this transmigration world.

The cardinal numbers in the Vedic universe are Two, Three, Five and Seven. The cardinal numbers pertain to ever-greater levels of subtly: As the numbers progress to higher levels, so does physical matter become ever subtle and so intensify the worshiper's journey to liberation. These numbers are coordinates which are incorporated into the structure of the universe. The microcosm and macrocosm can be interpreted with reference to these cardinal numbers. The Vedic path to liberation and salvation, traverses these stages of creation, these manifestations of the possible universes. The spiritual progression is very much an upward climb through these universes, from the duality present in the Two-Dimensional world to the transcendent world of the Seven-Dimensional Universe. The many possible worlds are born from the single, unitary, One (Ekam). As quoted in the Tao Tse Ching, "One produced two; two produced three; three produced ten thousand."

These are the Vedic multiple universes reflect the material world:

- The Two-Dimensional Universe which the material world itself.
- The Three-Dimensional world is the gateway, inching towards the Five-Dimensional Universe.
- The Five-Dimensional Universe is the subtle aspect of the material world. It is at this point that the spiritual journey the Agni, the principle of Change accomplishes the world yajna in five movements, three and seven threads. (RV 10.52.4.)
- The Seven-Dimensional Universe which that which transcends the material world.

There will be references in these epithets to the Two-Dimensional, Three-Dimensional, Five-Dimensional, and Seven-Dimensional Universe. Soma, sacrificially and as a philosophical construct, plays its own part in defining these dimensions.

Having set up the fabric of the universe, a method was required to be used to describe the fundamental energies which was present in and powered hat universe. Specifically, the Rishiis attempted to describe the fundamental presence which permeated the universe. The Rishiis concluded that Consciousness permeates the universe and of which it was imbued. The Rishiis could not simply say that everything was Consciousness and consisted of Consciousness and leave it like that. They were mandated to describe this Consciousness as minutely as possible without falling into absurdity. That the universe consists of and is perceived by Consciousness is relevant to Soma, because Soma is an active agent on Consciousness.

The Rishiis were practically compelled to describe this Consciousness in symbols. Symbols abound in the Vedas, and two of the most prominent are the Horse and the Cow, both of which described different aspects of Consciousness.

This line of interpretation is also coupled with the fact that at their inception the Vedas were recited to a population who were most at ease with an agrarian culture. Thus, reference is made throughout the Vedas of "cow" or "horse," to a populace who understood these words from their animal livestock, and not to the different levels of knowledge. The same could be said of Soma. Thus, Soma is at once a plant, but also a deity and a state of mind. Vedic literature and scripture does not often distinguish between Soma the plant, Soma the deity, or Soma the State of Mind. This work is an attempt to present a full picture of Soma and distinguish one of its functions from the other.

The Horse

If you conclude by now that Vedas speak in symbols, you are one-hundred percent correct. The Vedas are replete with symbols. Things are not what they appear, and the Vedas may say one thing but mean quite another. We mentioned Water; water is a good example. The horse is another. The horse, by and large, in the Vedas do not specifically means the four-legged animals, but something completely different. Luckily, the Upanishads provide a very, very good clue as to the meaning.

The Horse is a manifestation of the terrestrial Fire of Agni. (BD, 1.109.) There are no shortage of interpretations as to what the "Steed" or "Horses" signify.

The noted Vedic scholar, R.L Kashyap, has interpreted the "Horse" to mean "energies." Through linguistic and textual analysis of the Sanskrit word for Horse which links it to the Ashvins, Yogi Baba Prem interprets as signifying prana, karma and Speech. (*http://vedicpath.com/Articles/ Ashvamed-ha.html.*)

Subhash Kak, in his book, *The Asvamedha, the Rite and its Logic*, offers a few other interpretations. According to Kak, the Horse and the Horse Sacrifice represent

- Prana, the Sun, and time.
- The Universe. The Horse has thirty-four ribs, and according to RV 1.162.18, thirty-four represents the twenty-seven Nakshastras, the five planets, the Sun and the Moon.
- The process by which Time progresses and transcends all else.

16

Horses pertain to "Equine Knowledge." Equine Knowledge is best stated in the Katha Upanishad. (Kath. U., 3.3 - 10.) In that famous passage, the Katha Upanishad states:

Know the Self to be sitting in the chariot, the body to be the chariot,
the intellect [i.e., Buddhi] the charioteer,
and the mind the reins.
The senses they call the horses,
the objects of the senses their roads.
When he [i.e., the Highest Self] is in union with the body, the senses, and the mind,
then wise people call him the Enjoyer.

He who has no understanding and whose mind [i.e., the reins]
is never firmly held, his senses [i.e., horses] are unmanageable,
like vicious horses of a charioteer.
But he who has understanding and whose mind is always firmly held,
his senses are under control, like good horses of a charioteer.

He who has no understanding, who is unmindful and always impure,
never reaches that place but enters into the round of births.

But he who has understanding, who is mindful and always pure,
reaches indeed that place, from whence he is not born again.

But he who has understanding for his charioteer,
and who holds the reins of the mind, he reaches the end of his journey,
and that is the highest place of Vishnu.

Beyond the senses there are the objects, beyond the objects there is the mind,
beyond the mind there is the intellect, the Great Self is beyond the intellect.

This highly influential passage accomplishes much to the esoteric understanding of the symbol of the horse and its place in its cosmological structure. It delineates the various elements within which the consciousness resides:

- The Self, the subject, sits with the charioteer.
- The Chariot is the body
- The intellect (Buddhi) is the charioteer.
- The mind, Manas, is the reins.
- The senses, the indriam, are the horses.
- The object of the senses is the road.
- So is the image of the horse in the Veda.

This passage defines the esoteric meaning of horses in the Veda. Horses in the Veda have the metaphorical meaning of the "senses," sight, touch, hear, smell, and feel. Horses represent the senses, the mind's perception of the senses, in all their unbridled glory. Unyoked, the Horses represent the Monkey Mind, distracted, unfocused, confused, going from one thought to another.

There is yet another level to this esoteric meaning. When the worshiper perceives the surrounding world, that sense data creates a mental impression on the worshiper's mind. This mental impression is the vrttis about which Patanjali in his Yoga Sutras makes the goal in yoga. Just as there is a small fingerprint remaining once a thumb is lifted from a clump of cookie dough, these mental impressions remain long after the worshiper undergoes any kind of mental activity — perceiving the sensible world, feeling happy, sad, joyous, depressed, the memories, hearing a tune in your head that you heard earlier in the day and which you liked. All these mental events are impressions lodged in the consciousness. When you stop to think of the dynamics involved here, it all makes perfect sense. The object of yoga is not to eliminate the vrttis; the worshiper would be brain-dead if the mental impressions were eliminated. The goal is to *manage* the vrttis, control them in such way that they are not an impediment to the spiritual or mental growth of the worshiper. The passage from the Katha Upanishads emphasizes the consequences of and need to yoke — i.e., restrain, control — the senses and vrttis, metaphorically represented by horses, to achieve liberation and salvation. "Yoked horses" thus becomes a metaphor for the yogic practice of pratyahara, withdrawal of senses and the organs of sense perception creating the mental impressions in the worshiper's mind.

Soma operates to confound the worshiper even further.

- The dynamic Vedic energy of divine union (Soma) acts to "unyoke" the horses. (RV 3.32.1.) This is in Soma's nature. After the experience — any experience — of divine union, the worshiper's perception of the world is different. Instead of viewing the world in black and white, the world is suddenly, as in the Wizard of Oz, in living color. The worshiper experiences what Alan Watts states any seeker must do — get "out of your mind." In the language of the Veda, the horses are unyoked.
- Thus, when the experience of divine union is experienced after consumption of the Soma juice at the sacrifice, the senses flow, like Soma, like a rapid horse. (RV 9.16.1; 9.23.2; 9.26.1; 9.36.1; 9.59.1; 9.62.6; 9.72.1; 9.74.1; 9.93.1; 9.96.20; 9.97.18; 9.101.2.)

The epithets in this collection include samans (mantras) that show Soma to be the charioteer, the horses, the reins, and, yes, the chariot itself. Rather than indicating inconsistency, these references demonstrate the ubiquity of Soma and its pervasion to the worshiper. Soma provides the reins to yoke the Monkey Mind which constitute the horses. (RV 1.28.4.) The zoological references do not stop with Horses.

The Cow

The cow, however, represents more than an animal. The Cow is normally a very placid mammal, interested more in chewing cud than in anything else. It takes a lot to infuriate a cow, and once riled, quickly calms down. The ancients no doubt superimposed their own aspiration on the cow's demeanor. Its stoic calm indisputably indicated a deeper understanding which stood as a stark contrast to the great penchant for mischief in humans. In keeping with these aspirations, cows were subsequently interpreted as these:

19

- Cows represent the inner illumination of the rays of knowledge. (RV 2.24.6; 4.1.16 (glory of the cow of light discovered after meditation of the supreme name of the milch cow).

- Cows represent consciousness as knowledge. (RV 3.30.20; 3.39.6 (Indra finding meath (empirical knowledge) in the cows); 10.92.10 (inspired knowledge); 3.31.10; 3.31.11.)

- According to Sri Aurobindo, cows represent the power of consciousness, discrimination, and discernment. (See also, RV 2.11.2; 2.15.10; 2.16.9; 2.34.15 (right-thinking); 3.31.11; 10.92.10.) In recognition of this meaning, some English translations render gobhir, as "Ray-Cows," signifying the rays of knowledge. (See, RV 1.7.3; 1.16.9; 1.23.15; 1.53.4; 1.62.5; 1.95.8; 1.151.8; 2.15.4; 2.30.7, 20; 2.35.8; 3.1.12; 3.50.3; 3.3.3, 4; 8.7; 2.24.6; 2.20.5; 6.19.12; 6.45.20, 24. 6.66.8; 6.64.3 (red rays); 10.92.10; 4.5.5; 4.17.11; 4.23.10; 4.27.5; 4.30.22 (Indra, lord of the ray-cows); 4.31.14; 4.32.6, 7, 18, 22; 4.40.5; 4.42.5; 4.57.1; 5.1.3; 5.2.5; 5.3.2; 5.45.8; 5.80.3; 6.44.12; 6.47.27; 6.53.10; 3.55.8; 3.30.10, 21; 2.55.8; 3.35.8; 1.36.8; 9.31.5; 6.1.12 (herds of light); 6.17.2; 6.17.6; 6.43.3 (ray-cows within the rock); 6.28.1 (ray-cows bringing bliss); 6.28.3; 9.31.5 (ray cows yielding light and the milk of knowledge); 7.18.2; 7.41.3; 7.54.2; 7.90.2; 8.2.6; 8.20.8; 8.24.6; 9.62.12 (Soma pours the ray-cows and life-energies upon us); 9.67.6; 10.7.2; 10.16.7; 10.31.4; 10.68.2; 10.108.7; 10.111.2.)

- Gobhir, the ray-cows, figured prominently in the Ninth Mandala, is the presiding divinity of Soma Pavamana. (RV 9.2.4; 9.6.6; 9.8.5; 9.10.3; 9.14.3; 9.32.3; 9.43.1; 9.50.5; 9.61.13; 9.66.13; 9.68.9; 9.74.8; 9.85.4; 9.85.5; 9.86.27; 9.91.2; 9.97.15; 9.103.1; 9.107.2, 2, 9, 18, 22.)

- Kine, generally referred to in the Vedas as the milking cow, is the source of truth, essence, and knowledge. The imagery is inescapable. Just as just as there is the milk of knowledge, so is the Kine, the milking cow, its symbol.

- Kines are also representative of the union of heaven and earth.

The Jaiminiya Brahmana (JB 1.19) makes the following correspondences of cows to knowledge:

- The agnihotra cow is speech.
- The calf of agnihotra cow is mind.
- The milk of the mother cow flows to her calf.
- The milk of agnihotra cow produces the speech that causes the mind to flow
- This mind of the calf is followed by speech.
- For this reason, the mother cow runs after the calf who walks in front.

These correspondences pertain to Speech. But speech contains a hidden meaning. Speech is the articulation of the world, attaching a word to an object in the world. For the worshiper to assign the word "tree" to the actual object implies knowledge of that object, albeit through the sense perceptions. This is the hidden meaning of "speech" in the Vedas. The agnihotra cow is that knowledge of the world, and that knowledge is attained through the sacrificial rite.

This portion from the Jaiminiya Brahmana explains the many similes found in the Rg Veda of the mother cow running after or tending to her the calf.

- From RV 1.32.9, which says that after Indra struck while she was tending to her son Danus, Vrtra was above Danu like a cow with her calf.
- From RV 1.38.8, the Marut's lightning roars like a cow for her calf.
- From RV 1.164.9, Heaven (the mother) sustains the Earth (the child), the seed resting in the clouds, the same way the calf bellows for her mother, the cow. This simile emphasizes that the mind is the child of speech.

The correspondence continues:

- the milk post is the heart.
- The rope is the breath.

21

With this correspondence the author of the Brahmana makes the following conclusions concerning the relationship of breath, the vital life force, and the mind:

- With the breath the mind and speech are tied to the heart.
- The rope (breath, prana) ties (binds) the cow (speech) and the calf (mind) to the heart.

The cows represent knowledge, wisdom and illumination, most likely because these are representative of their products: milk, butter and ghee. Because the cows produce several by-products, different cows in the Vedas represent different aspects of knowledge or the mind:

- The barren or immature cow is taken to mean the lack of consciousness, incomplete or faulty knowledge, because of its unripe milk. (RV 3.30.14 (unripe milk); 2.7.5; 1.112.3; 1.116.22; 1.117.20; 1.61.9 (raw cows); 6.72.4; 4.19.7; 7.68.8.)
- The ray-cows represent Aditi, the infinite consciousness. (RV 4.58.4; 4.1.6.)
- The Ray-Cows also represent hidden or occult knowledge. (RV 4.53; 4.58; 4.5.10.)

Soma reaches its highest level of physical appearance in the sacrificial context. The sacrificial, ritualistic component to Soma is mentioned but not emphasized. There is a definite ritualistic component to Soma, and epithets will occasionally be made to ritual and sacrifice. But Soma is primarily a mental and spiritual construct. Soma is a means for us mere humans to experience the divine, to become like gods, to achieve liberation and salvation. The Soma Sacrifice is the social setting for achieving this goal, and this is all it is. While a correlation exists between the spiritual experience on the one hand and the sacrificial setting on the other, attempts to equate the two should be avoided, and it is not the approach taken in this book. That approach will be taken in another book in this series.

It's one thing to name these epithets of Soma, but it is quite another to place these epithets in an understandable context. This is where comes in the second portion of the subtitle, "Explorations in the Natural Order (*Rta*)." According to the Vedic view of the universe, the process and evolution of creation is not the result of a chance, random series of events. There is an order to the universe, and the Vedas are the Rishi's attempt to reveal that Order. The Vedic deities serve to reveal the categories of that Order. The Vedas are so shrouded in an obscurity hidden by the progression of time, that finding that Order is problematic. It should come as no surprise that the categories of the Natural Order (*Rta*) are best set forth in the Hexagrams found in the I Ching, a compatible work of comparable obscurity, of similar antiquity, and belonging with the same Zeitgeist which prevailed at the time the Vedas were developed and communicated. Soma and its epithets harmonize beautifully with the Hexagrams of the I Ching.

The imagery, the wording, the application of the words to the images of the Vedas and particularly of the Ninth Mandala are highly symbolic. Some scholars have theorized intended to be very obscure to hide the true meaning from those not properly prepared to accept their meaning. This is very plausible, given the ubiquitous injunction of yogic texts that the contents should be kept secret and not share with those who have not been initiated to the rites of yoga through a guru.

What's in a Name?

More on the title of this book. According to the dictionary an "epithet" is defined as a "word or phrase accompanying or occurring in place of the name of a person or thing." In the Vedic world, "name" has a more precise meaning. A "name" in the Vedas tell something about the very nature of an object. In other words, in Sanskrit, and to a lesser degree in English and other languages, the intrinsic meaning of an object is reflected in the name of the object. Take, for example, the names of common objects we have encountered in this introduction, such as Cow, Horse, Water. They all have their everyday meaning used by everyday people every day. There are different meanings attached to these and other words in the Veda, and the deeper one delves into the meaning of these words, the farther away from everyday speech they are applied. The entire process is much like the words from an early Pink Floyd song: "The words have different meanings."

This book contains the many epithets, names, of Soma. Many of these epithets consist of the names for Soma, the subject of this book. This book consists of expressions, rcs (chants from the Rg Veda) and samans (songs from the Sama Veda) and other phrases about Soma which give meaning to a different aspect of Soma. As with everything in the Vedic dharma, a "name" has its own specific, complicated, meaning. In the Vedas a name has meaning, it is something with power. This notion is contrary to the notion in other traditions, philosophical or otherwise, which hold that the assignment of a name is purely arbitrary. On the contrary, in the Vedas, a Name has an inherent power to effect transformation and change. The Name is foundational to the worshiper's understanding of the world and is related to the Word (vak). Articulation, Name and the Word, are born from OM, the most auspicious of names. Articulation is Name and Word bound together, and they are inextricably related to the creation of the cyclic evolution and dissolution of the universe. Whenever the universe is dissolved and subsequently evolves, the Divine Sound, OM, resonated. (JUB 1.7.1; 1.9.1; 1.10.1.)

There are many types of "names" in the Vedic dharma.

- There is nama, the common name whose utterance invokes the powers inherent in the Vedic divine force, such as Soma bearing the name of Indra. (RV 9.109.14.)
- There is guhyaani, the secret, occult, hidden name. (RV 9.95.2.)
- There is Mahat, the "great name" that permits a divine force to assume the role of other forces. It is ultimately a secret name, as in RV 3.38.1 and 3.38.4, which state that by this great secret name creatures were born in the past and will continue to be created in the future.
- There is *turiya*, the transcendental name which is incomprehensible and is only known in Heaven or revealed to the Rishiis.

We are principally concerned with this fourth classification. It is in this highest category names that the true power of Soma is found.

- In RV 9.96.19, where Soma, by proclaiming his name ascends to Heaven.
- In RV 9.14.5, where by proclaiming his name Soma gives shape to forms according to the knowledge obtained therefrom.
- In RV 10.67.1, where the Rishiis reveal the transcendental nature of Articulation, Name and the Word, which gives meaning to the objects in the material universe.

It is here that the transcendent nature of the categories contained in this book originate. Soma's transcendental nature gives rise to the Elements to the spiritual aspect of the Vedic dharma.

The Elements of the *Rta*, the Vedic Dharma

The names for Soma provide the raw material for the Elements of the subtle, spiritual aspect of the Vedic dharma. We see the Vedic dharma, *Rta*, as vast and all-encompassing. It consists of the entire universe, the macrocosm, and all that which turns inward, the microcosm, to the smallest atom. Soma has its own unique role to play in this wonderful universe. As an herbal substance, it is representative of the microcosm; as a means for experiencing divine ecstasy, it is the carrier to the macrocosm. It is for this reason that Soma, in its omnipresent capacity, can manifest both as a Vedic divine force, an entheogen, and a simple deity, and to its many other forms.

Existence is a very complex thing. Just as there are many levels of existence in the Vedic multi-universe, so are there many aspects to the Vedic dharma. Soma is one such aspect. Soma is the unifying force to the spiritual aspect of the Vedic dharma. There are other aspects to the Vedic dharma represented by the Vedic deities. Soma, however, is most fundamentally a Vedic divine force. It is an energy block which permeates and regulates the operation of the universe, or *Rta*, at every level. In this respect Soma is no different than the other Vedic forces present in the universe, such as Agni, Indra, and the remaining members of the Vedic Pantheon.

Just as the material aspect of the Vedic dharma consists of atoms, neutron, electrons, protons, and the like, the categories described in this book consists of the constituent parts of the spiritual aspect of the Vedic dharma. Those Elements, those categories creating the spiritual aspect of the Vedic dharma are:

- Abundance.
- Approach.
- Arousal (Sound).
- Awakening (Enlightenment).
- Conflict.
- Consciousness.
- Consumption.
- Contemplation (Deliberation).
- Deliverance.
- Difficulty (Water and Thunder).
- Discernment.
- Dispensation.
- Divine Vision.
- Duration.
- Earth (The Receptive).
- Efficient Cause.
- Energy (Impulsion).
- Enthusiasm.
- Establishment (Material Support).
- The Falcon.
- Family.
- Fellowship.
- Fire.
- Flood.
- Flow.
- Food.
- Glorification.
- Heaven (The Creative).
- Increase.
- Inner Essence.
- Insightful Knowledge.
- Intelligent Design (Will).
- Joy, Bliss.

- Knowledge.
- Liberation.
- Light (Illumination, Grace).
- Lordship.
- Luminosity.
- Motion.
- Nourishment.
- Overcoming Adversity.
- The Path.
- Perfection.
- Pervasion.
- Physical Integrity, Improvement.
- Pressing.
- Protection.
- Possession in Great Measure.
- Purification.
- Rapture.
- Release.
- Replenishment (The Showerer, the Bull).
- Sense Perceptions (The Horse).
- Soma Pavamana.
- Streaming.
- Strength, Might.
- Surrender.
- Urging.
- The Vast.
- The Vedic Dharma.
- Vegetation.
- Vrtra.
- The Waters.

Conspicuously absent from this list is "Sacrifice." Soma, remember, is a complex divine entity. It is a physical plant and a state of spiritual consciousness; these two "Somas" are bound together for a sacrificial rite specially designed to achieve the rapture needed for liberation. Sacrifice very much is implied by its absence in this present work. A discussion of the Soma Sacrifice could easily take up a separate book and will be covered at length in a future volume.

These categories are the "Elements" of the subtle aspect of the Vedic dharma. These separate categories could have just as easily been called Platonic "Forms" or "Ideas." These are intangibles which shape the subtle world of spiritual life, the region where Soma dwells. Just as children's' building blocks that can create a large wall, these individual ideas and actions build the structure describing the spiritual aspect of Soma. These are not walls that separate. Instead, these Elements create steps to spiritual development. Their function is peculiar to Soma. These individual categories can be extrapolated to be applied to the constituent elements of spirituality generally and the application of the spirituality to the worshiper in general. They are Soma's special contribution to the Natural Order. And yet Soma plays no greater role than to facilitate the liberation of the worshiper's soul.

Soma's Path to Liberation and Salvation

The Vedic dharma is very systematic. Due to the great antiquity of the Vedas, doctrines have been formulated for millennia and have settled to precise methods to achieve liberation. Soma has its own role to play in this framework, of course. Remember, a big part of Soma's role in the Vedic dharma is to enable the worshiper to achieve liberation and salvation.

There are three stages to the accomplishment of liberation and salvations.

In the first stage the worshiper achieves an elevation of consciousness. There is an old French proverb which says, "To know all is to forgive all." This is the thought behind the achievement of liberation through Consciousness. The raising of consciousness is accomplished in seven stages:

- The Awakening is the first step in the journey towards salvation and liberation.
- From the Awakening, or Enlightenment, the worshiper acquires Knowledge.
- From Knowledge, he worshiper gains Consciousness.
- From Consciousness, the worshiper has the capacity to be engaged in Contemplation or Deliberation.

- From the act of Contemplation or Deliberation the worshiper gains Insightful Knowledge.
- From this Insightful Knowledge, the worshiper obtains Discernment.
- From Discernment, the worshiper obtains Divine Vision.

In the second stage, the worshiper experiences rapture and bliss.

- From Divine Vision, the worshiper experiences Joy.
- From Joy, the worshiper is completely overcome by Rapture.
- From there, Rapture, the worshiper gets a taste of Liberation.

In the final third stage, the worshiper is saved through Soma's ability to expiate sins. This is not an uncommon power. Many Vedic divine forces, including Agni, the Vedic force of Change and Transformation, possesses this specific power. As some of the epithets in this book state, Soma's power to expiate sins is expressly inherent in its divine force. It is a net result of Soma's powers to induce an elevated level of consciousness and to produce its powers of elation and ecstasy.

These stages taken together are roughly equivalent to the path of liberation formulated millennia later with Vedanta. Satcitananda is a method of uniting with Brahman. It consists of three elements: Reality, "Sat" + Understanding, Consciousness, "Cit" + Ananda, "Bliss." The last two elements are the first two methods to liberation as far as Soma is concerned. It is a recognition that the final liberation of the worshiper's soul is ultimately an act of Grace.

And yet it is equally plausible that given the great antiquity of the Rg Veda the exact or intended meaning of Soma will never be learned, let alone the identification of the Soma plant. To a certain extent divining the meaning of the Rg Veda is a matter of pure interpretation and hence so too with this book. Great effort has been made to conform the interpretation with subsequent Vedic thought to make it consistent with the great Vedic scriptures that followed the Vedas. Such an interpretation would not only be consistent with the lines of thought which followed, but more accurately reflect the preoccupation of the many thinkers, Rishis and Sages which looked at wonder with the contents of the Vedas.

There is no representation that the discussion in this book is exhaustive. An extensive discussion, if one is possible, would require a treatment many times longer than the one that is presented here, so vast is the subject of Soma. Nor will it be that this interpretation conforms to the conventional or academic wisdom. It is meant to be an introduction of one vision of Soma. References will be made as much as possible to the vast array of literature about Soma in the Rg Veda. This book is intended to think outside of the box with respect to Soma.

This present interpretation of Soma is idiosyncratic. But aren't all English commentaries idiosyncratic? To coin the expression of attributed to Winston Churchill about Russia, the Vedas are "A Riddle Wrapped in a Mystery Inside an Enigma." Winston Churchill's comment about Soviet Russian could also be said of Soma. There are several levels in which Soma can be understood. Soma can be read as a mythological narrative, as a history persona, as an alchemical, astronomical or astrological treatise. Sometimes what is said of Soma is downright contradictory. Soma is so diverse, it is mentioned in so many scriptures, it is applied to so many disciplines, that it defies concrete definition.

This work will touch on those sacrificial, mythological, historical, alchemical, astronomical, and astrological aspects of Soma, and make the subject more understandable, in the context in which Soma is most prominent, the Ninth Mandala of the Rg Veda. This work is an attempt to think outside the box and explain, truly explain, Soma for what it is, the most diverse of Vedic energies. Whenever possible, assertions about this natural order are supported by doctrinal support. It is the author's sincere hope that you, dear Reader, will not be intimidated by the citations. The presence of the citations in this text are as much for the benefit of those curious for additional knowledge. There is nothing more frustrating than to read a factual assertion or reference from a scripture without a citation referencing the quote. These citations are as much for the reader's benefit as it is for the author's own assurance that he is not falling into error.

Agree or disagree, it is hoped that this work will stimulate interest and increase your understanding in Soma in the same way the Soma juice stimulates the spiritual experience. If the interpretation is incorrect, outlandish, audacious, unfounded, unorthodox, or simply mistaken, or if there is some other inadequacy, the fault lies not in the rcs (chants from the Rg Veda) and samans (songs from the Sama Veda) in this marvelous, moving, piece of wisdom called the Vedas, but belongs solely to the author.

ONE THOUSAND NAMES FOR SOMA

The Elements for the Natural Order (*Rta*)

The Meaning of Divine Ecstasy

ABUNDANCE

Abundance is an element of the Natural Order (*Rta*). Abundance, fullness, is what distinguishes the Vedic religion from Buddhism. Voidness in Buddhism is genuinely empty, with various gradations of nihilistic vacuity. In the Vedas dharma sunya, emptiness, implies a fulness which includes empty spaces and spaces with matter. Soma was born of this abundance, is imbued with this fulness, and conquers this fullness for the benefit of the worshiper.

The Sanskrit word for this category is *vaaljaM*. Like many categories in the Vedic dharma *vaaljaM* cannot be reduced into one English word. Abundance is related to other categories in this definition. *VaaljaM* connotes "fullness," in that it does not lack of any other quality, and "plentitude" because of its abundance and because it is vast. The category does not simply imply vastness such that it is transcendent, outside common experience. The most complete description of the category from the Vedic dharma is the "Fullness of the plentitude."

The best explanation of Abundance, *vaaljaM*, can be found in RV 1.27.5. There the Rishii spoke of the powers of Agni, in his manifestation of the ability to grant awareness of abundance to the worshiper. The Rishii made clear that there was abundance, a fullness of plenty, in the three levels of the Three-Dimensional Universe consisting of the Earth, Mid-World and Heaven. Abundance is not limited to one level of existence or to one dimension; it is a characteristic common to every level of the Vedic dharma. As RV 1.27.5 recites, there is a richness in every level.

This is an important rc (mantra) for the worshiper to keep in mind, because while traveling along the Vedic path towards salvation and liberation, the worshiper should not become down-hearted if progress is not as anticipated or expected or not enough. Soma Conquers the Abundant Vastness for Humans. (Epithet No. 5.) Soma conveys, flows the Fullness of Plenty to the Worshiper. (Epithet No. 7.) Endowed with knowledge and the plenitude, the worshiper is purified by Soma to proceed on the spiritual journey. (Epithet No. 6.) Soma provides the Elements required to provide the experience of abundance. This abundance fosters the spiritual development of the worshiper. Endowed with knowledge and the plenitude, Soma conveys the radiance of the Vedic dharma, the natural order to the worshiper. (Epithet No. 4.) Soma is the worshiper's source of inspiration to experience the abundance of the universe. The reason? Soma is Full of Plentitude. (Epithet No. 1.)

1. Soma is Full of Plentitude. (RV 9.94.1.)

The Plentitude is the fullness of the Vedic dharma. Think of the experience of life as a spectrum. In a band of light, there is visible light and there is ultra-violet light, which is essentially not visible to the human eye. The experience of Soma covers both the visible light and ultra-violet light --- the full spectrum. The Plentitude, the Vast, these are synonyms for the Vedic dharma, taken as a whole.

2. Soma was born in the vast fulness of plenty (*vaaljaM*). (RV 9.61.10.)

This epithet is another way of identifying Soma with the vastness of the Vedic dharma.

3. Soma joins (*saMgathel*) the worshiper to the Fullness in Plenty (*vaaljasya*). (RV 1.91.16.)

The experience of the Soma at the Soma Sacrifice is one method of liberation and salvation. The experience mimics what it is like to be divine, itself a code-word signifying liberation and salvation.

4. Endowed with knowledge (*golmantam*) and the plenitude (*vaal jaM*), Soma conveys (*akSaran*) the radiance of the Vedic dharma, the natural order (*shukraal Rtalsya*) to the worshiper. (RV 9.63.14.)

The worshiper may achieve liberation and salvation through meditation or by drinking the Soma juice at the Soma Sacrifice. In either instance, the worshiper receives Knowledge of the Vedic dharma. With this Knowledge the worshiper learns how to live in accordance with the Vedi dharma.

5.   Soma Conquers the Abundant Vastness (*vaaljaM*) for Humans. (RV 9.61.20.)

One of the functions of Soma is to increase the mental and spiritual powers of the worshiper to appreciate the Vastness, the inner essence of the Vedic dharma and convey that Knowledge to the worshiper.

6.   Endowed with knowledge (*golmantam*) and the plenitude (*vaaljaM*), Soma conveys (*akSaran*) purity to the worshiper. (RV 9.63.14.)

This is a by-product, not only of the Soma experience, but of any acquisition of Knowledge or, as the Vedantin say, discrimination. With Knowledge the worshiper is purified.

7.   Soma conveys, flows (*pavasva*) the Fullness of Plenty (*vaaljaM*) to the Worshiper. (RV 9.63.18.) *Pavasva*, flowing, is the act of conveying Knowledge, or any spiritual endowment.

8.   The food of Soma (*alndhasaa*) dwells in the light (*dyukSalH*), the area of the vast (*bhalrad*) fullness of plenty (*vaaljaM*). (RV 9.52.1.)

Food in this context is the inner essence, and the food of Soma is the inner essence is located at the region of light, the highest region of the Vedic dharma.

APPROACH

Approach connotes the forward motion nearing towards a goal. There is a sacrificial aspect to this category. In a sacrificial context, Approach is symbolized sacrificially by the bringing the Soma plant to the pressing stones for crushing. In the language of performance art this is symbolic of heaven meeting with the earth so that the two may unite. This is reflected in the reverent tone of the Ninth Epithet. There, the Seven Seers represent Heaven as they approach Soma, the Body, Earth. (Epithet No. 9.) The power and wisdom of the Natural Order, *Rta*, is conveyed to the worshiper. For one brief moment, during the ritual peace and harmony prevail. This is so reflected in the Eleventh Epithet. In this profound peace is found in the rapture experienced from Soma. In this spiritual context approach is representative on the beginning of the worshiper's journey to liberation. This liberation is symbolized by the Rays of the Sun. Soma both provides the means and the context for the inner purification the worshiper obtains upon learning the inner essences of the Natural Order. (Epithet No. 10.) The Approach is more a sign of reverence. The meaning of Approach is reflected in these samans (mantras):

9. The Seven Seers Approach Soma in the Body. (RV 9.91.2.)

10. Soma Approaches the Rays of the Sun (*suu/ryasyo/pa rashmi/m*). (RV 9.97.33.)

11. Flowing in rapture (*ma/daH*) Soma approaches in true order (*devaayuSa/g*) to Indra, the Articulation of Form. (RV 9.63.22.)

These epithets describe three different movements. One, the Seven Seers approach Soma. This epithet indicate that the Soma plant is imbued with transcendental powers of the Seven-Dimension Universe. Two, Soma approaches the light of the Sun. This is for illumination, both subtle and gross. Three, having been enlightened Soma approaches the greater Vedic dharma, to be used for all sentient and non-sentient objects therein.

AROUSAL (SOUND)

Sound is important in the Vedic dharma, because it is the first physical event of creation. This is reflected in the very name modern cosmology theory assigns for the start of the universe — the Big Bang. There is a subtle reflection of this phenomenon. The Gospel of John, 1.1 states that in the beginning there was the "Word." Here, "Word" signifies not only verbal articulation of physical objects in the Natural Order, but their subtle basis. For this reason, John continues to clarify that the Word was God and with God. "Word" in the case for John is an unfortunate rendering. The original Greek is written as "logos," to which there is no easy translation. Logos means many things, which include "word" and "speech," but also includes "reason," "meaning," "cause," "basis," and "reason for being or existence." Essentially, Logos, the Word, is another word for the natural order, the Vedic dharma.

The traditional divine Vedic force is Saraswati. Saraswati is the representation of Vak, Logos, the First Principle, Paratman. As RV 1.164.45 teaches, there are four elements to Vak, and they correspond to the four, broad, dimensions of the multi-universe.

Level of Vak	Corresponding Dimension of the Universe
Vaikhari	Two-Dimensional Universe
Madhyama	Three-Dimensional Universe
Pasyanti	Five-Dimensional Universe
Para	Seven-Dimensional Universe

This is the overview-representation of the Vedic dharma, the natural order (*Rta*).

- The natural order begins at Vaikhari, the underlying basis of material existence present in the Two-Dimensional Universe, where the worshiper experiences the insane tug and pull of maya.
- Beginning to break free of the chains of maya, the worshiper begins to live and experience in the material world reflected in the Three-Dimensional Universe.
- Through meditation the worshiper discovers the subtle basis of the material world in the Five-Dimensional Universe.
- Through intense worship, ritual and meditation (*Tapas*) the worshiper, if lucky, transcends to the liberation of the Seven-Dimensional Universe. Salvation has been achieved.

This simple sentence from John 1:1 provides a good working definition for the Natural Order and describes the relationship between Sound and that Order. Just as in the beginning there was the Word and the Word was with God and the word was God, the Aitareya Brahmana, 5.3, identifies Sound, crystallized in "AUM," with the three stages of the creation of the universe, which are further identified with the three Vedas. This is indicated when the epithets states that "Soma is the Word." (Epithets Nos. 27 and 28.)

No discussion of Sound in this connection can be complete without some mention of AUM. Arousal is an appropriate word to classify Sound or especially AUM, because it is through Sound that the Vedic dharma as a whole is aroused. The universe was created by Sound, manifested in the Sabda Brahman. (BU, 4.12.) Brahman is associated with Speech, Vak (RV 10.114.8), and Vak is associated in turn to the creator of the universe. (RV 10.71.7.) So it is with AUM. Whenever the universe is dissolved and subsequently evolves, the Divine Sound, OM, resonates. (JUB 1.7.1; 1.9.1; 1.10.1.) A little-known, minor, Upanishad, the Ekakshara-Upanishad, is wholly devoted to the explanation of AUM. In this Upanishad, the Rishiis establish a correspondence between Soma, AUM, the primal sound of the universe, and the creation of the Vedic dharma. AUM is the sound of the primeval Brahman emitted when the Vedic dharma arose from the indeterminate mass at the beginning of this cycle of creation. (BU, 5.1.1.)

Soma is the link between Sound and the Natural Order. A source no less than the Chandogya Upanishad says in the very beginning at 1.1.2 that

- The essence of all beings is the Earth.
- The essence of the Earth is Water.
- The Essence of Water is plants.
- The Essence of plants is man.
- The essence of man is Speech.
- The essence of Speech is the Rg Veda.
- The essence of the Rg Veda is the Sama Veda.
- The essence of the Sama Veda is the Udgīta (which is AUM).

The Vedic force of Soma originates the Sound and finds the voice of the Vedic dharma by finding the Sound of the Universe. (Epithet No. 22.) This is very close to what was written in the Mandukya Upanishad millennia later concerning the divine Sound, Aum, in relation to the Atman. Quoting from this Upanishad:

- This identical Atman, or Self, in the realm of sound is the syllable OM, the above described four quarters of the Self being identical with the components of the syllable, and the components of the syllable being identical with the four quarters of the Self. The components of the Syllable are A, U, M. (MU, 8.)
- Vaisvanara, whose field is the waking state, is the first sound, A, because this encompasses all, and because it is the first. He who knows thus, encompasses all desirable objects; he becomes the first. (MU, 9.)
- Taijasa, whose field is the dream state, is the second sound, U, because this is an excellence, and contains the qualities of the other two. He who knows thus, exalts. (MU, 10.)
- Prajna, whose field is deep sleep, is the third sound, M, because this is the measure, and that into which all enters. He who knows thus, measures all and becomes all. (MU, 11.)

- The fourth is soundless: unutterable, a quieting down of all relative manifestations, blissful, peaceful, non-dual. Thus, OM is the Atman, verily. He who knows thus, merges his self in the Self – yea, he who knows thus. Om śantih; śantih; śantih Om Peace! Peace! Peace! (MU, 12.)

These passages from the Mandukya Upanishad are significant. Not only do they equate AUM with the Atman, but they equate AUM with the very fabric of the Vedic dharma, the macrocosm, and the worshiper's states of consciousness, the microcosm. As we will see later in these pages, Soma will be seen as the precursor to the Atman. Soma is also equated as the very Sound of the universe, like AUM. This is shown when the epithets state that Soma makes a "Sound," or "utters a cry." (Epithet No. 15.) Soma communicates Sound when the forms for physical objects in the universe appear and articulates the names for those objects. This is indicated when the epithet states that in making its sound Soma is placed in our thoughts. (Epithet No. 24.) It is the divine representative. Thus one Epithet states that Soma is the Divine Spokesman. (Epithet No. 16.) The divinity of Soma is shown in many ways. It is implicated when the epithet states that Soma is the Cosmic Articulation. (Epithet No. 13.) Soma's divine communication pervades throughout the three levels of the existence. This is spoken when the epithet states that Soma "speaks with three heads." (Epithet No. 14.) The "three heads" are the three existential levels of Earth, Mid-World, and Heaven. On a sacrificial level, the Sound articulated by Soma is represented by the noise made while the juice races through the purifier and sieve. This is stated when the epithet states that Soma makes a sound when it rushes out of the filter. (Epithet No. 20.) The epithet states that as Soma moves forward it makes a sound. (Epithet No. 21.) As it passes through the filters and other sacrificial implements the wisdom of the Sound is conveyed to the worshiper when it enters the worshiper's Words and Utterances. (Epithet No. 28.) The worshiper must be ready to receive this blessings. The hope is that the worshiper may somehow obtain a bit of that wisdom. It is indicated when the epithet states that Soma arrives to the "seekers of gold" --- the worshiper --- when Soma makes a sound. (Epithet No. 18.) But, let's read the epithets to see what they say.

12. Soma Carries the Utterance. (RV 9.86.48.)

Soma is the conveyance of the Articulation in the Vedic dharma. Articulation in this context pertains to all four levels of Speech outlined in the introductory part.

13. Soma is Displays Cosmic Articulation (*visvat*). (RV 9.10.5.)

This is a reference to the subtle sound of AUM which created all being at the beginning of the dharma's creation and continues to pervade.

14. Soma Speaks with Three Heads. (RV 9.73.1.)

With "Three Heads" the implication is Soma plays a role in the Articulation of forms and beings in the Three-Dimensional Universe.

15. Soma Utters a Cry. (RV 9.74.5.)

Vedic scholars such as R.L. Kashyap theorize that portions of the Rg Veda mentioning that Soma "utters a cry" or makes a noise is figurative language for the sound the Soma pap makes during the distillation process.

16. Soma is the Divine Spokesman (*na/raa ca sha/MsaM*). (RV 9.86.42.)

This is again figurative language indicating the divine nature of Soma.

17. The Word Is Born of Soma. (RV 9.25.5.)

Soma is not the only Vedic force responsible for providing the subtle basis of the Word. The Vedic forces of Agni and Indra also claim this privilege. The role of Soma plays more in the divine aspect of the Word.

18. Soma Comes to the Seekers of Gold (*hiranyayuh*) Making a Sound (*gavyu/r*). (RV 9.27.4.)

Gold is symbolic of the highest level of purity and divine experience. This is why Soma is associated with Gold.

19. Soma Sounds like a horse leading a chariot. (RV 9.10.1.)

The Horse leading a chariot is symbolic imagery for the enlightened mind. Soma is associated with the enlightened mind.

20. Soma, the luminous one (*ha/rir*), rushes (*arSati*) out of the filter (*pavi/tre*), making a sound (*ka/nikrada*). (RV 9.3.9.)

A double level of meaning. There is a ritualistic meaning, of course, and the epithet refers to the distillation process. "Passing through a filter" is symbolic of inner mental and physical purification. "Rushing" refers to the intensity of the Soma experience. "Making the sound" is the articulation of the worshiper's new life.

21. Soma moves forward making sounds. (RV 9.33.4.)
This is another reference to the Soma experience.

22. Soma finds (*vida*) the sound (*shra/vo*) of the universe. (RV 9.20.3.)
Soma finds the cosmic sound for the benefit of the worshiper. Soma finds the lost chord.

23. Soma makes a sound (*ka/nikradat*). (RV 9.5.1.)
Soma is Articulation.

24. In making its sound (*ka/nikradat*) Soma is placed in our thoughts (*dhiyaa/*). (RV 9.25.2.)
Finding the lost chord, personifying Articulation, Soma conveys that Sound to the worshiper.

25. Soma emits the powers of Indra (*indriya/m*) when it makes a sound (*ka/nikradat*). (RV 9.30.2.)
The Vedic force of Indra embodies the principle of Articulation. Soma acts in unison with Indra in communicating this Sound to the Worshiper.

26. Soma moves making a sound (*ka/nikradat*). (RV 9.33.4.)

27. Soma Is Possessed of the Luminous Word. (RV 9.74.3.)

28. Soma Enters the Worshiper's Word's and Utterances. (RV 9.20.5.)

AWAKENING, ENLIGHTENMENT

The Awakening is the first step in the elevation of consciousness during the worshiper's journey towards salvation and liberation.

- From the Awakening, or Enlightenment, the worshiper acquires Knowledge.
- From Knowledge, he worshiper gains Consciousness.
- From Consciousness, the worshiper has the capacity to be engaged in Contemplation or Deliberation.
- From the act of Contemplation or Deliberation the worshiper gains Insightful Knowledge.
- From Insightful Knowledge, the worshiper obtains Discernment.
- From Discernment, the worshiper obtains Divine Vision.

From there, the worshiper gets a taste of Liberation in Rapture. Each separate level of this spiritual awakening has its own separate category. Soma informs each category. Soma is also the vehicle which takes the worshiper through all these different points of entry.

The Awakening is sometimes described in terms of simile. The Ninth Mandala likens the Awakening as the Dawn (Epithet No. 29), personified by the divine force of Usas. It is also described as Illumination. (Epithet No. 31). Since the Awakening is symbolized in terms of light and illumination, in cosmological terms it is found in the Svar, (Epithet No. 33), the intermediary region of light, between Heaven and Earth. All these aids the worshiper in the journey to salvation and liberation. The following provides a brief picture of this spiritual journey.

29. Soma is the Creator of the Dawn. (RV 9.86.19.)

The Dawn Usas, is representative of the first stage of liberation through Soma --- the Awakening.

30. Soma enlightens (*ruce/*) the worshiper though the divine powers of godhead (*na/ryo*). (RV 9. 105.5.)

31. Soma creates illumination (*vi/praH*). (RV 9.84.5.)

The Awakening starts with the first glimmer of Illumination.

32. Soma is a Sage (*vipra*). (RV 8.79.1.)

Soma is the Great Guru, a Sage communicating the occult knowledge of enlightenment.

33. Soma envisions (*dRshe/*) the region of the Svar (*sva\r*). (RV 9.61.18.)

Are we surprised that Soma lives in the uppermost regions of the Vedic dharma?

34. To the young (*yuu/na*), Soma provides the discrimination (*da/kSaM*). (RV 1.91.7.)

The "young" refer to both age and mentality. Soma provides discrimination to the worshiper just beginning the spiritual journey.

CONFLICT

When conflict arises between two or more opposing forces, when they meet and converge, resolution cannot be achieved. The Rig Veda presents a black-and-white world in which the boundaries Good encounters Evil are definite, stark, and clearly defined. In the language of the Veda, there existed the Enemies on one hand and Vedic divine forces on the other. This category is elaborated on Conflict. There are the Enemies, as indicated in one of the epithets, on the one hand. There is, of course, Soma, on the other. Soma repels, drives out, the Enemies. (Epithet No. 37.) To combat the Enemies, Soma is fierce (Epithet No. 35), Soma is powerful (Epithet No. 38), and Soma is heroic. (Epithet No. 39.) For every conflict there is a point of convergence where the two or more opposing forces meet. This category therefore also describes the result of this conflict. The epithets therefore state that Soma is fierce and heroic and repels the enemy forces.

35. Soma is the Fierce One. (RV 9.109.22.)

36. Soma is fierce (*ugraa/N*). (RV 9.66.16.)

37. Soma repels (*baa/dhase*) the enemies. (RV 9.94.5.)

38. Among the forceful (*ugre/bhyash*), Soma is the most powerful (*o/ jiiyaa-n*). (RV 9.66.17.)

39. Among heroes, Soma is the most heroic. (RV 9.66.17.)

40. Soma creates the weapons for Indra. (RV 9.96.12.)

These epithets collectively pertain to the epic battle between Indra and the serpent Vrtra. One of the results of this battle is the release of Waters. This is symbolic language for the beginnings of Consciousness in the Vedic dharma, which is discussed next.

CONSCIOUSNESS

We have just become familiar with other categories which describe specific levels of spiritual awareness and consciousness, such as Discrimination and Awakening. These epithets deal only with Consciousness itself. From the Awakening, or Enlightenment, the worshiper acquires Knowledge and from Knowledge, he worshiper gains Consciousness. Soma plays a huge role in the elevation of consciousness. (Epithet No. 47.) The epithets give a clear picture of Soma's role in the field of consciousness. The worshiper becomes conscious by consuming Soma. (Epithet No. 46.) Thought and thinking are by nature subtle. (Epithet No. 45.) Thought and thinking may be viewed as electrical impulses traveling through the synapses in the brain. Soma can be viewed as the Bull which fertilizes the seed which invigorate those electrical charges. (Epithet No. 43.) Soma is consciousness itself. (Epithet No. 41.) Through Soma the worshiper acquires the Universal Consciousness of Atman. (Epithet No. 42.)

41. Soma is conscious (*jaalgRvir*). (RV 9.106.4.)

This is true whether this saman (mantra) refers to the Soma plant, the Soma experience, or the Soma principle. A bedrock principle in the Vedic dharma is that every object, sentient or non-sentient, possesses some level of consciousness. It is a question of degree only. Soma is conscious and consciousness personified.

42. Soma makes the universal consciousness (*vilshvaani celtasaa*) flow in the thoughts (*matii*/) of the worshiper. (RV 9.20.3.)

This is the primary spiritual endowment bestowed on the worshiper.

43. Soma is the Bull Who Fertilizes the Force of Consciousness. (Nir., 3.3.)

The Bull is a familiar metaphor for Soma. This epithet explains one function of the Bull, to fertilize, start the process which creates consciousness.

44. Soma is Illuminated in Consciousness (*jaj-naana/M*). (RV 9.86.36.)

By supplying consciousness Soma becomes conscious.

45. Soma moves by the force of subtle thought (*dhiyaa/ a/Nvyaa*). (RV 9.15.1.)

The movements of Soma travel through the different existential levels. Here, it travels with the force of subtle thought.

46. Soma elevates the consciousness of both the worshiper (*yaata/yann*) and chanter. (RV 9.86.42.)

This is the practical result of the worshiper's realization. The power of the mind on the world around it is great. The sounds of the chanting rcs (mantras of the Rg Veda), samans (mantras of the Sama Veda), and chhandas (mantras of the Yajur Veda) of the Vedas during the sacrifice (yajna) literally mold the fabric of space-time. (RV 10.130.1.) The alterations work on a gross, material, level and on a subtle, intangible level. Materially space-time is altered by the very vibration of the sound waves themselves acting on the fabric of the universe. On an intangible level space-time is altered by the profound power of the revelations of the Rishiis on the Vedic astrologer's mind and soul.

47. By drinking Soma, the worshiper becomes fully conscious. (RV 9.108.2.)

This, of course, is the method by which the worshiper becomes conscious --- through consumption of the Soma juice. This is explained more fully in the next section.

CONSUMPTION

Consumption is very basic to the spiritual experience of Soma. Consumption has a long history. The epithets indicate that Manu, the first human, consumed Soma that the worshiper may take advantage of its spiritual qualities. Without consumption of the Soma, its powers cannot be enjoyed.

Note that Soma the beverage is consumed by the Vedic divine forces. It is consumed by Mitra, Varuna, Vayu, the Maruts, and a host of other Vedic divine forces, most of all Indra. (See, Epithets Nos. 47 – 57.) Foremost, of all the Vedic divine forces, the majority of the rcs (chants from the Rg Veda) and samans (songs from the Sama Veda) mention the consumption by Indra of Soma. (Epithet No. 48.) In this regard, pay attention to the consumption of Soma by Bhaga. (Epithet No. 55.) According to the Mahabharata Bhaga is a Vedic force inhering six divine qualities, some of which are contained in this collection: Lordship, Righteousness, Glory, Wealth, Skills, Wisdom, and Detachment. Note too that Soma is consumed by the worshiper, and that when the worshiper consumes Soma, the worshiper assumes the powers of Indra. Consumption, imbibing Soma, is an internal, volitional action, whether by Vedic divine forces or the worshiper. In this way, Consumption may thereby be seen as an internalization of divine powers, whether by Vedic divine powers or the worshiper. If consumed by the worshiper, the implication is that the worshiper becomes divine and acquires the powers of the other Vedic divine forces who consume Soma. This is indicated when the saman says that by consuming Soma, the worshiper is the Knower of the Sun world. (Epithet No. 58.) The worshiper "Knows," on an experiential level and becomes one with the members of the Sun World, metaphorical for

Heaven, where the Vedic forces congregate. The worshiper thereby may assume either specific Vedic divine qualities or general spiritual qualities. Not here, but there is an epithet which states that the worshiper becomes immortal when Soma is consumed. This does not mean that the body of the worshiper will never die. The worshiper becomes god*like*, similar to but not exactly the same as, a Vedic force or energy and will meet the moment when the body will cease to be. However, in the meantime, the worshiper's soul, perhaps, will attain salvation and liberation, which is the functional equivalent. It is the worshiper's soul that becomes immortal.

Consumption is related to Food. It is a product of Food. More significantly, it is related to the method of the worshiper's spiritual development. The salient feature of Soma is that it is consumed by the various Vedic dynamic forces, from Mitra to Varuna. (Epithets Nos. 50 through 57.) The truly telling set of epithets are 48 and 49. By far the most notorious consumer of Soma is Indra. (RV 9.56.2; 9.64.13; 9.71.5; 9.108.9, 13; 9.113.1 - 11.) Epithet No. 49 confirms that when Indra consumes Soma, the powers of Indra are conveyed to the worshiper. It could validly be concluded that by the consumption of Soma the worshiper acquires the power of the other Vedic dynamic forces which consume Soma.

48. Soma is consumed by Indra. (RV 9.108.14.)

The most frequent prerequisite for one of the most iconic passages in the Rg Veda --- the battle between Indra and Vrtra --- has Indra consuming Soma prior to the battle. Soma is consumed to give energy --- spiritual and physical --- to do battle with the serpent.

49. When the Soma juice is consumed the worshiper acquires the powers of Indra. (RV 8.48.10.)

Straightforward wording in the saman, but what are these powers? The Vedic force of Indra represents the Principle of Increase in the Vedic dharma, which subsumes several other vital forces: Conjunction and Unity, Strength and Force, Maker of Forms, Articulation of Mind and Matter, Pure Energy Light, and the Force of Mind, Consciousness, and Discernment. These are all characteristics shared by other Vedic forces; Indra is distinguished from these other forces in his combination of principles, not with the principles themselves. These principles are imparted to the worshiper in consuming Soma.

50. Soma is cherished (*ju/STo*) by Mitra. (RV 9.70.8.)

The Vedic force of Mitra is an Aditya. In the Vedic dharma, the Adityas represent the various houses of the Zodiac. Mitra belongs to the Zodiacal house of Scorpio. That Mitra "cherishes" Soma is coded language which signifies that Soma powers the Zodiacal house of Scorpio.

51. Soma is cherished (*ju/STo*) by Varuna. (RV 9.70.8.)

The Vedic force of Varuna is an Aditya. In the Vedic dharma, the Adityas represent the various houses of the Zodiac. Varuna belongs to the Zodiacal house of Aquarius. That Varuna "cherishes" Soma is coded language which signifies that Soma powers the Zodiacal house of Aquarius.

52. Soma is cherished (*ju/STo*) by Vayu. (RV 9.70.8.)

The Vedic force of Vayu is an Aditya. In the Vedic dharma, the Adityas represent the various houses of the Zodiac. Vayu belongs to the Zodiacal house of Libra. That Vayu "cherishes" Soma is coded language which signifies that Soma powers the Zodiacal house of Libra.

53. Soma is consumed by the Maruts. (RV 9.108.14.)

Even though they are known to be closely associated with the divine force and energy of Indra, the Maruts are essentially aligned with and obtain their energy from Vanaspati, a Terrestrial manifestation of Agni. (BD, 1.103.) Consumption implicates the incorporation of Soma's properties into a Vedic force or to the worshiper. Here, those properties are incorporated into the Maruts and is conveyed to the Vedic forces and to the worshiper upon consumption.

54. Soma is consumed by the Aryaman. (RV 9.108.14.)

The Vedic force of Aryaman is an Aditya. In the Vedic dharma, the Adityas represent the various houses of the Zodiac. Aryaman belongs to the Zodiacal houses of Leo and Virgo. Consumption implicates the incorporation of Soma's properties into a Vedic force or to the worshiper. Here, those properties are incorporated into Aryaman and is conveyed to the Vedic forces and to the worshiper upon consumption.

55. Soma is consumed by the Bhaga. (RV 9.108.14.)

The Vedic force of Bhaga is an Aditya. In the Vedic dharma, the Adityas represent the various houses of the Zodiac. Bhaga belongs to the Zodiacal houses of Leo. Consumption implicates the incorporation of Soma's properties into a Vedic force or to the worshiper. Here, those properties are incorporated into Bhaga and is conveyed to the Vedic forces and to the worshiper upon consumption.

56. Soma is consumed by the Mitra. (RV 9.108.14.)

Mitra is an Aditya and presides over a zodiacal house, and that Mitra consumes Soma implicates that Soma's properties are incorporated into this Vedic force and zodiacal house and is conveyed to the Vedic forces and to the worshiper upon consumption.

57. Soma is consumed by the Varuna. (RV 9.108.14.)

Varuna is an Aditya and presides over a zodiacal house, and that Varuna consumes Soma implicates that Soma's properties are incorporated into this Vedic force and zodiacal zodiacal house and is conveyed to the Vedic forces and to the worshiper upon consumption.

58. By consuming Soma, the worshiper is the Knower of the Sun world. (RV 9.108.2.)

The consumption of Soma results in a higher level of knowledge. Here, the worshiper knows the "Sun World," which is coded language for the Svar.

59. Soma instilled Food in Manu, the earliest man, and later bringing these riches to the worshiper. (RV 9.96.12.)

In the Vedic dharma Manu is the equivalent of the Vedic Adam, the first man. In the first instance, when the human race first appeared, the properties of Soma imbued Manu, the individual all humans can point to as their ancestor.

60. After consumed by the body Soma is resplendent (*hari*) and ruddy (*aruSol*). (RV 9.8.6.)

"Resplendent" and "ruddy" are Vedic coded language. Resplendent implicates the highest level of enlightenment and illumination. Ruddy is a darker shade of red and implicates a level of awareness lower than complete self-realization, but at a level of awakening beyond the beginning of the spiritual journey.

CONTEMPLATION, DELIBERATION

Contemplation and Deliberation are an important part of the worshiper's journey to liberation and salvation.

- From the act of Contemplation or Deliberation the worshiper gains Insightful Knowledge.
- From this Insightful Knowledge, the worshiper obtains Discernment.
- From Discernment, the worshiper obtains Divine Vision.

Contemplation is defined in the epithets as that activity of *Tapas* or askeseis, which are defined as intense thought or meditation. (Epithet No. 69.) In this way, the epithets clearly indicate that contemplation has an obvious mental aspect. Soma is responsible for providing for the capability of humans to think, deliberate and become aware. (Epithet No. 61.) In addition, Soma gives birth to human thoughts and *is* that human thought. Soma is the Contemplator of Men. (Epithet No. 62.) This is a very telling Epithet. The Veda recognizes that the worshiper is a thinking subject. However, the worshiper is a thinking subject because Soma superimposes the worshiper's thoughts for the worshiper. If this sounds like Classical Vedanta, you're correct. Soma thereby becomes the subject and the object of human thought. This reconciles the epithets in which Soma impels --- is the Efficient Cause --- humans' thoughts, the Contemplator of humans and is inside human thought. (Epithet No. 66.)

61. This Soma (*pappivaa/Msam*) makes the human thinking mind (*dhii/ro*) more aware. (RV 6.47.3.)

62. Soma is the Contemplator of Men (*nRca/kSasaM*). (RV 9.8.9.)

63. Soma Contemplates on All the Forms (*ruupaa/*). (RV 9.85.12.)

64. May Blissful Discrimination (*dakshina*) come to the worshiper. (AV 18.4.50.)

65. Soma is the wise thinker (*dhii/raas*). (RV 10.25.5.)

66. Soma Impels the Thoughts of Human Beings. (RV 9.21.7.)

Impulsion is an important concept in the Vedic dharma and an important concept to Soma. Impulsion is a defining feature of Soma. Impulsion supplies the very impetus for consciousness, Mind, thoughts, indeed, to all forms of mental activity. According to the Vedas, the subtle energies which kick-start the living force of the worshiper is called, isas, translated as "impulse" or "impulsion." Not to be confused with a related topic, "life Force," more commonly known as "breath" or "prana," isas is the ignition that starts a motor vehicle; so the impulse provides those energies required to run the many other physiological functions of the worshiper. So without the impulse, prana, breath and the other bodily functions of the worshiper would be impossible, or, so to speak, stuck in neutral.

67. Soma Generates Humans' Thoughts. (RV 9.96.5.)

This is another aspect of Impulsion. The generation, the creation, of human thought is a prime example of Impulsion.

68. Soma is inside (*anta/H*) human thought (*dhiinaa/m*). (RV 9.12.9.)

69. Soma is the great one (*mahe/*) in *Tapas* or askeseis.

DELIVERANCE

There are two parts to Deliverance. The first part concerns the conflict and tension which gives rise to the need for deliverance. This is implicated in the first epithet that indicates that the conflict is between evil and sin and sacrifice. (Epithet No. 70.) The implication is that participation in the sacrifice. The last two epithets indicate the result of the resolution of the conflict. When that conflict between evil and sin and sacrifice is resolved, Soma wipes away the sin and debts of the worshiper. (Epithets Nos. 71 and 72.)

> 70. Soma (*indu*) protects the worshipers and everyone connected with the sacrifice from evil and sin (*srava*). (RV 9.56.4.)

Soma's protection is available to all sentient beings.

> 71. Soma protects the worshiper from sin. (RV 10.25.8.)

This saman (mantra) explains how Soma provides for the worshiper's salvation.

> 72. Soma wipes away the worshiper's debts. (RV 9.110.1.)

One of the many insights of David Graeber's book, *Debt, the First 500 Years*, is the connection between becoming indebted and guilt. A universal theme in world religion is that humans are born indebted, that is, with a burden of some stain on the human character. In Christian religions, that concept is known as Original Sin. Soma erases the burden of Original Sin.

58

DIFFICULTY, WATER AND THUNDER

The path to salvation and liberation is beset with difficulties. These difficulties are symbolized by Thunder. The category of Difficulty consists of two elements: Thunder is symbolized by Thunder and Water. Soma thunders. (Epithet No. 73.) Like the thunder, the ground will shake, the nerves will rattle, and an immense sound will fill the heavens. The earthly force is formidable; as a spiritual force it is equally so. Soma's thunder is eternal because it does not decay. (Epithet No. 74.) Like water, this commotion will be followed by the downfall of water, reassuring the jarred nerves. While there will always be disturbances and conflicts along the path to salvation and liberation, final salvation must be achieved with a clear mind and soul. As a result of these disturbances, the worshiper receives the fulness of the vast plenitude. (Epithet No. 80.)

This phase of spiritual development is symbolized sacrificially when the Soma juice passes through the pressing stones and sieve. The collective message from the Ninth Mandala is that while it passes through the sieve, Soma "roars." (Epithet No. 75.)

73. When purified Soma thunders (*stanalyann*) in front of the worshiper. (RV 9.86.9.)

74. When Soma thunders (roars) he is free of decay. (RV 9.72.6.)

75. Reaching the peak of heaven (*divol*) Soma roars and cries out. (RV 9.86.9.)

76. Soma passes through the sieve roaring. (RV 9.106.14.)

77. Soma Holds the Thunderbolt. (RV 9.53.1.)

78. Soma thunders like the Maruts (*maru/taam*). (RV 9.70.6.)

79. As the thunderer, Indra presses out Soma. (RV 9.51.2.)

80. Soma Bestows the great plenitude (*vaa/jaaya*). (RV 9.86.34.)

DISCERNMENT

Discernment is another stage of consciousness which leads the worshiper to liberation in the spiritual journey. This is an important stage. From Discernment, the worshiper obtains Divine Vision, the precursor stage to rapture and ultimate liberation. (Epithet No. 85.) Soma has penetrating Wisdom. (Epithet No. 82.) The worshiper receives discernment from Soma. (Epithet No. 85.) Soma has this discernment. (Epithet No. 83.) That discernment is eternal. (Epithet No. 84.)

81. Soma is the Sage among the wise. (RV 9.95.3.)

82. Soma Has Penetrating Wisdom (*nRca/kSasaM*). (RV 9.1.9.)

83. Soma has discernment (*da/kSa*). (RV 8.48.8.)

84. Soma's discernment (*da/kSam*) is eternal (*sa/naa*). (RV 9.4.3.)

85. Soma brings the happy discernment (*da/kSam*) to the worshiper in its rapture. (RV 10.25.1.)

DISPENSATION

There is a decided sacrificial element to this category. Dispensation is the category dealing with one of the two elements in the greater category of Sacrifice. The Vedic sacrifice ritual is intended to demonstrate a fundamental truth of the universe: that there is a give-and-take between the Microcosm (humankind) and the Macrocosm (the universe), of every object therein, encompassing the process from creation to dissolution. This give-and-take is the essence of how the natural order (*Rta*) operates.

This give-and-take is an outgrowth of the binary, dualistic Two-Dimensional Universe. On the one hand, the worshiper seeks and offers obligations to the chosen Vedic force or energy. On the other hand, the force and energy of the chosen Vedic force is channeled to the worshiper. On a rudimentary level, this give-and-take is the bargained for exchange for the condition of life in the universe: One being dies so another may live. The dynamics of the exchange takes many forms and is premised on a fundamental assumption that if it is accurately performed sacrifice has a secret power to produce the desired effect. The dynamics in this new level demonstrates the give-and-take process which has been operating every moment in the material universe for eons.

This give-and-take is reflected in several ways. In the sacrificial level, an offering is made to receive blessings. The left-handed movement of the giving is based on a simple premise. Divine powers are associated with and inherent to the action of giving. The right-handed movement of discernment is reflected in and a product of the sacrifice itself, which establishes consciousness, mind and thought.

This give-and-take is carried out in the simple act of giving of an offering and the invoking of a divinity so that the sacrificer may also take his or her reward, which is redemption, being born again, purification, or obtain the divinity's grace. In the Soma sacrifice this give-and-take is played out by the "killing" of the Soma plant, the giving its own life literally squeezing its life out through the pressing process, so that the sacrificer receives spiritual redemption and divine bliss.

On an individual level, the essence of yajna, the sacrifice, is the interchange between the embodied soul and conscious human nature and the eternal spirit. It is stated plainly in the Vajaseneyi Yajurveda Samhita that by worshiping Bala (Indra) the worshiper acquires and Increases their own Indra-powers (*Indriyam*), specifically by giving powers of knowledge for the worshipers willing to put forth the effort.

Dispensation is instrumental in this grand, cosmic interplay. Soma is the grand puppet-master. Just as in traditional Christian liturgies, bread is given to the congregation to symbolize the sharing of the body of Christ, the distilled Soma juice is consumed by the worshiper to experience the ecstasy of liberation with the Universal Atman. Consumption, though, is one Element, dispensation is another. Dispensation is the subtle element of the act of giving. The Epithets in this category further explain the thought behind the act of Giving. The act of Dispensation is calculated to elevate the consciousness of the worshiper. (Epithet no. 88.) It enables the worshiper to enter the realm of heaven. (Epithet No. 89.) It is through this act of Dispensation that the worshiper unites with the Universal Consciousness. (Epithet Nos. 90 and 91.) On a broader note, the act of Giving dispenses energies to the worshiper. (Epithet No. 101.) Specifically, through the act of this Dispensation, Soma

- Conveys vigor. (Epithet No. 94.)
- Gives Health. (Epithet No. 95.)
- Fosters physical strength. (Epithet No. 96.)
- Gives long life. (Epithet No. 97.)

Viewed though these Epithets, Soma can be seen as a precursor to the art of Ayurveda. Also, through the act of Dispensation, Soma

- Confers the Life-Force for the Sun. (Epithet No. 106.)
- Supports the Cows, (Epithet No. 107), symbolic speech for Inspired Knowledge.
- Supports the waters, (Epithet No. 109), representative of the Vedic dharma.
- Yoked the horses (Epithet No. 111), the metaphor of the Monkey Mind.

Soma is the active agent of the first element of the act of Dispensation, as demonstrated in these epithets:

86. Soma is the most generous dispenser. (RV 9.66.17.)

In the Vedic dharma, dispensation is the active movement of conveying the spiritual endowments and benefits to the worshiper and other sentient beings.

87. Soma is Always Keen to Distribute Food. (RV 9.90.1.)

Food is another code word. In the coded language of the Veda, to say something is food is to refer to the entire universe and all that exists in it. (BU 1.5.1.) The entire Natural Order, in fact, is divided into two parts, the eater and the eaten. (SPB 10.6.2.1.) In the Veda, food, that which is eaten, takes several forms. For our purposes, Soma is food. (RV 9.55.2; 9.41.4; 9.61.1, 3; 9.9.63.2; 9.64.13; 9.65.13; 9.66.4, 23, 31; 9.71.8; 9.74.2, 3; 9.85.3; 9.91.5; 9.97.5; 9.99.2; 9.101.11; 9.104.) Soma is food of the gods. (10.94.6.)

88. This Soma (*pappivaa/Msam*) elevates the level of human speech (*vaa/cam*). (RV 6.47.3.)

This saman (mantra) demonstrates an entirely different dimension to Soma's capability to provide Articulation to the Vedic dharma. There are different levels of Speech in the Vedic dharma (*Rta*); indeed, the Vedic dharma is represented by Speech. (JUB 1.2.1, 2.) It is only through speech that the articulation of names is obtained (SA, 5.4), and thereby making the sensible world intelligible. The material and esoteric are then harmonized in the Saman chant. Saman is the Word (Vak). Without Speech no form could exist. (SB, 2.5.) Without speech, any form could not be known, and the worshiper would be bereft of intelligence. Soma acts in conjunction with Indra to dispense Speech to all sentient and non-sentient beings The Vedic forces of Indra and Soma create the "regions" (read: the cosmos) but does not say how. It is through the Articulation of Mind and Matter. Having obtained information from the sensory organs; the worshiper obtains all names, through smell all odors through speech with intelligence; all sounds, through the tongue with intelligence all taste through sight with intelligence all forms, through hearing with intelligence; all feeling, through the body with intelligence all pleasure and pain through the hands with intelligence; all "dalliance" and joy through the generative organ with intelligence; all motion through the feet with intelligence; and all thoughts through the mind with intelligence. (SA, 5.7)

89. Through the help of Soma humans ascend to heaven. (AB 1.19.)
This is another way in which Soma provides the salvation of the worshiper.

90. Soma conveys the spiritual riches (*raaya/H*) from four oceans (*samudraa/Msh catu/ro*) to the worshiper. (RV 9.33.8.)

91. Soma grants Universal Consciousness (*vi/shvaani ce/tasaa*) to the worshiper. (RV 9.20.3.)
Soma and its consumption is one method of achieving Universal Consciousness.

92. Soma provides the Fullness of Plenty (*vaa/jaaM+ iyarti go/mataH*) to the Wise (*vi/praa*ya). (RV 10.25.11.)
This is another reference to the Plentitude. The Plentitude is actually a significant theme with Soma in the Vedic dharma. The Plentitude provides a picture of the fullness of the Soma experience.

93. Soma provides illumination to the worshiper's eyes. (RV 7.91.4.)
Illumination is a separate building bloc which will be discussed later.

94. Soma provides vigor (*o/jo*) to the worshiper. (RV 7.91.4.)
Vigor is needed to embark on the spiritual journey.

95. Soma Provides Health (*ayus*). (RV 9.80.2.)

65

Health and physical integrity is another Element to religious ecstacy. A healthy body is a requirement due to the intensity of the Soma experience.

96. Soma supplies the physical strength (*uu/rjaM*) in human beings. (RV 9. 80.2.)

97. Soma Provides Long Life. (RV 9.64.14.)
Long life is an occasional result of spiritual and bodily purity.

98. Soma Provides Food. (RV 9. 80.2.)
Continuing on the meaning of this code-word, "Food" in this context is the body of Soma itself. It is the ultimate form of self-sacrifice: Soma is consumed by the worshiper that the worshiper may incorporate the spiritual endowments of Soma.

99. Soma conveys (*pavasva*) golden riches (*hi/raNyavad*) to the worshiper. (RV 9.63.18.)
Ayurvedic texts frequently refer to the "killing" of a substance such as gold or mercury. (R., 2.216.) The Vedas and Brahmans also speak of the "killing" of Soma. (K.B., 3.32; SPB 3.2.6.6; 3.9.4.3; 3.9.4.8; 3.9.4.23; 4.3.4.1.) According to the Ayurvedic sciences, Soma is "killed" when it is pressed by the pressing stone. The "killing" presupposes a prior, impure, state. The thought that underlies this process is just as a human being once killed cannot be brought back to life, so a metal or substance once "killed" cannot return to its original, previous state. The only distinction here is that when Soma is killed when the Soma juice is distilled (i.e., purified) during the Soma Sacrifice, through the self-sacrifice of Soma its properties are endowed to the worshiper.

100. Soma conveys (*pavasva*) Energies (*a/shvaavat*) to the worshiper. (RV 9.63.18.)
These are the energies that power the Vedi dharma.

101. Soma conveys (*pavasva*) the energy of life (*viira/vat*) to the worshiper. (RV 9.63.18.)
These energies are those which sustain the worshiper's body.

102. Soma conveys (*pavasva*) Articulation of Light (*go/mantam*) to the worshiper. (RV 9.63.18.)

The Saman --- the mantras of the Ninth Mandala --- is the Word. (CU, 1.1.5.) In this sense the Word is the articulation of the universe. In its gross form the Word becomes Speech. Speech, the Word, is the light of prana. (TS, 5.3.2.3.) Both are endowed to the worshiper during the Soma Sacrifice.

103. Soma is the Giver of the Life-Force for the Lord of the Vedic dharma (*varunaya*), the Natural Order (*Rta*). (RV 9.84.1.)

104. Soma is the Giver of Bliss (*ma/dhor dhaa/raabhir*). (RV 9.5.3.)
Bliss is the principle property of the endowments of Soma.

105. Soma is the Giver of the Life-Force for the Sun (*indraya*). (RV 9.84.1.)
Soma gives strength before Indra sets out to fight Vrtra.

106. Soma is the Giver of the Life-Force for the Wind (*vayava*). (RV 9.84.1.)
Vayava is the functional equivalent to prana, the life-force of the worshiper.

107. Soma is the Giver of Cows (*gosaa*). (RV 9.2.10; 9.55.3.)
All the properties of Cows, Knowledge, et al., are dispensed to the worshiper.

108. Soma is the Giver of Strength (*vayodhaa/s*). (RV 8.48.15.)
Similar to vigor, strength is a prerequisite to embarking on a spiritual journey.

109. Soma is the giver of waters (*apsaa/M*). (RV 1.91.21.)
The waters are the inner essence of the Vedic dharma. This is a spiritual endowment of Soma.

110. Soma is the Giver of Strength (*vajaasaa*). (RV 9.2.10; 9.55.3.
Vayaasaa is a higher degree of the strength in Epithet 108.

111. Soma is the Giver of Horses (*ashvasaa*). (RV 9.2.10.)

Discussed in the Introduction, the properties of the Horse is a spiritual endowment from Soma.

112. Soma crushes the negative forces (*ni*) so that the worshiper may recover riches of inspiration (*rayi/M shravaa/yyam*). (RV 9.63.23.)

This is one way in which Soma dispenses its spiritual endowments to the worshiper.

113. Soma enhances the inherent nature (*svadha*) of the divine Vedic forces. (RV 3.47.1.)

Svadha is defined as an inherent power which upholds its own nature, following its own law or nature. Svadha also refers to the essential nature of Change and the other dynamic forces in the Vedic pantheon. On a personal level, svadha implicates the means by which the qualities present in the Vedic divine forces may be implementation into the life of the worshiper. Soma not only dispenses its own svadha to the worshiper, and, as it says here, the svadha from the other Vedic forces.

114. Soma Brings Universal Life (*vishva-ayu*). (RV 9.4.10.)

This is equivalent to Self-Realization.

115. Soma is Makes Everyone in the Universe Noble. (RV 9.63.5.)

116. Soma makes the unmanifested powers become manifested. (RV 9.67.11.)

DIVINE VISION

Divine Vision is an important Element in the spiritual aspect of the Vedic dharma. Not only is it an important stage of liberation but is also a symbol of the pervasion which is the natural order, the Vedic dharma.

Soma not only permeates all creation, it permeates *Rta* itself. *Rta* is the underlying principle which empowers the entire Vedic dharma. Soma is *Rta/van*, born or possessed of *Rta*. This is no mean characteristic, as the only other Vedic force possessed of *Rta* is Agni, the personification of the element of the fire of Change. (RV 1.72.1, 2, 5; 2.35.8; 3.13.2; 3.20. 4; 4.2.1; 4.6.5; 4.2.1; 4.7.7; 5.1.6; 5.25.1; 6.12.1; 6.15.1; 6.15.13; 7.3.1; 7.7.4; 5.28.2; 10.2.2;10.6.2; 10.7.4.) Agni is also *Rta/jata*: 1.36.19; 1.144.7; 1.189.6; 3.6.10; 6.13.3.)

One of the most common characteristics assigned to Soma is *vi/shvaa*, or "pervasion," its ability to pervade and permeate the cosmos, the sacrificial hall and the world. (RV 9.1.10; 9.3,4; 9.4.2; 9.8.7; 9.14.8; 9.16.6; 9.18.6; 9.20.1, 3; 9.21.4; 9.23.1; 9.25.4; 9.28.2, 5; 9.29.4;9.36.5; 9.40.1, 4; 9.42.5; 9.43.2; 9.9.54.3; 9.55.1; 9.57.2, 4; 9.59.3, 4; 9.61.19, 24, 25, 28, 30; 9.64.6, 8, 18; 9.65.2, 9, 10; 9.66.1; 9.73.8; 9.80.3, 4; 9.84.2; 9.85.11; 9.86.6, 15, 24, 26, 30, 41, 48; 9.87.6; 9.88.2; 9.89.6; 9.90.1, 6; 9.94.3, 5; 9.97.51; 9.98.7; 9.100.2; 9.102.1; 9.107.23; 9.108.11; 9.109.4, 8, 9, 14; 9.9.110.9; and 9.111.5.) Not only does it permeate or pervade the universe, it is "all pervading," *vishvacakSa*. In this regard a common adjective used in connection with Soma is *sahasra*. Subject to several meanings, Wilson translates *sahasra* as "thousand" but it can also mean "innumerable." Keshav Dev Verma has given this word in the Vedas a gloss in terms of modern particle physics and interprets *sahasra* simply as "the universe." (Verma, *Vedic Physics* (2008 Motilal Banarsidass). A rendering with this gloss gives much more meaning to ordinary translations, for example, in RV 1.10.11, Soma is said to give the worshiper a "thousand gifts." Those "thousand gifts" point to the enormity of the specific spiritual benefits originating from the Vedic dharma. Having drunk the Soma Juice, the worshiper is given the essence of the world, the universe, the Vedic dharma.

In addition to being identified with the Vedic dharma, Divine Vision is a beginning stage towards liberation. Soma is the great Guru. The epithets which follow all elaborate on the characteristics of the Great Guru and barely needs commentary:

117. Soma is Divine (*divyam*).

118. Soma is the Secret Seer (*kavi\r giirbhi/H*). (RV 9.96.17.)

119. Soma possesses divine vision. (RV 8.48.15.)

120. Soma is all seeing (*sva\rcakSaa*). (RV 9.97.46.)

121. Soma Has the mind of the Seers (*kavi*). (RV 9.96.18.)

122. Soma is Many-Eyed. (RV 9.26.3.)
This is a code word for omniscient. Soma is omniscient.

123. Soma Has a Thousand Eyes (*saha/sracakSasam*). (RV 9.60.1.)

124. Soma is the Seer (*Rishir*). (RV 9.87.3.)

125. Soma is the Sage (*vi/praH*). (RV 9.87.3.)

126. When the Soma juice is consumed the worshiper acquires the powers of Indra. (RV 8.48.10.)

127. Soma Is Gandharva, Divine in Vision. (RV 9.86.36.)

128. Soma has penetrating vision (*kavi/H*). (RV 9.62.30.)

129. Soma is the greatest among the Sages (*vi/praaNaam mahiSo/*). (RV 9.96.6.)

DURATION

Duration is the subtle category of Time. Time is everywhere around us. At any given moment of the day, Time is everywhere, displayed on our cell phones, on the computers, on our watches. This inadvertently creates the impression of absolute time. But this is not necessarily so. In the Vedic dharma, Time is the Sun, the creator of the flow of Time. It is for this reason that the Vedic astrologer knows Time to be relative. As with space, this is due not only to the relative position of the observer, but to the fundamental makeup of the natural order of things. All units of Time reside in the Waters, and the Waters reside in the Sun. The Vedas love paradox, but the worshiper knows there is no paradox to assert the Waters reside in the Sun. The Sun is the source of all life, and the Waters is the source of the essential nature of the Vedic dharma, the mechanism which winds the watch of life. Specifically, "the Waters" is coded language for that element of the Vedic dharma whose essential nature is a flowing or field. Examples of this use of the Waters are found in the following fields:

- The current or field of consciousness present in the natural order.
- The expanse or field of Immortality.
- The current, flow or field of energy present in the universe.
- The field of pervasion (*prnita*).

Time flows. Time pertains to the sequential ordering of things and percolates through different existential levels. For that reason, the quality, quantity and appreciation is relative to the existential level occupied by

71

the observer. In this case, that observer is the worshiper and Soma is the purveyor of Time. There is an order or sequencing that regulates the movement of physical objects and the sequence in which that movement occurs. The Vedic dharma, the natural order of things, receives the flow of Time thus created and operates and regulates that movement. One element of this sequential ordering is *Rta* itself. Remember *Rta*? *Rta* is the active principle that

- controls the regulation of time and the temporal sequence of everyday life.
- maintains the balance between the cosmic and microcosmic levels.
- the macro- and microcosmic and all the levels of existence found therein.

All these properties of *Rta* are reflected in the constituent parts of Time. Time is both existence and all possible other existences. It is for this reason that there is a multiplicity of universes in the Vedic dharma. This in part in the past, present and future existences. The Surya Siddanta analyzes time in the following elements:

- There are two types of Time, finite and infinite.
- Infinite Time is that which there is no beginning nor end.
- Finite Time is that which is capable of being measured, where we can know its beginning and end.

The Surya Siddanta analyzes Time in these most essential elements:

- There are two types of Time, finite and infinite.
- Infinite Time is that which there is no beginning nor end.
- Finite Time is that which is capable of being measured, where we can know its beginning and end.
- Finite Time is further divided into Real and Unreal Time.
- Real Time is that which can be quantitatively measured.
- Unreal Time is that which is so instantaneous that it cannot be measured.

Time operates relative to these qualities. An exposition of time is found in the Atharvaveda. The description in the Atharvaveda emphasizes the influence of Time on the material regulation of the material world:

- Time generated the sky and the earth. (AV 19.53.5.)
- In the very beginning of the universe Time created the Lord of Creation, the Progenitor which created all other creatures. (AV 19.53.10.)
- Time created all those things which were and shall be. (AV 19.54.3.)

Soma continues this Vedic tradition regarding time. Soma is invoked at Dawn. This is taken to mean the physical start of the day and the dawning of understanding. Dawn becomes day, day becomes night, and so on and so forth. Soma creates the days and nights. Soma is Chandra, the Moon. The days and nights shape the Moon, and the Moon shapes the monthly cycles. Those cycles become seasonal and morph into years. Thus, regulatory and sequential order of things are informed with a foundation of Soma.

130. Soma shapes the months (*maa/sa*). (RV 10.85.5.)

131. Soma is Associated with the Seasons (*rtubhih*). (RV 9.66.3.)

132. Soma shapes the years. (RV 10.85.5.)

133. Soma Is the Night. (SPB, 3.4.4.15.)

134. Purified Soma Appears Silvery During the Night (*na/ktam Rjra/H*). (RV 9.97.9.)

135. Soma is the Creator of the Days and Dawn. (RV 9.86.19.)

136. Soma is invoked at dawn. (RV 7.41.2.)

137. Soma is the Moon. (YV 12.112; 10.30; SPB, 10.4.3.1.)

Soma receives its power and in turn presides over these members of the stellar population: Soma is the presiding deity and personification of the Moon; Soma is the presiding deity, in alignment with the Lunar houses of Agni and Prajapati, of ruling the zodiacal houses of Vrsabha (Taurus) and Mithuna (Gemini); Soma rules over the spiritual endowments from the asterism of Mrgashirsha.

The Vedic astrologer knows that Soma occupies a position much exalted in the astrological Vedic dharma. Soma is situated in the Lunar mansion of Mrghashira, which is itself in an exalted position. The eminent Vedic scholar, Bal Ganghadar Tilak, postulated in The Orion, of the Antiquities of the Vedas, that Mrghashira was identified by the ancients as the Orion Star, signified the beginning of the Vernal Equinox, and subtly was associated with the devayana, the Northern Path trod by the worshiper's soul after death. (Tilak, Orion, or the Antiquities of the Vedas (1898), p. 107.) In an interpretative note, in much the same way that the Big and Little Dippers are represented as bears, Tilak deduces that the references in the Vedas of deers and antelopes are references to Orion or the Mrghashira asterism. (RV 2.34.3, 4; 2.36.2; 4.21.8; 5.53.1; 5.55.6; 6.75.11; 7.40.3; 7.87.6; 8.2.6; 8.7.36.) Tilak's deductions further a deeper understanding to the message of the Vedas. The reason the Vedas reveal that the Maruts in their dazzling, blazing, glory traveled the skies on the deer was because Orion itself is the brightest Star in the evening sky. (RV 1.37.2; 5.58.6; 5.60.2.) The deer is identified with Soma. (RV 10.94.5.) The deer is mrgam (RV 8.5.36), so it is not a huge stretch to call Soma's Lunar house "Mrghashira." Mrgam --- which references either collectively or individually the Vernal Equinox, Orion, the devayana, the Northern Path, the Lunar house of Soma, Mrghashira, or Soma itself --- is found in many other passages in the Rg Veda. (RV 1.80.7; 1.105.7; 2.33.11; 5.29.4; 8.1.20; 8.2.6; 8.5.36; 8.69.15.) But we are getting ahead of ourselves.

EARTH, THE RECEPTIVE

In the category of Approach, Soma is instrumental in uniting the two opposing poles of Earth and Heaven. Soma is the image is the earth. In this capacity, it is the perfect complement of Heaven, the Creative Principle, discussed a little later. Heaven, the Creative Principle, is the complement, not the opposite, for the Receptive Principle, the Earth, which does not combat the Creative; it completes and complements the Receptive Principle. In this category, Soma symbolizes one part of that union, Earth. This interchange is symbolized by the Falcon bringing Soma to the Earth, Epithet No. 139. The Receptive Principle is accomplished by the Earth receiving Soma from the Falcon; that the Falcon arrived from the Heavens symbolize the Heaven/Earth duality. It represents nature in contrast to spirit, earth in contrast to heaven, space as against time, the female-maternal as against the male-paternal. However, as applied to human affairs, the principle of this complementary relationship is found not only in the relation between man and woman, but also in that between prince and minister and between father and son. Indeed, even in the individual this duality appears in the coexistence of the spiritual world and the world of the senses. But strictly speaking there is no real dualism here. There are laws that Earth observes, just as Heaven, and Soma sustain the Earth through its laws (Epithet No. 144), because there is a clearly defined hierarchic relationship between the two principles.

138. Soma is the Holder of Earth. (RV 9.89.6.)

139. Soma is Brought to Earth by a Falcon (*shyenabhRta*). (RV 9.71.1; 9.87.6.)

140. Soma is the Bull of Earth. (RV 9.44.28.)
The Bull is another symbol, the symbol for the principle of Regeneration.

The Bull is *vrsanaa*, the Showerer of benefits. For its many regenerative properties, a Vedi force closely related to Soma, Agni (Fire), is described as the "Bull (*vRSabha*) of the Standing Waters." (RV 7.5.2; 2.35.13.) This is a quality and capacity shared by other Vedic forces: Indra; (RV 1.7.6,7; 1.52.23; 1.108.3, 7, 8, 9, 11, 12; 2.17.8; 4.50.10; 5.33.2; 6.22.8; 6.33.1; 6.44.20; 7.31.4; 8.85.7; 10.153...2.); Agni, of course, (RV 1.112.8; 3.27.25; 6.1.1; 8.73.10; 10.191.1); Agni-Soma, (RV 1.93.6); Indragni, (RV 1.108.3, 7, 8, 9, 11, 12); Indra-Soma, (RV 7.104.1); Indra-Varuna, (RV 6.68.11; 7.60.9; 7.82.2; 7.83.9); the Asvins, (RV 1.112.8; 1.116.22; 1.117.3, 4, 8, 12, 15, 18, 19, 25; 1.118.1, 6; 1.119.4; 1.157.5;1.158.1; 1.180.7; 1.181.8; 1.183.1; 1.184.2; 2.41.8; 5.74.1; 5.75.4, 9; 6.62.7; 7.70.7; 7.71.6; 7.73.3; 7.74.3; 8.5.24, 27, 36; 8.22.8, 9, 12, 16; 8.26.1, 2, 5, 12, 15; 8.35.15; 10.39.9); Mitra-Varuna, (RV 1.151.2, 3; 1.151.2; 7.60.9, 10; 7.61.5); and the Maruts. (RV 2.33.13; 7.56.18, 20; 7.58.6; 8.20.16; 10.93.5). And of course, Soma. (RV 2.40.3; 8.93.19; 9.5.6; 9.19.5; 9.64.2.)

141. Soma is Reposed on the Earth. (RV 9.85.11.)

142. Soma's glories (*dhamani*) are in Earth (*pRthivyaa/M*). (RV 1.91.4.)

143. Soma makes the Earth (*prthivii/*) mighty (*mahii/*). (RV 10.85.2.)

144. Soma upholds earth with his laws (*dha/rmabhiH*). (RV 9.86.9.)

EFFICIENT CAUSE

In the *Timaeus*, Plato posits that for any object there are two causes. One is the cause which results from the mechanical contact of one object against another. The other, which is discussed next is Element, that cause which originates from the laws of Providence. The first type is where the first object is the Efficient Cause of the other.

The role of Soma as the Efficient Cause is of utmost importance to the Natural Order, *Rta*.

In any action there are two components. There is first the Causation agent, that which effects the action, and there is second, an object which is the recipient to that which causes, i.e., the result. If A causes B, A is the causal agent and B is the result. In the same way, there are two sides to Efficient Cause. One is the cause itself, and two is the result of that cause. As the causal agent, Soma is the Efficient Cause, in other words, A. This category, Efficient Cause, lists those qualities which are the result of Soma's essential nature.

145. Soma is the First-Born. (RV 9.5.9.)

146. Soma is the Efficient Cause (*iSa/yann*) which brings humans near (spiritual) riches (*u/paavasuH*). (RV 9.84.3.)

147. Soma is the Efficient Cause (*i/saH*) of things Golden (*hi/raNyavat*). (RV 9.61.3.)

148. Soma is the Efficient Cause (*i/saH*) of the Brilliance of Knowledge (*go/mad*). (RV 9.61.3.)

149. Soma is the Efficient Cause (*i/saH*) of distributed food (*ksa/traa*). (RV 9.61.3.)

150. Soma is the Efficient Cause (*i/saH*) of an Oblation of Food to Deceased Ancestors (*Kavi*). (RV 9.74.2.)

151. Soma is the Efficient Cause (*i/saH*) of Revealed Knowledge (*jaj~naano/ jana/yann*). (RV 9.3.10.)

152. Soma is the Efficient Cause (*i/saH*) of the desire of Food (*pracakraaNa/m*). (RV 9.15.7.)

153. Soma is the Efficient Cause (*i/saH*) of Lenten Food (*prajaa/ vatiir*). (RV 9.23.3.)

154. Soma is the Efficient Cause (*i/saH*) of Sacrificial Food (*yaata/ yann*). (RV 9.39.2.)

155. Soma is the Efficient Cause (*i/saH*) of Food Measured in the Thousands (*vidaa/H sahasri/Niir*). (RV 9.40.4.)

156. Soma is the Efficient Cause (*i/saH*) of Abundant Food (*pa/vasv patho/ ra/jaH a bRhatii/r*). (RV 9.42.6.)

157. Soma is the Efficient Cause (*i/saH*) of Abundant Wholesome Food (*ayakSmaa/ bRhatii/r*). (RV 9.49.1.)

158. Soma is the Efficient Cause of Speech (*vaa/cam iSiraa/m*). (RV 9.84.4.)

159. Soma Causes the Sun (*suu/ryam*) to Radiate (*dhaa/man*). (RV 9.28.5.)

160. Soma Causes the Sun (*suu/ryam*) to Shine. (RV 9.37.4.)

161. Soma Causes Heaven and Earth (*ro/dasii*) to Shine Out. (RV 9.85.12.)

162. Soma is the Efficient Cause of clarity of mind (*ghRta/vaanti*). (RV 9.63.13.)

163. Soma Causes the Sun (*suu/rya*) to Move Up to Heaven (*devavii/tama*). (RV 9.107.7.)

164. Soma causes happiness (*mayobhu/va*). (RV 1.91.9.)

ENERGY, THE IMPULSION

Impulsion is the second type of Cause in the Vedic dharma. Impulsion describes Soma's role in providing the Cause of the Vedic dharma. In the *Timaeus*, Plato posits two causes concerning any one object. The last discussion presented the first type, the mechanic cause of one object making contact with the other. Plato always insisted that the teachings in his writings are not his own but have been handed down from the Eastern Mysteries. It is easy to imagine then that the idea of two causes existing at the same time originated in the Indus Valley and that the "laws of Providence" can be translated as the "laws according to the Vedic dharma," or *Rta*. Impulsion is the result, Soma's energy which propels the communication of the essential qualities of the Vedic divine forces to the worshiper. The difference between the Efficient Cause and Impulsion is one, the former, is the gross appearance of cause and movement, and the other, the latter, is the subtle basis of cause and movement. Soma is both.

Impulsion supplies the very impetus for consciousness, Mind, thoughts, indeed, all forms of mental activity. According to the Vedas, the subtle energies which kick-start the living force of the worshiper is called, isas, translated as "impulse" or "impulsion." "Impulsions" are defined as the consciousness of knowledge of the thoughts of sentient beings.

- The horses (Strength, and the power of knowledge) which were held by Vrtra. (RV 3.30.2, 6, 20; 3.34.9; 3.35.1 – 5.)
- Indra releases the power of impulsions in the vastness of the Vedic dharma which were held by Vrtra. (RV 3.30.11.)

- Indra Creates the impulsions in all sentient beings, including the worshiper, which were held by Vrtra. (RV 3.34.5.)
- In creating the impulsions in all sentient beings, Indra, as a result of the death of Vrtra, creates the words in the worshiper's speech (vi/vaaco/), which were held by Vrtra. (RV 3.34.10.)

An "Impulsion" is the medium through which the thoughts, feelings, and desires of the worshiper and all other sentient being make their presence in the mind. When Vrtra was overtaken by Indra the worshiper and sentient beings gained their thoughts. The thoughts of the worshiper and sentient beings are symbolized in different ways by the Veda. "Impulsions" are frequently described symbolically in watery terms.

- Indra releases the Rivers, symbol of the flow of Consciousness, which were held by Vrtra. (RV 3.33.1, 4, 6, 8, 10, 12.)
- Indra releases the Ocean, symbol of higher Consciousness, which was held by Vrtra. (RV 3.32.16; 3.33.2, 3.)

Indra yokes, restrains, the thoughts of the sentient beings and worshiper which while held by Vrtra were uncontrolled and unrestrained. (RV 3.35.4.) This is of course after having consumed Soma.

Impulsions are not to be confused with a related topic, "life Force," more commonly known as "breath" or "prana," isas is the ignition that starts a motor vehicle, so the impulse provides those energies required to run the many other physiological functions of the worshiper. So without the impulse, prana, breath and the other bodily functions of the worshiper would be impossible, or, so to speak, stuck in neutral. The bodily function focused in the Vedas concern Consciousness and mental activity.

These are the stages of spiritual development: The Vedic divine forces have their own essential natures. These divine natures are urged upon the worshiper. Soma is a prime catalyst for this urging, as will be explained with epithets later in this text. Urging relates to the ability of Soma to communicate the essential qualities of the divine Vedic forces to the worshiper. Impulsion is the energy fueling Soma's energy. Impulsion is an inherent characteristic of Soma. The epithets make clear that Soma flows with impulsion, and impulsion is what Soma grants to the worshiper. This is due to Soma being full of Strength, another characteristic and a separate category. The Urging is a personal action from Soma, and the Impulsion is the action itself towards the worshiper.

Soma's impulsion is a wide and an all-pervasive force. The results of Soma's impulsions are reflected in the various epithets which specify those actions for which Soma is responsible. Soma provides the impulsion which gives us the Word, for the Brilliance of Knowledge (go/mad), for the purity of thoughts (iSe/ *pavasva* dhaa/rayaa), discrimination, the worshiper's thoughts, the very vastness of the Natural Order, *Rta*. Soma, as with Urging, acts as a mediator. Soma is powered by the life energy of the universe (a/shvaavad), through the Seers (Rishiis), and Soma thereby communicates this life energy, conveyed by impulsions, to the worshiper.

The selections here are the most representative about the impulsions, where they originate, how they act, and how they affect and influence the worshiper:

165. Soma conveys perfect energy (*suvii/ryam*) to the worshiper. (RV 9.66.21)

166. Soma Flows with Impulsions (*i/saM*). (RV 9.63.2.)

167. Soma is Full of Strength. (RV 9.90.3.)

168. Soma Grants Impulsions (*iso*). (RV 9.72.9.)

169. Soma is Impelled by the Ray-Cows. (RV 9.85.5.)

Now is a good time to discuss the Ray-Cows. The Ray-Cows correspond to the Sanskrit *Go*, or *Gobhir*. The Vedic scholar R.L. Kashyap renders *go* or *gobhir* as "rays of light." He and other scholars follow this meaning first ascribed by Sri Aurobindo, and render go or gobhir "ray-cow," "rays of intuition," "rays of knowledge," or the like.

The Cow is symbolic of Knowledge in all its permutations. The Ray-Cows are no different. Indra, the incarnation of the Fire of Agni and powered by Soma, is instrumental in conveying knowledge obtained, derived, and learned from the stellar population:

- RV 1.7.3: So, in a Sukta in which Indra, as the incarnation of the Fire of Agni, presides, Indra destroys the mountain, releasing the cattle, gobhir, which, in the fire of the zodiacal house of Vrscika (Scorpio), release not simply cattle, but happiness and bliss.
- RV 1.16.9: For these same reasons, Indra, as the incarnation of the Fire of Agni, provides happiness and bliss to the worshiper.
- RV 1.53.4: Indra, as the incarnation of the Fire of Agni, in conjunction with the fire of the zodiacal house of Vrscika (Scorpio), releases happiness and bliss held by Vrtra.
- RV 1.62.5: Indra, as the incarnation of the Fire of Agni, dispels the darkness with the light shining from the planet of Jupiter and the asterisms of Jyestra.

This is Impulsion on an inter-stellar level.

170. Soma impels all the Hymns Upwards. (RV 9.86.41.)

171. Soma Gives Birth to the Force of Impulsion (*I/sa*). (RV 9.3.10.)

172. Soma Impels the Word (*Vac*). (RV 9.85.7.)

173. Soma is Impelled to the Lap of Aditi by the Ten Fingers. (RV 9.71.5.)

174. Soma Impels (*tu–njaana*) the forces which support life. (RV 9.57.2.)

175. Soma Impels the Worshiper towards the Fullness of Plenty. (RV 9.35.4.)

176. Soma Teaches humans about Impulsions (*iso*). (RV 9.87.9.)

177. Soma impels the purity of thoughts (*iSe/ pavasva dhaa/rayaa*). (RV 9.64.13.)

178. Soma gives human the powers of impulsions (*i/sas*). (RV 3.62.14.)

179. Soma flows with impulsions (*i/saM*) and energy (*uu/rjaM*). (RV 9.63.2.)

180. Soma is impelled by the Seer. (RV 9.37.6.)

181. By drinking Soma, the worshiper moves (*a\kramiid*) towards the impelling forces. (RV 9.108.2.)

182. Soma is impelled to the Supreme with a mind-set (*matii/*) of discrimination (*dhiyaa/*). (RV 9.44.2.)

183. Soma is the impeller of the journey (*gayasphaa/no*). (RV 1.91.12.)

184. The impulsive force of Soma (*i/saM*) is powered by the Brilliance of Knowledge (go/mad). (RV 9.41.4.)

185. The impulsive force of Soma (*i/saM*) has the luster of gold (hi/raNyavat). (RV 9.41.4.)

186. The impulsive force of Soma (*i/saM*) is powered by the life energy of the universe (a/shvaavad). (RV 9.41.4.)

187. The impulsive force of Soma (*i/saM*) has the Fullness of Plenty (*vaa/javat*). (RV 9.41.4.)

188. By drinking Soma, Indra, the divine force of articulation of forms, with fully conscious (*supra/keto*) to the impelling forces (*i/so*). (RV 9.108.2.)

189. Soma brings the impulsions (*i/saM*) to the chanters and the worshipers at the sacrifice. (RV 9.20.4.)

190. Soma impel, subjects (i/yarti) the world to heavenly words (*diva/ i/yarti vaa/caM*). (RV 9.68.8.)

191. Soma is possessed of the Maruts' energies (*marutvat*). (RV 6.47.5.)

192. Soma is full of energy and force (*o/jiSTho*). (RV 9.67.1.)

193. Soma is thousand-energized (*saha/sravarcasam*). (RV 9.43.4.)

194. Soma provides the energy which powers the mind (*indriya/M*). (RV 10.36.8.)

195. Soma Pavamana (*pavamaanaabhy*) is propelled (*a\rSasi*) to provide impulsion and energy (*i/sa*). (RV 9.86.35.)

ENTHUSIASM

The Element of Enthusiasm is best understood by the original derivation of the English word. "Enthusiasm" is borrowed from the Greek *enthousiasmos*, meaning "inspiration or possession by a god." For the first two hundred or so years that it was used in English, enthusiasm was primarily employed to refer to beliefs or passions that related to religion. By the beginning of the 18th century, however, the word began to be used to describe having strong feelings or interest in secular matters. Now the word can be applied to anything.

With regards to the worshiper's spiritual journey, enthusiasm is derived from the fact that the time is eminent to embark on the journey and wherein the worshiper acts in accord with it. Hence the worshiper begins. To arouse enthusiasm it is necessary for a worshiper to make the necessary adjustments and act in accordance with those adjustments.

This category is clearly related to Bliss, the quality most associated with Soma.

196. Soma is the Desire of the Gods. (RV 9.11.7.)

197. Soma is the One to Be Rejoiced In. (RV 9.24.4.)

198. Soma is Inspires Good Qualities. (RV 1.91.3.)

199. Soma is Inspires Noble Actions. (RV 1.91.3.)

200. Soma is the Fulfiller of Aspirations. (RV 9.11.7.)

ESTABLISHMENT
(MATERIAL SUPPORT)

At its basis the Vedic dharma is an organic whole. There are various parts to the Vedic dharma. By definition, in the Vedas, dharma is the totality of the natural order. (VaS, 1.1.1.) The Greek language has a wonderful word, συμπαν, meaning the vast cosmos. The word consists of two separate words, συν, meaning addition, plus, conjoining, and παν, everything. In other words, the cosmos and the Vedic dharma is "that which includes everything." That is the Vedic dharma. The Vedic dharma is everything, all together. These parts must be united with others in some sort of order that all may complement and aid one another through their mutual interaction. But the holding together calls for a central figure around whom other persons may unite. What is required is that this entire organism be united someway, somehow, by a unifying agent. To become a center of influence holding people, things and objects together is a grave matter and fraught with great responsibility. It requires greatness of spirit, consistency, and strength.

This is the function of Soma with regards to the Vedic dharma. Soma is suited for this task. In the language of the Veda, Soma provides the establishment of the Vedic dharma as whole. (Epithet no. 218.) Soma established the worlds. (Epithet no. 201.) On one level this can be interpreted to mean that Soma establishes the three levels of existence. (Epithet no. 217.) On another deeper level this explains the epithet that Soma is established in the Waters. (Epithet no 203.) The Waters in many ways is symbolic for the nature of the Vedic dharma as a whole. Soma's function in this dynamic order is two-fold. Soma establishes the Vedic dharma in many ways. (Epithet no. 212.) First, Soma provides for the material support of the

Vedic dharma. Soma established the material world (Epithet no. 215), as well as establishing the other levels of the Vedic cosmos. (Epithet no. 216.) Soma's establishment is not simply material. The second function of Soma is to provide the subtle, intangible glue to hold the Vedic dharma together. This is how Soma sustains all. (Epithet no. 210.)

The following Epithets list those objects and concepts that Soma provides their existential basis. Soma provides the gross and subtle foundation for these desperate objects and concepts.

201. Soma Established the Worlds. (RV 9.86.14.)

202. Soma is established by the chants during the Sacrifice. (RV 9.62.15.)

Mentioned earlier, the chanting at the Sacrifice --- whether they are the rcs (mantras of the Rg Veda), samans (mantras of the Sama Veda) --- plays a significant role in the creation of subtle basis for the Vedic dharma. Pursuant to RV 10.130.1. The sounds of the chanting rcs (mantras of the Rg Veda), samans (mantras of the Sama Veda), and chhandas (mantras of the Yajur Veda) of the Vedas during the sacrifice (yajna) literally mold the fabric of space-time. The alterations work on a gross, material, level and on a subtle, intangible level. Materially, space-time is altered by the very vibration of the sound waves themselves acting on the fabric of the universe. On an intangible level space-time is altered by the profound power of the revelations of the Rishiis on the Vedic astrologer's mind and soul. The power of the mind on the world around it is great. The siddhis, or supernatural powers in the Yoga Sutras, are predicated on the ability of the focused, concentrated mind to bend the physical laws of physics. All this, of course, had been revealed in the Vedas and is known to the Vedic astrologer:

- The recitation of the rcs (mantras of the Rg Veda), samans (mantras of the Sama Veda), and chhandas (mantras of the Yajur Veda) of the Vedas vibrate the very fabric of the Vedic dharma. From the vibration of these acts of worship the realm of worship was born, as well as the two aspects of Time, the Past and the Future. (RV10.90.10.)

- In this way the Purusa became this entire universe and everything in it, all of what has been, and what is to be. (RV 10.90.1; TA, 3.12.2.)

203. Soma is established in the waters (*apsu*). (RV 9.97.47.)
It bears repeating, the Waters are the basis of the inner essence of the Vedic dharma.

204. The abode of Soma is surrounded by seven allies (*sapta/jaamayaH*) and seven invokers (*ho/taaraH*). (RV 9.10.7.)
The "Seven Invokers" is representative of the Seven-Dimensional Universe.

205. Soma Establishes the Ecstasy in the Sacrificer. (RV 9.3.6.)
Ecstasy is Soma's principle spiritual endowment to the worshiper.

206. Soma is the Foundation of Indra. (RV 9.85.3.)
A very common image is Indra consuming Soma. He thereby is established of Soma.

207. Soma is Seated in the Human Body (*dronani*). (RV 9.3.1.)
Soma is established in the human body after it is consumed.

208. Soma Enters Within Becoming Aditi. (RV 8.48.2.)
This establishment is in Aditi, the leader of the Adityas, the houses of the Zodiac.

209. Soma Enters the Web of the Northern Path (*uttamaa/yyam*). (RV 9.22.6.)
The Northern and Southern Paths play a crucial role in the Vedic path to salvation and liberation. The Northern and Southern Paths are intricately tied to the most important aspects of the worshiper's spiritual journey. In fact, it concerns the greatest of all issues, whether concerning the Vedic astrologer, the worshiper, or any other person's life — the destination of soul after death. There are only two places the soul may travel upon — the Northern Path or the Southern Path. The Northern Path has these properties:

89

- It is the devayana.
- It is the Path of the Gods.
- The destination is the liberation of the worshiper's soul such that the soul does not transmigrate to the material world after death.

210. Soma sustains (*dhartaal*) all. (RV 9.76.1.)

211. Soma is manifested during the sacrifice (*bhareSujaalM sukSitilM*). (RV 1.91.21.)

212. Soma establishes the universe in many ways. (RV 10.25.8.)

213. Soma is the supporter of the Supreme Good (*varivodhaaltamo*). (RV 9.1.3.)

214. Soma is placed in the midst of the constellations (*nal kSatraaNaam*). (RV 0.85.2.)

215. Soma is established in the world (*bhulvaneSv alrpitaH*). (RV 9.86.39.)

216. Soma is established (*alrpitaH*) in the worlds (*bhulvaneSv*). (RV 9.86.39.)

217. Soma is Established in the three regions (*tridhaaltv*). (RV 9.108.12.)

218. Soma Establishes. (RV 9.78.4.)

THE FALCON

The Falcon holds a special place for Soma. It is with a Falcon that Soma descends to the world. The Falcon is closely related to the Earth element, which in the Vedic dharma is the Receptive Principle. As explained earlier, the Receptive Principle is accomplished by the Earth receiving Soma from the Falcon; that the Falcon arrived from the Heavens symbolizes the Heaven/Earth duality. It represents nature in contrast to spirit, earth in contrast to heaven, space as against time, the female-maternal as against the male-paternal. The Falcon is not just mentioned in the Ninth Mandala, but in other places in the Rig Veda, in RV 1.80.2, RV 1.93.6, RV 4.26.4, 7, RV 4.27.3, 4, and others.

The reader might wonder what all this has to do with the Falcon or with Soma. Soma is described here as the Golden Bird. (Epithet No. 221.) This is no doubt a reference to the Falcon but also is a nod to the entire concept surrounding Gold and its inner meaning. Not just here, however, but elsewhere Soma is identified with Gold. Soma itself is golden. (Epithet no. 557.) Soma, in its manifestation as Vanaspati, is golden. (Epithet no. 953.) Soma discovers the golden inner aspect of the worshiper (Epithet no. 641), thus "winning" the worshiper's gold. (Epithet no. 628). These and other mentions should not be interpreted as the worshiper hitting the lottery but achieving salvations and liberation. This is achieved through the falcon and received by the Earth, wherein the worshiper resides.

219. Soma is Brought to Earth by a Falcon (*shyenabhRta*). (RV 9.71.1; 9.87.6.)

220. Soma Looks down at the World like a Bird. (RV 9.71.9.)

221. Soma is a Golden (*hiraNya/yaM*) Bird. (RV 9.85.11.)

222. The hawk came down bringing Soma for a thousand pourings and a thousand more. (RV 4.26.4.)

223. Soma is the Falcon among Vultures. (RV 9.95.3.)

224. Well-winged, Soma Looks down on the World. (RV 9.97.33.)

FAMILY

A family consists of a mother, father, and child. In the Vedic dharma Soma is all three.

The foundation of the family is the relationship between husband and wife. This is the Feminine Principle that hold the family together lies in the loyalty and perseverance of the wife. That relationship is indicated in Epithet number 233, where the Waters is said to be the mother of Soma. The basis for this statement is based partially on the sacrificial procedure during the Soma Sacrifice. In this sacrifice, the juice of the Soma plant is distilled and purified and made ready for the worshiper. Water is an indispensable base for the finished product, Soma Pavamana. At that point it is ready for consumption by the worshiper and progression for the spiritual rapture. The spiritual rapture continues to be described in symbolically fluid terms. Soma is also described as the child of the Ocean (Epithet no. 232), implying that the Ocean is Soma's mother. This symbolic image should be taken to mean that the Ocean is the Atman, the Absolute Self, and that the worshiper is informed of the Absolute Self through the Soma Sacrifice.

That water provides the nurturing for Soma is significant, given the symbolic significance of the Waters. The Waters provide the very basis for the Vedic dharma. However, from there something paradoxical occurs. Yes, the Water is the mother for Soma; however, through a subtle, reflexive process, the power and essence of Soma is communicated back to the Waters, the Vedic dharma.

The place of the mother is within, second in line, but equal in importance, to the husband (father). Within the family structure a strong authority is needed; this is represented by the parents. If the father is really a father and the son a son, if the elder brother fulfills his position, and the younger fulfills his, if the husband is really a husband and the wife a wife, then the family is in order. In this capacity, Soma asserts its influence. Here, it is stated that Soma is the father of the Vedic dynamic forces (i.e., Gods). (Epithet no. 225.) In this capacity, Soma is the father, progenitor of the gods in that it supplies the subtle foundation, the energy, for all the Vedic dynamic forces. This is reflected in Epithet number 252, where it is said that Soma is in all the Vedic dynamic forces. The Vedic dynamic forces would lose their dynamism without the presence of Soma. For an idea of just how Soma supplies the dynamic fuel for the Vedic forces, Epithet number 256 provides that the force of Soma is "internalized" in Indra. Soma thereby becomes the pith and marrow of Indra. But this internalization is by no means limited to Indra but applies to all the dynamic Vedic forces in the dharma. Indeed, it is for this reason Soma is identified with Visvedevas, all the Vedic dynamic forces. (Epithet no. 246.) Soma provides the girding for the entire Vedic network.

Once the family is in order, all the dynamic relationships of the Vedic dharma will be in order. Fellowship should not be a mere mingling of individuals or of things --- this would be chaos, not fellowship. If fellowship is to lead to order, there must be organization within diversity. Soma provides this leadership to spiritual order. The family is a society in the embryo; it is the native soil on which performance of moral duty is made early through natural affection, so that within a small circle a basis of moral practice is created, and this is later widened to include human relationships in general. In the language of the Vedas, Soma is the embryo of the Waters, the vast pantheon of the dynamic Vedic forces.

225. Soma is the father (*pitaa/*) of the gods. (RV 9.87.2.)

226. Soma is one of the Rishiis. (RV 10.134.1, 5 - 9.)

227. Soma is Brahman among devas. (RV 9.95.3.)

228. Soma is Indra. (SPB 2.2.3.22.)

229. Upon Soma entering the worshiper becomes Aditi. (RV 8.48.2.)

230. Soma is the Child of the Waters (*naptam apsu/*). (RV 9.16.3.)

231. Soma is the child of heaven (*diva/H shi/shum*). (RV 9.33.5; 9.38.5.)

232. Soma is the child of the ocean (*si/ndhumaataram*). (RV 9.61.7.)

233. The Waters is the Mother of Soma. (RV 9.61.4.)

234. Soma is the Embryo (*ga/rbho/*) of the Waters. (RV 9.97.41.)

235. Soma is Approached by the Seven Mothers and Sisters. (RV 9.86.36.)

236. Soma Stimulates the deeds (*ka/rmaaNi*) of the Fathers (*ptr*). (RV 9.96.11.)

237. Soma is Brings the Delightful Chant to the Daughter of the Sun. (RV 9.72.3.)

238. Soma is pressed for Indra. (RV 9.33.3.)

239. Soma is pressed for Vayu. (RV 9.33.3.)

240. Soma is pressed for Varuna. (RV 9.33.3.)

241. Soma is pressed for the Maruts. (RV 9.33.3.)

242. After Being Pressed Soma Descends and Goes to Indra. (RV 9.39.2.)

243. Soma and Pusan together create spiritual treasures (*rayiiNaa/m*). (RV 2.40.2.)

244. Soma has the Vedic dynamism of Rhbus (*Rbhu/r*). (RV 9.87.3.)

245. Soma Is the Gandharva and Guards His Place at the Sacrifice. (RV 9.83.4.)

246. Soma is All Deities (*Visvedevas*). (SPB 1.6.3.21.)

247. Soma is the son of Vivasvati (Surya, the Sun). (RV 8.52.1.)

248. Soma Is Prajapati. (SPB 5.1.5.26.)

249. Soma is Tvastr, the architect of the Universe. (RV 9.6.9.)

250. In His ecstasy the Force of Soma Goes with Vayu. (RV 9.7.7.)

251. In His Ecstasy the Force of Soma Goes with Ashvins. (RV 9.7.7.)

252. Soma Is all the Vedic divine forces. (SPB, 1.6.3.21.)

253. Soma makes the Adityas Strong. (RV 10.85.2.)

254. With Soma control over the senses (*a/vidaama devaa/n*) is achieved. (RV 8.48.3.)

255. The Maruts milk the Soma juice. (RV 9.34.5.)

256. Soma is internalized inside Indra (*e/ndrasya kukSaa/*). (RV 9.80.3.)

257. Soma is like Brahma among the gods (*brahmaa/ devaa/naam*). (RV 9.96.6.)

258. Soma rests on the tip of Varuna's tongue (*va/ruNasya maaya/yaa*). (RV 9.73.9.)

FOOD

The political philosopher Costas Douzinas has an interesting theory about Food. In his book, *Syriza in Power,* he observed that food and words are eternally at odds. Both are engaged and compete for the same orifice --- the mouth. The mouth, the tongue, saliva; when one takes over the other withdraws. Words replace food; eating replaces words.

Douzinas made these observations in connection with political philosophy. The application was to hunger strikes and what they signify. They apply equally well with religiosity and, by extension, with Soma. The different levels of the Vedic Dharma (*Rta*) are represented in speech. Word is the articulation of the material universe. This Word is represented by the divine sound, nada, and is established at the beginning of the universe's creation. With articulation, the indiscriminate mass which existed before the beginning of time is given form. The evolution from the divine sound to creation is represented by Om, the divine sound, to Saman, the articulation and manifestation of form, the Word. Among many other things, Saman are songs from the Soma Veda, the repository of Soma. On a physical level the vibration in the universe is made in the articulation of the original sacred syllable, OM. Thus, it is only through speech that the articulation of names is obtained, thereby making the sensible world intelligible. This is a dynamic symbolized through Food.

Food is a central, foundational Element, mentioned in previous categories. It is an Element which crosses over other categories. For example, as part of the abundance of the universe, "the food of Soma (*a/ ndhasaa*) dwells in the light (*dyukSa/H*), the area of the vast (bha/rad)

97

fullness of plenty (*vaa/jaM*)." (Epithet No. 8.) Soma is the Efficient Cause (*i/saH*) of Abundant Food (*pa/vasv patho/ ra/jaH a bRhatii/r*). (Epithet No. 156.) Indeed, Soma is the Efficient Cause (*i/saH*) of Abundant Wholesome Food (*ayakSmaa/ bRhatii/r*)(Epithet No. 157.)

We saw earlier and will see elsewhere in this text that Consumption is associated with Food and Food is associated with Soma. In the Element of Consumption, consuming "Soma instilled Food in Manu, the earliest man, and later bringing these riches to the worshiper." (Epithet No. 59.) Prior to Consumption, Soma provides food (Epithet No. 98) and is keen to do so. (Epithet No. 87.) Soma is Lord of the Foods. (RV 9.97.22, 27; 9.108.9, 13.) Food is the principal produce of the efficient power which Soma represents. Because of this efficient power, Soma is the Efficient Cause (*i/saH*) of distributed food (*ksa/traa*) (Epithet No. 149), and Soma is the Efficient Cause (*i/saH*) of the food to offered to deceased ancestors (*Kavi*)(Epithet No. 150.) Soma thus produces the desire of Food (pracakraaNa/m)(Epithet No. 152.) In a ritualistic context, Soma is the producing agent of Lenten Food (*prajaa/vatiir*)(Epithet No. 153) and Sacrificial Food (*yaata/yann*) (Epithet No. 154.) In this context, Soma as Food is Measured in the Thousands (*vidaa/H sahasri/Niir*)(Epithet No. 155.) This ritualistic aspect is contrasted with Soma in an ordinary sense. As a part of the ritualist sacrifice, Soma is food for the gods; otherwise, it is an intoxicant, Sura, given to the worshiper. (Epithet No. 276.) This is so important it needs to be said twice. "While Soma is food for the gods, Sura, unpurified Soma juice, is for human beings." (Epithet No. 721.)

What is the worshiper to make of all these cryptic epithets? The immediate benefits accruing to the worshiper are many. The worshiper understands the Vedic dharma, the natural order (*Rta*), with food (*psa/ raH*) obtained from the sweet Soma juice (*su/kRtaM somya/m*) and the rays of Aditi (ga/vyuutir a/diter)(Epithet No. 935.) One should not be taken aback with the Epithet referring to the intoxicant, Sura. Sura is no common, ordinary intoxicant. When thinking of Sura the worshiper should not think of an alcoholic beverage like Wild Turkey, but instead view the concoction in the general terms of mind expansion. There is a clear line of distinction between entities divine and individual humans. It is the human aspiration to become divine and to be liberated from the endless cycle of transmigrations and rebirth. Sura is thus considered the means to an end, that final liberation. Tasting the food through Sura thus gives the worshiper the understanding to achieve that liberation.

The many references of Food elsewhere in this collection are far more reaching. Millenia later Vedanta was developed as the "end of the Vedas." Just as modernly, a once-common but now repudiated phrase, "the end of history" became the conventional wisdom, Vedanta became known as "the end of the Vedas." Fukuyama devised his phrase "the end of history" with a political agenda. Vedanta has no pretentions. This phrase the "end of the Vedas" meant that Vedanta owed its philosophical and spiritual inspiration to the Vedas and that it was the highest, most refined crystallization of the wisdom laid down in its rcs (chants from the Rg Veda), samans (songs from the Sama Veda), and yajurs (formulas for conducting sacrifices from the Yajur Veda). Vedanta itself underwent much further development after its most articulate expression in the works of Adi Sankara.

Sankara summarized the philosophy of Vedanta in a single stanza in his short work, Dg-Drsya Viveka. In the opening stanza, Sankara states, "The form is perceived, and the eye is its perceiver. The eye is perceived and the mind is its perceiver. The mind with its modification is perceived and the Witness (the Self) is verily the perceiver. But it, the Witness, is not perceived by any other." The import of the samans (mantras) dealing with Food is similar. Soma is both the food, the enjoyment of food and the provider of food. In other words, it is the Self, the Mind, and the objects the Mind perceives, all wrapped up in one existential package. Soma is the Self; this is what the epithet that follows, Epithet No. 262, Soma is the Enjoyer, means. As the Showerer, the enjoyer of food, Soma provides the substratum by which the forms of the material existence may be presented in front of the mind, as well as providing the basis for the Mind to perceive those forms. These shapes, figures, and forms are provided by the Self and thrown in front of the Mind as rain during a rain shower. Soma the enjoyer can be read different ways. As simply the "enjoyer" in Epithet No. 260 Soma is also the Mind itself, enjoying the kaleidoscope of shapes, figures, and forms in front of it, as if watching a movie at the Cinema or watching TV at home. Finally, the Epithet No. 259 says Soma is the "food of the Gods."

The triad found in this particular Element shows itself in other Elements in this collection. It will be found in Regeneration, the Showerer, and others.

259. Soma is the Food of the Gods. (TB 1.3.4.4.)

260. Soma is the Enjoyer. (RV 9.62.11.)

261. Soma Creates the enjoyment (*Bha/gam*) at dawn. (RV 9.10.5.)

262. Soma is the Enjoyer, Showerer (*vR/SNas*). (RV 9.64.2.)

FELLOWSHIP (WITH
THE WORSHIPER)

True fellowship among men must be based upon a concern that is universal. It is not the private interests of the individual that create lasting fellowship among men, but rather the goals of humanity. That is why it is said that fellowship with the worshiper in the open is so important.

Soma is the perfect friend. (Epithet No. 263.) The Swami Paramhansa Yogananda says of a related issue, Friendship, the following: "Friendship is the universal Spiritual attraction which unites Souls in the hand of the Divine love and may manifest itself in either two or in many [ways]. The Spirit was One. By the Law of Duality it became two[,] positive and negative. Then, by the Law of Infinity applied to the Law of Relativity, it became many. Now the One in the many is endeavoring to unite the many and make it one. ... When Divine Friendship reigns supreme in the temple of your heart, your Soul will merge with the one vast Cosmic Soul." In the language of the Vedas, with Soma's friendship the worshiper overcomes (saasahyaa/ma) all enemies. (Epithet No. 265.)

If unity of this kind prevails, even difficult and dangerous tasks, such as crossing the great water, can be accomplished. But in order to bring about this sort of fellowship, a persevering and enlightened leader is needed --- a man with clear, convincing, and inspiring aims and the strength to carry them out.

263. Soma is the perfect friend (*sumitra/H*). (RV 1.91.12.)

264. Soma is Anointed by Ten Friends. (RV 9.98.6.)

Vedic scholar R.L. Kashyap has an interesting interpretation to the "Ten Friends." The "Ten Friends" is related to the "Ten Fingers," sometimes mentioned in the Ninth Mandala. The "Ten Fingers" relate to the hands which process and distill the Soma juice during the Soma Sacrifice. RV 5.47.4 speaks of ten directions. RV 1.164.14 speaks of the "ten which yoke the wheel." Here, the "ten" refers to the senses, Indriyas, or it could mean Prana is the source of energy that operates the ten Indriyas. (*http://www.awaken.com/2018/09/process-of-kundalini-awakening-part-i-2/.*) There is no shortage of possible and permutations. The common denominator in all references is that the fingers, the directions, the yoke, and the senses, all act in unison and forward towards the goal, which would not be possible if these components do not act with fellowship.

265. With Soma's friendship the worshiper overcomes (*saasahyaalma*) all enemies. (RV 9.61.29.)

FIRE

The spiritual experience has long been compared to fire. Agni is commonly associated with Fire. In Sanskrit "Agne" means "fire." Agni is traditionally mentioned as the god of fire. Agni is more, so much more so, that simple fire. Classical grammarians, however, derive Agni's name from the root, "ang." From the root ang the word angara for "charcoal" is derived. The charcoal is the remnants of the Sacrificial or any Fire, which is representative of Knowledge and Self-Sacrifice. Just as fire consumes wood, leaving its essential elements in the form of charcoal and ash, that same process is in operation and reduces the form and substance of the universe to its essential elements. Embers are the heated coals once the fire has subsided, and after the embers have subsided, charcoal remains after the Sacrificial Fire has been ignited. If the Sacrificial Fire represents knowledge, charcoal represents the final irreducible essence of that knowledge.

Soma is like Agni. (Epithet No. 272). Agni is in the active Principle of Change and Transformation. Agni is associated with this material world. In his dominion over this world, Agni rules as the Principle of Change, encompassing the constant change and flux of the sensible world and informs the mental and spiritual transformation of the mind and soul of the worshiper. Soma addresses change and transformation as well. The change involves the spiritual transformation of the worshiper. That transformation is facilitated through consumption of the Soma elixir at the Soma Sacrifice. The link between Soma and Agni exists as well through the Sacrificial Fire alight during the Soma Sacrifice.

The Upanishads identify four principal forms of fire. Agni Vaisvanara, the aspect of the Principle of Change, the fundamental nature of Agni, is

103

defined as the Terrestrial Fire and is produced from the Aerial Fire and Celestial Fire. The Bhagavad Gita defines Vaisvanara as the digestive fire. The Aerial, Celestial and digestive fire are the processes by which the Principle of Change is powered and regulate the other aspects of Agni's divine cosmic force. Soma is the Vegetative Fire, the aspect of Fire which rejuvenates living organisms, such as the worshiper, after they have been reduced to their irreducible elements though the cleansing properties of fire.

Fire is a necessary component to the spiritual journey. That journey is made in convert of other Vedic forces associated with fire. That fellowship associated with fire is indicated in Epithet no. 271. There, Soma serves as the host for the Maruts, a group of dynamic forces closely associated with Indra. RV 1.19 lists the seven qualities of the Maruts. Those qualities are:

RV 1.19.3: Divine (deva) and know how to cause the waters to descend (purification).

RV 1.19.4: Fierce (ugra) and know how to cause the descent of waters (Vigor and purification). Ugra, not only meaning "fierce," also connotes heat, passion, intensity, a close relative to *Tapas*.

RV 1.19.5: Radiant and powerful (Vigor and Consciousness).

RV 1.19.6: Live in the heaven above the Sun.

RV 1.19.7: Moves mountains (purification), where mountains are symbolic of dead inner matter.

RV 1.19.8: They spread and expand with the rays of an ocean (higher consciousness)

RV 1.19.9: They drink Soma (purification).

Soma is also represented by a host of related principles derived from the common root, ang. Ang relates to the connection between change (Agni) and consciousness is reflected in a Sanskrit root associated with Agni, Ang.

- Anga, signifying brilliance or effulgence, specifically to describe the aspect of Change in the light of consciousness.
- Angdh, the attribute of resplendence, again, expressed in association of consciousness.
- Angdhve, signifying the flash of revelation.
- The Angiras, the family of Vedic Rishis.

- Angirastama, the mystic essence of the Agniras Rishis.
- Angiraso, that aspect of Angiras in possession of super-human intellectual powers, a siddhi.
- Angiro, the divine reflection of Angiras imbued with the glory of Change.

Fire thus is the principal medium for change. Its principal nature is Change. Fire changes not only in its own form and appearance, but irretrievably changes whatever it comes into contact. A huge part of the capacity of Change is to purify. As a physical phenomenon fire constantly changes shape and form, and it is one of the few agents which changes another substance to another and reduce it to its most elemental physical substances. Agni is Fire, the image of a flame of fire constantly flickers and palpitates which is why Agni is the principle of Change and transformation.

It is the nature of fire to flame up to the heaven. Thus, Soma is said to "blaze like the Heavens." (Epithet No. 170.) Further, The fire in heaven above shines far, and all things stand out in the light and become manifest. Fire is therefore in the nature of light, and in this manner illuminates the worshiper. (Epithet no. 269.)

Fire is the metaphor of spiritual liberation. Soma is Enkindled. (Epithet No. 267). Soma illuminates the worshiper like fire. (Epithet No. 269). Soma Blazes like the Heavens. (Epithet No. 270). Heaven has the same direction of movement as fire, yet it is different from fire. Just as the luminaries in the sky serve for the systematic division and arrangement of time, so human society and all things that really belong together must be organically arranged. Soma is the agent for Agni, the fire of spiritual liberation. Indra drinks the ecstasy of spiritual revelation with the tongue of Agni. (Epithet No. 273). Soma is Praised by Jamadagnina, the Spiritual Blaze of the Sacrificial Fire. (Epithet No. 269). The spiritual processes of Agni and Soma are, however, mutual. Soma is poured on Agni like light. (*GhRta*). (Epithet No. 274). Accordingly, when Change (Agni) consumes and is conjoined with Soma, he conveys the offerings to the divine sphere. (RV 3.29.16.) Not only is this an explanation of the power which propels the stars and constellations, it is another example of the give-and-take process which permeates the Sacrifice.

266. Soma is Praised by Jamadagnina, the Spiritual Blaze of the Sacrificial Fire. (RV 9.62.24; A.S.S., 8.9; N., 1.17; 7.24.)

267. Soma is Enkindled (*Samidhdha*). (RV 9.5.1.)

The important word in that passage is "Kindled." Physical fire is "ignited," but the Sacrificial Fire is "kindled." Soma is like Agni. In Agni, "kindling" imparts all those qualities and energies from the universe and channeled those qualities and energies into the Fire. The Sacrificial Fire of Agni plays a central role in the Sacrificial ritual, it is the center of attraction. Once kindled it is beheld by the worshiper, or, as in the Soma Sacrifice, the principal means of producing the Soma juice to be consumed by the worshiper. In all sacrificial settings, the central fire is the means by which the worshiper is transformed spiritually. The Sun is the source of all life. It is the agent which destroys the old life of the worshiper, and like the phoenix rising from the ashes, a new worshiper emerges. Breath in this above passage is prana, the subtle essence of the life force permeating the universe and sustaining the life of the worshiper. In other words, in part, the Fire of Agni is powered by and empowers the elements of the Vedic dharma, the natural order (Rta).

268. Soma is like Fire (*agnir*) Running Though a Forest. (RV 9.88.5.)

269. Soma illuminates the worshiper like fire. (RV 8.48.6.)

270. Soma Blazes like the Heavens. (RV 9.17.5.)

271. Soma is the Host of the Maruts (*marudgana*). (RV 9.66.26.)

272. Soma Is like Agni. (RV 9.22.2.)

273. Indra drinks the ecstasy of spiritual revelation (Soma) with the tongue of Agni. (RV 3.35.9.)

In an interesting rc (mantra), the Vedic force of Indra is said to drink the Soma juice with the tongue of Agni. (RV 3.35.9.) This rc (mantra) continues the mutual identification of the three Vedic forces of Agni, Indra, and Soma. It also further clarifies that relationship. By drinking the Soma juice for Indra, Agni becomes the agency by which the power of Soma is conveyed to Indra. A number of levels of meaning exist when this is accomplished through Agni's "tongue." The "tongue" of Agni is commonly interpreted as flames of fire, and so the Rishiis' meaning is that the efficacy of fire is the mechanism by which the benefits of Soma are incorporated into Indra's being. The tongue is associated with speech, and so by drinking Soma for Indra's benefit, Agni is giving articulation to the purpose of the Soma juice. It also underscores a theme which will be repeated several times in this book. When fighting the serpent Vrtra, Indra acts as the incarnation of Agni, thereby effectively providing two mighty Vedic forces to fight Vrtra.

274. Soma Is Poured on Agni (Transformation) like Light (*GhRta*). (TB 1.4.2.3.)

FLOW

In the context of Soma and the Soma Sacrifice, Flow or Flowing refer to the stream of purified Soma juice flowing along the ducts of the distillery into the cups, to be given to the worshiper. This is translated to the Vedic dharma in a different context.

In the Vedic dharma, flow serves many functions. On a surface level it refers to the flowing of the Soma juice extracted from the plant during the Soma Sacrifice. On a deeper, more significant level, it is a metaphor for Consciousness itself, a key recipient of the benefits of Soma. The metaphors do not stop here, as the flowing nature of Consciousness is further articulated as watery carriers: rivers, streams, and the like. All these levels of metaphor originate from Soma and its flowing nature.

Consciousness is by its nature in motion. It is transformative, which is why Agni presides over consciousness. The thoughts, feelings, experiences, memories, impressions and beliefs mentioned above ebb, flow and meander, one after another, one changed into another, yet originating from one thinking, conscious subject.

This attribute for the Vedic dharma is mentioned many times in the Rg Veda with the simile of a flowing river. There are generic references of the flow of rivers and waters symbolizing the eternal flow of Consciousness. As a river which ebbs and flows along its course (RV 1.32.12 (the seven rivers); 1.52.7 (rivulets); 1.72.8 (seven rivers flowing from heaven); 1.73.6; 1.83.1; 2.11.1; 2.38.2; 2.28.4; 3.1.3; 3.7.1, 4; 3.33.4, 6, 12, 13; 4.22.6; 3.46.4; 4.22.6, 7 (Indra setting the rivers to flow freely); 4.22.6, 7 (same); 5.49.4; 5.62.4; 5.83.8; 6.19.5; 6.20.12; 9.31.3), this simile depicts the thoughts flowing one after another in the conscious mind much like water flowing through a waterway. This is the eternal flow of individual Consciousness. The thoughts and sensations flow one after the other, seemingly and hopefully to and with a specific goal. The transformative nature of Consciousness then is its malleability, its constantly changing nature. This quality of transformation is captured in sindhavah, the Eternal Law of the flow of the rivers (1.61.11; 1.73.6; 1.90.6; 1.101.3; 1.105.12; 1.168.8; 3.36.6; 5.53.7; 5.62.4; 6.52.4; 7.35.8; 8.6.35; 8.44.25; 8.54.4; 8.69.12; 8.96.1). This is a prominent theme in the Ninth Mandala. (RV 8.6.35; 8.44.25; 8.54.4; 8.69.12; 8.96.1). Sindhavah is representative of Consciousness.

The movement of consciousness is the attribute of Flow, the Element in this category. This is exhibited in the individual mind's consciousness. The flowing of Soma is found elsewhere in other Mandalas in the Rg Veda. (RV 1.84.4; 1.91.8; 1.135.2; 1.151.2; 3.32.15; 3.44.5; 3.45.3; 3.52.2; 4.22.8; 4.28.1; 4.47.2; 4.50.3; 4.58.9; 5.51.7; 6.37.2; 6.41.1; 6.42.3). It is also found in the Flow to divine union, bliss, and joy, symbolized with the flow of Soma during the Agnistoma ritual. (RV 9.1.1; 9.2.1; 9.3.9; 9.3.10 (producing food) 9.4.6; 9.5.1 - 4, 6, 7, 9; 9.6.1, 7, 8; 9.7.1, 5, 8; 9.8.2, 3, 7; 9.12.8; 9.13.1, 3, 6, 7; 9.14.1; 9.16.4, 5; 9.17.2 - 4; 9.18.1; 9.19.6; 9.20.2, 3 (producing food); 9.21.1, 6; 9.23.1, 4, 5, 6; 9.24.1, 2, 4 - 6; 9.25.1, 5, 6; 9.27.5; 9.28.1, 2; 9.29.1, 4; 9.30.1, 4; 9.31.1; 9.36.2, 4; 9.41.5, 6; 9.42.2, 3; 9.43.3, 6; 9.44.4; 9.46.1, 2, 5, 6; 9.49.2, 5).

Water and waterways also flow. The Sanskrit "sindhavah" ---- "River" --- illustrates in metaphor the full import of the flowing characteristic of Consciousness. With the addition of the "avah" suffix, it conveys the "down from, off" or "away" action of Consciousness. Thus beliefs, impressions, and thoughts are carried off, "away" or "down from," the river, sindhu, and carried down or up stream. Sindhavah, the rivers, thus govern the flow of locomotion which carry the beliefs, impressions, and thoughts which constitute the subject's Consciousness.

Soma presides over sindhavah, the flow of Consciousness. (RV 1.101.3; 9.31.3; 9.31.3; 9.62.27; 9.66.6; 9.66.13; 9.108.16). Soma presides over Sindhu, the river of consciousness, as Agni-Soma and Indra-Soma. (RV 1.93.5; 4.28.1). Sindhava is related to Sindhu, which is simply a river. The river incorporates the meaning of sindhava and conveys it in the individual capacity. Sindhu, the river, incorporates two flowing actions. Sidhu implicates the eternal flow of Energy in two respects. First, according to

Yaska, the Vedic grammarian, it represents the susumna, the central nadi wherein the kundalini sakti travels upward towards the upper chakras. Second, it is represented by the spark or kindling expressing, literally, the striking of the match which creates the Light of Consciousness. This, in turn, motivates the eternal flow of Consciousness. This eternal flow is implicated by the presence of smoke. Smoke implies the presence of fire, and fire is the symbol, the origin, of Consciousness. This series of implications merge to produce the energy of mental functioning or Consciousness.

They are indeed carried somewhere, or to some destination.

275. Soma flows with a thousand spiritual riches (*sahasri/NaM rayi/M*). (RV 9.63.1.)

276. The Sura Drink Is for the Worshiper, While Soma Is Food for the Gods. (TB 1.3.3.4.)

277. Soma gives us the kingdom of Varuna. (TB 1.4.2.11.)

278. Soma flows with rapture (*ma/daH*). (RV 9.63.22.)

279. Soma is pure-flowing (*pa/vamaanaa asRkSata*). (RV 9.63.25.)

280. Soma flows like the unlimited (*ivora/vaH*) wind. (RV 9.22.2.)

281. Soma moves (*a\rSanti*) towards the chants spoken at the Sacrifice. (RV 8.62.3.)

282. Soma flows swiftly (*asRkSata*). (RV 9.63.26.)

283. Soma flows (*srava*) for Indra. (RV 9.61.12.)

284. Soma flows (*srava*) for Varuna. (RV 9.61.12.)

285. Soma flows (*srava*) for the Maruts. (RV 9.61.12.)

286. Soma flows (*srava*) for Indra, Varuna and the Maruts to provide the worshiper with the supreme good (*varivovi/t*). (RV 9.61.12.)

287. Soma Makes the Three Times Seven (*tri sapta*) Rivers Flow. (RV 9.71.4.)

288. Soma is purity flowing (*pa/vamaano*). (RV 9.5.3.)

289. Soma Flows through the Vedic Field. (RV 9.107.6.)

290. Soma is seated in the Svar above the ocean (*samudra/sya*). (RV 9.12.6.)

291. Soma flows within (*anta/r*) the worshiper like lightning caused by the clouds. (RV 9.87.8.)

292. Soma flows (*agru/vo/*) like the rivers. (RV 9.66.9.)

293. Soma flows (*puuSNe/*) to Bhaga. (RV 9.61.9.)

294. Soma flows (*puuSNe/*) to Mitra. (RV 9.61.9.)

295. Soma flows (*puuSNe/*) to Pusan. (RV 9.61.9.)

296. Soma flows (*daanupinva/*). (RV 9.97.23.)

297. Soma flows for Indra (*i/ndraayendo*). (RV 9.106.4.)

298. Soma rushes to the bodies. (RV 9.17.4.)

GLORY, GLORIFICATION

This category is a panegyric to Soma. The glory of Soma is widespread, it reaches to the very edges of existence, to all levels of existence. Significantly, it reaches the very foundations of the Vedic dharma, the Waters. In all its glory, the following is said of Soma.

299. Soma is the most glorious of the glorious (*yasha/staro yasha/saaM*). (RV 9.97.3.)

300. Soma is Worthy of Praises (*iiLe/nyaH*). (RV 9.5.3.)

301. Soma's glory (*dhaa/ma*) is profound (*gabhiira/M*). (RV 1.91.3.)

302. Soma's glories (*dhamani*) are in Heaven (divi). (RV 1.91.4.)

303. Having Glory, Soma is like Indra. (RV 4.28.1.)

304. Soma's glories (*dhamani*) are in the mountains (pa/rvateSv). (RV 1.91.4.)

305. Soma's glories (*dhamani*) are in the Waters (*apsu*). (RV 1.91.4.)

306. Soma upholds the glory (*ratnadhaa/*) of the divine Vedic forces (*deve/Su*). (RV 9.67.13.)

307. The Ray-Cows praise Soma. (RV 9.26.2.)

HEAVEN, THE CREATIVE

Heaven in the Vedic dharma is the Seven-Dimensional Universe. Heaven, the Seven-Dimensional Universe, is the Creative Principle. It is so because the spiritual endowments and emoluments rain down from Heaven to the existential levels below. In order to fully understand Soma's role in the Creative Principle found in Heaven, there must first be a crash-course on Vedic cosmology. The Vedic dharma is grounded on triads, groups of three:

- There are three levels to the lowest level of the material world.
- There are three levels to the atmosphere, the mid-world, firmament.
- There are three levels of heaven, dyaus. The three divisions of heaven are:

Uttamam, or uttame; madhyama or madhyame; and avama or avame.

- There are also three levels of heaven in the Atharva Veda. The highest level is that level where the ptrs (fathers) and angirasas reside. The second level is the "starry" heaven, and the third, lowest, level is the "watery" heaven.

Matters are further complicated in that there are several synonyms for heaven which pop up in the Vedas. These designations are not true "synonyms" because they have special meanings that apply to different situations that do not concern us right now. We are only concerned with

Soma, and as far as Soma is concerned, the following words are synonyms for "heaven": Rocani, Diva, and Svar.

These designations perform the same function. Heaven is above; Earth, movement, is below. When the movement of the material world is in accord with and follows the law of heaven, worshiper is innocent and without guile and receptive to profit spiritually in his journey. In other words, the mind of the worshiper is natural and true, not shadowed by reflection or ulterior designs. For wherever conscious purpose is to be seen, there the truth and innocence of nature have been lost. Nature that is not directed by the spirit is not true but degenerate nature. Starting out with the idea of the natural, the train of thought in part goes somewhat further.

This and the two following categories are interrelated. Increase is the Creative Principle at action designed to uplift the worshiper's soul. Inner Essence refers to the innate ability of Soma to uplift that soul. Together they act to unite the worshiper's soul to Heaven.

- Soma resides in Heaven with Indra (Epithet No. 323), increases the strength of Indra (Epithets Nos. 355 and 356), and informs the power of articulation in Indra, the Vedic divine force of Articulation, among other powers. (Epithet No. 391.)
- Sacrifice plays an important role. Soma joins the transcendent world of Heaven at the completion of the Soma Sacrifice. (Epithet No. 311.) The powers of Indra are increased when Soma is consumed, conceivably at the Sacrifice. (Epithet No. 358.). The inner essence of Soma is released and created through the Soma Sacrifice. (Epithet No. 393.) Soma as Atman finds expression in the Soma Sacrifice. (Epithet No. 387.) Soma's essence is produced by the crushing stones. (Epithet No. 372.)
- Soma is the Bull of Heaven. (Epithet No. 315.) Soma is the "Bull with a Thousand Seeds." (Epithet No. 384.) This means that in establishing the inner essence of the Three-Dimensional Universe, Soma is the seed of that world (Epithet No. 394), located at the "Navel," or innermost locus, of the material world. (Epithet No. 370.)

The spiritual journey is basically a creative process. The worshiper re-creates a new self and fashions a new life. Throughout this process, there must be a unifying agent, some intangible impetus which allows the worshiper's mind to be receptive to this specific creative process. It is here that Soma plays its particular role.

The first group of Epithets describe how the subtle and gross endowments of Soma are introduced in the celestial realm:

308. Mighty (*vaajii/*) Soma rushes to the luminous heaven (*rocanaa/ diva/H*). (RV 9.37.3.)

309. Soma Upholds the Highest Level of Heaven (*dharu/No maho/ divo*). (RV 9.72.7.)

310. Soma Crosses the ends of Heaven and Earth. (RV 9.22.5.)

311. Soma Joins Heaven (*svadhvrah*) after the Perfected Sacrifice. (RV 9.3.8.)

312. Soma Joins the Heavens After Crossing the Worlds. (RV 9.3.8.)

313. Soma Gives Birth to the Worlds of Heaven (*rocanna divah*). (RV 9.42.1.)

314. Soma Enters Heaven. (RV 9.78.4.)

Next, Soma activates the Creative Principle possessed of the celestial realm:

315. Soma is the Bull of Heaven. (RV 9.44.28.)

Rasa is the source of higher mental and spiritual awareness and consciousness. (RV 5.53.9.) The rasa, or inner essence, of Soma sustains the process and principle of regeneration of the world (the Bull). (RV 8.72.13.)

Activating the Creative Principle in the celestial realm, the following Epithets identify the specific results of its activation:

316. Soma Manifests the Gods (*devaavii/r*). (RV 9.24.7.)

317. Soma flows from ancient times from heaven across different worlds. (RV 9.77.2.)

318. Soma is the progenitor of the gods (*devaa/naaM janitaa/*). (RV 9.87.2.)

319. Soma is the granter of heaven (*svarSaa/m*). (RV 1.91.21.)

320. Soma gallops (*sa/rgaa*) from heaven. (RV 9.97.30.)

321. Soma, the King, ascends to heaven on a pure chariot (*pavi/ traratho*) of consciousness (*va/saanaH*). (RV 9.83.5.)

322. The adharyus (priest at the sacrifice) secretly place Soma in heaven. (RV 9.10.9.)

323. Soma abides in heaven with Indra. (RV 3.40.5.)

324. Soma rushes across the worlds to heaven (*di/vaM*). (RV 9.3.7.)

325. Pure-Flowing Soma (*pa/vamaanaa*) is poured from heaven (*diva/s*) and the firmament (*anta/rikSaad*) to earth (*pRthivyaa/*). (RV 9.63.27.)

326. Soma Is in the Third Heavenly World. (TB 1.1.3.11.)

327. Soma makes his home in high heaven (*divy*). (RV 2.40.4.)

328. Soma is the leader of heaven (*sva\rNaram*). (RV 9.70.6.)

329. Soma Is the Supporter of Heaven (*divo/ dhartaa/si*). (RV 9.109.6.)

330. Soma Makes the Sun (*suu/ryam*) Shine (*aa/rohayo*) in Heaven (*divi*). (RV 9.86.22.)

331. Soma Makes the Realms of Heaven (*divo*) Shine (*rocanaa kavi*). (RV 9.85.9.)

332. The Gayatri Metre Brought Soma from the Third Heaven and Placed it in the Palasha Tree Leaf So its Juice Maybe Used for the Sacrifice. (TB 1.1.3.11.)

333. Soma bestows heavenly riches (*divyaa/ni*). (RV 9.63.30.)

334. Soma rests in the third realm (*rocane/*). (RV 9.86.27.)
Pursuant to its creative powers and endowments, Soma provides the subtle basis for other Vedic forces, energies, and principles.

335. Soma Gives Birth to Vishnu. (RV 9.96.5.)

336. Soma creates revelation (*kavi/H*). (RV 9.84.5.)

337. Soma has Cosmic Powers (*ha/rayo*). (RV 9.86.2.)

338. Soma Gives Birth to Agni. (RV 9.96.5.)

339. Soma Gives Birth to Surya. (9.96.5.)

340. Soma Gives Birth to Indra. (RV 9.96.5.)

341. The Svar (*sva\r*) where Soma resides is eternal (*sa/naa*). (RV 9.4.2.)

342. Soma is the Highest Heaven (*parame/ vyo\man*). (RV 3.32.10.)

343. Soma has given birth to all human beings. (RV 2.40.5.)

344. Soma extends the principle of Sacrifice to all edges of the Vedic dharma. (RV 9.86.8.)

INCREASE

This is one of the most esoteric, yet important, Element of the spiritual ascent upward in the Vedic dharma. There can be no spiritual development without Increase. Increase is the practical result of the worshiper gaining the spiritual endowments provided in the Vedas.

The concept is esoteric but not incomprehensible. The idea of increase is expressed in the fact that the spiritual development of the worshiper admits to the addition of qualities not present before of characteristics not previously exhibited. In many cases, previous views are modified, some are outright discarded. It is the very essence of sacrifice. Sacrifice is basically a giving and taking. Without Increase the spiritual journey to liberation and salvation would be impossible.

There is a central truth in the Vedic dharma. That truth is that there is a give-and-take between the Microcosm (humankind) and the Macrocosm (the universe), of every object therein, encompassing the process from creation to dissolution. (Sannyasi Gyanshruti, Sunnyasi Srividyananda, *Yajna, A Comprehensive Survey* (2006), pp. 84 – 85.) The giving and taking process is grounded in the Two-Dimensional Universe which serves as the basis for the material world. The rising of the Sun gives rise to the appearance of the Moon; Day rises to bring in the night; Hot is the flip side of Cold. This dynamic was not unknown in Vedic literature. The Chandogya Upanishad recognizes the dichotomy of pleasant and unpleasant smells; Truth and Falsity; pleasant and unpleasant sounds; and even pleasant and unpleasant thoughts. This dichotomy is grounded on the existence of Good and Evil; all dichotomies and juxtapositions have this polarity as their source. But even with these polar opposites there comes a point where there is unification. This is the purpose of Increase and implies the importance of Soma in the resolution of this push and pull.

This chaotic Two-Dimensional Universe is resolved with the worshiper's spiritual awakening. In the process of spiritual awakening, the world and its perception are different because the worshiper is different. The old worshiper is discharged in exchange of the new. The sacrifice of the higher element that produces an increase of the lower is called an out-and-out increase: it indicates the spirit that alone has power to help the world. Sacrifice thus becomes a prominent feature of increase, implicated in Epithet Number 346, because it is a product of a give and take process.

As Richard Wilhelm, commenting on the I-Ching, once observed, "Sacrifice on the part of those above for the increase of those below fills the people with a sense of joy and gratitude that is extremely valuable for the flowering of the commonwealth. When people are thus devoted to their leaders, undertakings are possible, and even difficult and dangerous enterprises will succeed. Therefore in such times of progress and successful development it is necessary to work and make the best use of time. This time resembles that of the marriage of heaven and earth, when the earth partakes of the creative power of heaven, forming and bringing forth living beings. The time of increase does not endure; therefore it must be utilized while it lasts."

Here however is where the I-Ching and Vedas depart. Where the I-Ching credits the worshiper for this increase, in the Vedic dharma, in the Vedas Soma is the agent for increase. Thus, it is said that Soma is the Increaser. (Epithets Nos. 346 and 360.) The spiritual development of the worshiper is increased by the qualities of Soma itself. (Epithet No. 350.) Increase occurs in the worshiper when Soma is consumed. (Epithet no. 358.) The epithets in this section contain the conditions for the worshiper's increase. They include the proliferation of inner illumination (Epithet no. 348), the worshiper's inner strength (Epithet no. 355), and increase in understanding (Epithet no. 361). The sum total of these increased powers is the worshiper's Immortality, which is the code-word for salvation and liberation.

The use of symbolic language dominates this Element. Soma increases the strength of Indra (Epithet no. 355) and Indra himself (Epithet no. 356). This is symbolic speech referring to the divine power possessed by Indra.

Indra is the dynamic Vedic force for speech and articulation; in Soma's ability to increase both Indra and the strength of Indra in the worshiper, it therefore the impetus behind the ability of the worshiper to channel these powers in the spiritual journey. Soma is also said to be the "Increaser of milk." (Epithet no. 366.) This is symbolic the poetic language of the "milk of knowledge." In this regard, in the later Epithet No. 436, Soma will be described as the "Milk of Knowledge." Soma is a primary provider of Increase as these Epithets indicate:

345. Soma Increases Towards Immortality. (RV 1.91.18.)

346. Soma is the Increaser. (RV 9.74.3.)

347. Soma Is Increased in the Sacrifice by Chants. (RV 9.17.6.)

348. Soma Is the Increaser of Light (*Dhymna*). (RV 9.31.2.)

349. Soma increases our nourishment (*puSTiva/rdhanaH*). (RV 1.91.12.)

350. Soma Increases Himself in Human Beings. (RV 9.97.39; SV 1359.)

351. Soma increases (*vardha/yann*) the life span of humans. (RV 3.62.15.)

352. Soma increases (*vardha/yann*) the power of humans to overcome enemies (*sadha/stham aa/sadat*). (RV 3.62.15.)

353. Soma Increases (*Va/rdhaa*) the Utterances Arising from the Inner Ocean (*samudra/m*). (RV 9.61.15.)

354. Soma increases (*va/rdhanto*) Indra to cross the waters quickly (*aptu/raH*). (RV 9.63.5.)

355. Soma Increases the Strength (*viirya\m*) of Indra. (RV 9.8.1.)

356. Soma is Increases Indra. (RV 9.106.8.)

357. Soma Increases the Capacity to Obtain Knowledge (*ja/nmane*). (RV 9.108.8.)

358. Indra is increased (*avRdhat*) in the worshiper when Soma is consumed. (RV 4.23.1.)

359. Soma increases (*va/rdhate*) the divine names (*naa/maani*). (RV 9.75.1.)

360. Soma is the Increaser (*va/rdhanaH*). (RV 1.91.12.)

361. Soma increases the understanding of the worshiper. (RV 10.25.10.)

362. Soma causes the increasings (*uuta/yaH*) which cause happiness (*mayobhu*) in the worshiper. (RV 1.91.9.)

363. Soma makes the increase (*vRdhe/*) of his power in the worshiper possible. (RV 1.91.10.)

364. Soma increases (*vardha/yaamo*) the knowers of Speech (*vacovi/daH*) in the worshiper. (RV 1.91.11.)

365. Soma increases (*aa/ pyaayasva*) with its radiances (*aMshu/bhiH*). (RV 1.91.17.)

366. Soma is the increaser of milk (*payovR/dhaM*). (RV 9.84.5.)

367. Once Soma is increased by the Truth, he gives shape to the perfect forms of the world (*bhu/vanaani nirNi/je*). (RV 9.70.1.)

INNER ESSENCE

This category aims at the inner essence of Soma. The characteristics listed here aim at the very core of Soma's being.

We were introduced to rasa a few pages ago. There, we found out that the rasa, or inner essence, of Soma sustains the process and principle of regeneration of the world (the Bull). (RV 8.72.13.) Rasa dwells in the inner subtle being of sentient and non-sentient beings and things. There are three basic characteristics to the inner essence of Soma. This is implicated in the Epithet No. 368 which states that Soma has a three-fold nature. One, Soma is the Knower of these two levels of existence. "Knower" in this context has a specific meaning. Before an object may be "known," that object must first exist in some tangible or intangible form so that it may be capable of identification. Once that object is available for cognition, the perceiving subject will attach a name to distinguish that object from others. Human Speech is the articulation of the world, attaching a word to an object in the world. For the worshiper to assign the word "tree" to the actual object implies knowledge of that object, albeit through the sense perceptions. It's all some heady stuff, but that in a nutshell is a very short description of consciousness. The essence of Vedanta is that the perceiving subject superimposes the objects of the world for mortals to perceive. As Adi Sankara opens in his Drg-Drsya-Viveka, "The forms are perceived and the eye is its perceiver. The Eye is perceived and the mind is the perceiver. The mind with its modifications is perceived and the Witness (the Self) is verily the perceiver. But it, the Witness or Self, is not perceived by any other." Error occurs when the perceiving object --- namely, us --- believe we are the subject responsible for the perception of the objects in the material

122

world, when in reality it is the Atman, the Self, superimposing itself on the universe.

Two, Soma is the bridge between these worlds. Many of the Epithets in this category note that Soma is found in and provides the subtle basis for Heaven and earth. On the one hand it operates on a purely terrestrial level to be the "Knower of Words." (Epithet No. 379.) Its capacity of Knower of the Words enables Soma to provide the basis of all things material. For example, Soma is associated with the seasons. (Epithet No. 385.) This can be taken to mean that Soma provides the terrestrial, climatological conditions to allow the seasons to occur. "Season" is also synonymous with Time itself. On the other hand, Soma is the Knower of the "Sun World," the Svar, a synonym used to connote the transcendental world of the Seven-Dimension Universe. (Epithet No. 380.) Soma is positively imbued with the supreme, most subtle, manifestation of articulation through Vac, the highest level of Speech. Soma thus is the grand unifier.

Three, the bridge between the material and transcendental worlds is informed through the Soma Sacrifice. The inner essence of Soma is released and created through the Soma Sacrifice. (Epithet No. 393.) Soma as Atman finds expression in the Soma Sacrifice. (Epithet No. 387.) Soma's essence is produced by the crushing stones. (Epithet No. 372.) As with everything Vedic, there is a ritualistic, material, meaning, and an esoteric, subtle, meaning. Ritualistically, the crushing stones are a metaphorical representation for the physical mind; esoterically, since the stones produce the juice to achieve a transcendent mental state, it is symbolic of the transformation of the worshiper's mind to a higher, spiritual, level.

- Soma is the inner essence. (Epithet No. 369.)
- That essence is in a pure form. (Epithet No. 373.)
- Soma establishes the inner essence of this Three-Dimensional Universe of the material world. (Epithets 388, 389.)
- Soma is the "Bull with a Thousand Seeds." (Epithet No. 384.) This means that in establishing the inner essence of the Three-Dimensional Universe, Soma is the seed of that world (Epithet No. 394), located at the "Navel," or innermost locus, of the material world. (Epithet No. 370.)

- The three-fold nature of Soma (Epithet No. 368), meaning that Soma provides the essence of the three levels of existence: The Three-Dimensional Universe of the material world, the Five-Dimensional Universe of the Mid-World, and the transcendental world of the Seven-Dimensional Universe.
- Through the dynamics of its own inner laws, Soma's inner essence is disbursed to both Heaven and Earth. (Epithet No. 382.)
- Based on this characteristic Soma is able to confer both earthly and spiritual benefits. (Epithet No. 375.)
- This is partially due to Soma being born of both mortal beings and the laws of Immortality. (Epithets Nos. 381 and 382.)

With these considerations in mind, the specific characteristics of the inner essence of Soma are these:

368. Soma Has a Three-fold (*tridhaaltur*) Essential Nature. (RV 9.86.46.)

Triads abound in the Vedic force of Agni. Soma is like Agni as we learned earlier. As in Agni, so in Soma, the triplets refer to various levels of the Vedic existential cosmos, whether Heaven, Mid-Earth, and Earth (RV 10.88.3), or any division within.

369. Soma is the essence (*ra/so*). (RV 9.77.5.)

The identification of rasa is significant. Rasa will be prove indispensable when describing the alchemical aspect of the Vedic dharma.

370. Soma is the Navel of the World. (RV 9.72.7.)

371. Soma the Essence is in the Chamasa Bowel. (RV 1.28.9.)

This is a ritualist appearance of the inner essence of Soma. The Chamasa bowl is wooden and used to drink Soma at the sacrifice. (RV 1.20.6; 1.110.3; 1.161.1; 8.82.7.)

372. The essence of Soma is released with swift stones. (RV 10.76.7.)

The Pressing Stones are another element to religious ecstasy and will be further discussed later.

373. Soma Is of a Pure Form (*nirni/jam*). (RV 9.99.1.)

374. Soma is yoked (*yugo*) by the Supreme Word (*Vac*). (RV 9.7.3.)

375. Bestows Heavenly and Earthly Benefits. (RV 9.63.30.)

376. Soma is the Highest Angirasa. (RV 9.107.6.)

377. Soma is the Knower (*vi/praa*) in the worshiper. (RV 9.86.39.)

378. Soma is the Knower. (RV 9.73.8.)

These last two Epithets will prove significant for the development into Vedanta. Soma is both the Knower and the Knower in the worshiper. The essence of Vedanta is that the perceiving subject superimposes the objects of the world for mortals to perceive. As Adi Sankara opens in his Drg-Drsya-Viveka, "The forms are perceived and the eye is its perceiver. The Eye is perceived and the mind is the perceiver. The mind with its modifications is perceived and the Witness (the Self) is verily the perceiver. But it, the Witness or Self, is not perceived by any other." The import of these last two Epithets, then, is that Soma is the subject responsible for superimposing the objects in the material world, the Atman, the Self, superimposing itself on the universe, and is also the agent responsible for the perception of those objects. The epithets then continue with specific objects and concepts in the Vedic dharma which are superimposed by Soma.

379. Soma Is the Knower of Words (*vacovi/d*). (RV 9.91.3.)

380. Soma is the Knower of the Sun World (*svarvi/d aa/*). (RV 8.48.15.)

381. Soma is born in mortals (*amRta*) in the law of Immortality (*aa/ M+ Rta/sya*). (RV 9.110.4.)

382. By Soma's own law (*dha/rmabhiH*) it flows to heaven and earth. (RV 9.107.24.)

383. Soma is Pressed Out by *Satya*, the underlying Truth of Existence (*Satye/na*). (RV 9.113.2.)

384. He is the Bull with a Thousand Seeds. (RV 9.109.17.)

385. Soma is Associated with the Seasons. (RV 9.66.3.)

386. Soma is Babhruh. (RV 9.31.5.)
According to Sayana, the Medieval scholar, *babhruh* (RV 2.33.8) is knowledge in the mortal mind, metaphorically one who upholds the worlds.

387. Soma is the Soul (*aatman*) of the Sacrifice. (RV 9.2.10.)
The following Epithets demonstrate not only is Soma the inner essence of the Vedic dharma, but Soma also establishes the inner essence. In other words, Soma is self-created or self-born.

388. Soma Establishes the Essence (*rasam*). (RV 9.23.5.)

389. Soma creates the Essence (*ra/so*). (RV 9.84.5.)

390. Soma is imbued with Essence (*rasaa/yyaH*). (RV 9.97.14.)

391. The essence of Soma (*i/ndur*) produced at the Soma Sacrifice (*somyo/*) informs the Articulation of Forms (Indra). (RV 9.67.8.)

392. The Essence of Purified Soma (*i/ndur*) Flows Through the Vedic Field (*avya/yaM*, filter). (RV 9.98.2.)

393. Soma is the Essence of the Soma Sacrifice (*somya*). (RV 9.67.8.)

394. Soma supports the seed (*retodhaa/*). (RV 9.86.39.)

INSIGHTFUL KNOWLEDGE (COWS)

From the Awakening, or Enlightenment, the worshiper acquires Knowledge; from Knowledge, he worshiper gains Consciousness; from Consciousness, the worshiper has the capacity to be engaged in Contemplation or Deliberation; from the act of Contemplation or Deliberation the worshiper is elevated to Inspired Knowledge. Cows are intimately related to Knowledge in general and the knowledge necessary for liberation and salvation.

The cows are an important part of the Vedic dharma. They represent knowledge, wisdom and illumination, most likely because these qualities are representative of their products: milk, butter and ghee. Cows are symbolic of the principle or precept of existence. Cows are also symbolic of some aspect of universality, usually in association with other Vedic divine dynamic forces. It is their aspect to this stage of liberation that interests us at this point. Because the cows produce several by-products, different cows in the Vedas represent different aspects of knowledge, mind, and/or consciousness. This was covered at length in the introduction but justifies repetition. The essence is the following:

- A barren or immature cow is taken to mean the lack of consciousness, incomplete or faulty knowledge, because of its unripe milk. (RV 3.30.14 (unripe milk); 2.7.5; 1.112.3; 1.116.22; 1.117.20; 1.61.9 (raw cows); 6.72.4; 4.19.7; 7.68.8.)
- Red or ruddy cows are said to represent the onset or beginnings of illumination. (RV 1.92.2; 10.68.6; 6.64.3; 1.49.1; 8.7.7).

- The ray-cows represent Aditi, the infinite consciousness. (RV 4.58.4; 4.1.6.)
- The Ray-Cows also represent hidden or occult knowledge. (RV 4.53; 4.58; 4.5.10).
- A cow's calf represents jiva, or the individual soul. (RV 4.33.4; 4.34.5; 1.110.8; 1.111.1; 1.164.5; 1.164.9, 17, 18, 27; 2.7.5; 2.16.8; 2.28.6; 2.24.8; 3.33.3; 3.41.5; 1.55.'4; 6.45.25; 5.30.10; 7.87.5; 8.43.17; 8.59.14, 15; 8.61.5; 9.41.14; 9.86.2; 9.100.1,7; 9.104.2; 9.105.2; 9.111.14; 10.8.2, 9; 10.53.11; 10.119.4; 10.145.6; 10.10.75.4;10.123.1).

The result of this insightful knowledge is the worshiper's ultimate liberation. This is again symbolically reflected in what the Vedas have to say about the Cows in the number Seven as contained in the Seven-Dimensional Universe. The Seven-Dimensional Universe is the transcendent world of Liberation and Salvation. The Vedas associate the Cows with this Seven-Dimensional Universe. Thus, to this level of existence the Cows symbolize the dawn of consciousness or truth. (RV 1.71.1). They represent the seven principles of existence. (RV 1.164.3), the seven rivers. (RV 1.32.12; 2.34.15), the "seven sisters." (RV 2.7.1), the very expanse of Heaven and earth itself. (RV 3.6.4; 9.86.2). The Cows --- and insightful knowledge --- are ubiquitous. The insightful knowledge of the Cows greatly aided the spiritual journey of the worshiper. For this there is little wonder. In gaining insightful knowledge the worshiper acquires the divine knowledge and wisdom of God which has obtained that insightful knowledge from the cows. Thousands, says the Satapatha Brahmana, are the number of cows taken from the gods. (SPB 3.3.1.13.) This is how the title of this book originated. Hence, this title.

What the Ninth Mandala has to say about the Cows and their connection with the worshiper's liberation and salvation follows.

395. When it is pressed and purified, Soma grants (*dhanva*) discernment (*go/Su*) to the worshiper. (RV 9.105.5.)

396. The rays of brilliant knowledge (*gaa/vaH*) mix Soma with the milk (*pa/yasaa*). (RV 9.84.5.)

397. Soma manifests (*ajanayas*) all the brilliance of knowledge (*gaa/H*). (RV 1.91.22.)

398. The Brilliance of Knowledge (*gaa/vo*) is encapsulated in the three Vedas (*tisro/*). (RV 9.33.4.)

399. Soma Pavamana gave birth to Illuminated, Inspired Knowledge (*go/jiirayaa*). (RV 9.110.3.)

400. Soma is surrounded by the inspiration of Illuminated Knowledge (*go/bhir*). (RV 9.107.18.)

401. Soma is endowed with knowledge (*go/mantam*) and life-energy (*ashvi/nam*). (RV 9.63.12.)

402. Soma Seeks the Ray-Cows (*gaa/*). (RV 9.89.3.)

403. Soma Works with Penetrating Wisdom (*kavi-kratuh*). (RV 9.9.1.)

INTELLIGENT DESIGN (WILL)

If a mental state can be attributed, not to the worshiper, then to Soma, but if not Soma, it would be to this category, Intelligent Design. The concept of Intelligent Design is commonly known as a theory of creation. Viewed as a compromise between Darwinism and Christianity, Intelligent Design states that a knowing God supervised the evolution of the animal and human species.

In a similar way, Intelligent Design is a spiritual roadmap for the worshiper, informed by Soma. The epithets regarding Intelligent Design list the spiritual characteristics of Soma as a spiritual entity. Those epithets merely contain simple characteristics. Implied among these epithets is the realization that those very same characteristics are carried over to the worshiper upon consumption of Soma and the elevation of the worshiper's state of mind. Those characteristics are:

- The worshiper acquires a developed mind. (Epithet No. 405.)
- The worshiper strives to find the Divine Will. (Epithet No. 406.)
- The worshiper finds the Divine Will through the rapture of Soma. (Epithet No. 408.)
- The worshiper strives to do good deeds. (Epithet No. 409.)
- The worshiper achieves correct wisdom through Soma. (Epithet No. 411.)
- Soma brings happiness to the worshiper. (Epithet No. 412.)
- The worshiper becomes most wise. (Epithet No. 413.)

- Through Soma the worshiper's soul acquires Immortality. (Epithet No. 410.)

Intelligent Design is an intrinsic characteristic of Soma, as these epithets indicate:

404. Indu, the purified Soma, is the Divine Will (*devamaa/danaH kra/tur*). (RV 9.107.3.)

405. Soma is a Seer Born with a Developed Mind (*ma/nasaa jaayate kavi/r*). (RV 9.68.5.)

406. Soma is the finder of the Divine Will (*kratuvi/ttamo*). (RV 9.108.1.)

407. Soma is full of Divine Will (*kra/tumaaM+ a/mena vi/shvaa*) like a King. (RV 9.90.6.)

408. Soma establishes the Divine Will (*kratum*) in the worshiper with its rapture (*vi/vakSase*). (RV 10.25.5.)

409. Soma is the doer of good deeds (*kra/tubhiH*). (RV 1.91.2.)

410. Soma's will (*kra/tum*) is eternal (*sa/naa*). (RV 9.4.3.)

411. Soma is the finder of the those having correct wisdom (*kratuvi/t*). (RV 9.63.24.)

412. Soma brings the happy will (*kra/tum*) to the worshiper in its rapture. (RV 10.25.1.)

413. Soma is the Most Wise. (RV 9.11.7.)

Sometimes, however, roadmaps are not enough. To start on the spiritual journey a car needs gasoline to start the engine. The fuel is Joy and Bliss.

JOY, BLISS

Joy, or Bliss, is the category most associated with Soma. Joy is the very essence of the aspect of Soma expounded in the Rg Veda. Soma is joyful (Epithet No. 416) and joyous (Epithet No. 415.) It is the very incarnation of Joy and Bliss. (Epithet No. 414.) Soma is rapture, a related Element. (Epithet No. 425.) Soma releases its rapture like waves (Epithet No. 418), and those waves makes the worshiper happy. (Epithet No. 417.) Mere happiness should be distinguished with spiritual bliss. Soma is not only possessed of Joy and Bliss, but it is also imbued with a higher expression of Spiritual Bliss. (Epithet No. 423.)

There is a fundamental misconception with regard to Joy or Bliss. Joy or Bliss are naturally associated with happiness, but many erroneously associate Joy and Bliss as a feeling. Joy and Bliss is not a feeling or sensation per se but refers to the quality of life, here, the spiritual life and is really considered the joy or bliss of living a spiritual life. It is possible to experience Bliss from the spiritual life. But as these Epithets testify, Bliss, the very personification of Soma, is much more than a fleeting sensation of happiness.

A significant part of the blissful aspect of Soma is the Word, articulation. In the bliss generated by Soma, the "rhythmic word" is spoken. (Epithet No. 422.) The meaning of this saman is that joy and bliss is generated simply by the chanting at the Soma Sacrifice.

As in all things Vedic, in its love of classification, there are different levels to Joy:

- There is *Mada*, the generic, ground level, category to Joy. It is the simple joy experienced by the worshiper, either as a result of a spiritual awakening or otherwise and associated with the Three-Dimension Universe of the material world. In the Rg Veda there are well over one hundred references to this type of Joy.

- There is *madhya*, the joy experienced as a result of a spiritual awakening. In the Rg Veda it is the joy experienced by the vast array of Vedic divine forces after consumption of the Soma juice. Again, there are upwards to one hundred and more references in the Rg Veda to *madhya* and its derivatives. Because it is associated with the Vedic divine forces, this is the form of Joy associated with the Five-Dimension Universe.

- There is *madhummatanam*, the highest form of Joy. *Madhummatanam* is that Joy experienced at the acme of spiritual development. Accordingly associated with the Seven-Dimension Universe, it is ananda of the three-part for the subjective experience, along with cit and sat, of the ultimate unchanging reality in Hinduism called Brahman. References to *madhummatanam* can be found in the following passages of the Rg Veda: 1.47.3; 5.11.5; 6.68.11; 7.42.2, 7; 7.102.3; 8.3.15; 8.9.7; 9.12.7; 9.30.5, 6; 9.51.2; 9.62.21; 9.63.16, 19; 9.64.22; 9.67.16; 9.80.4; 9.100.6; 9.101.4; 9.105.3; 9.106.6; 9.108.1, 15; 10.14.15; 10.122.7.

As far as the One Thousand Epithets of Soma is concerned, the experience of Joy is specifically defined and its scope is vast. Joy contains elements of Bliss (Epithets Nos. 420 and 423), Rapture (Epithets Nos. 418 and 425), Happiness (Epithets Nos. 417 and 424), Delight (Epithet No. 426), and Rapture (Epithet No. 418.) Least we delude ourselves we must be clear on the basis for Joy. It is not a hedonistic experience but one grounded from and the result of virtuous means. (Epithet No. 419.) The Source of Joy is Soma. Soma is Joy incarnate. (Epithet No. 414.) Soma is joyous (Epithet No. 415) and joyful (Epithet No. 416) by nature. The worshiper experiences Joy with two means. One, on a sacrificial level, the worshiper consumes the Soma Juice to experience the divine. This is the import of the saman which says that Soma makes the worshiper happy with "waves of Juice." (Epithet No. 417.) Two, the worshiper may experience Joy, Bliss, by hearing the "rhythmic word," the ritualistic chanting, at the sacrifice. (Epithet No. 422.)

414. Soma is Joy Incarnate (*priya/M*). (RV 9.108.8.)

415. Soma is joyous (*haryato/*). (RV 9.65.25.)

416. Soma is joyful (*haryata/M)*. (RV 9.98.7.)

417. Soma Makes us Happy with the Waves of Juice. (RV 9.63.5.)

418. Soma releases its rapture (madacyu/t) like waves of the river (*si/ndhor*). (RV 9.12.3.)

419. The Ecstasy of Soma Is Obtained by Virtuous Means (*kR/tvye*). (RV 9.76.1.)

420. Soma is Bliss (*mad*). (RV 9.5.10.)

421. Soma increases (*vRSaayate*) the bliss (*sukRtya/yaa*) in its intoxication. (RV 9.47.1.)

422. The bliss generated by Soma speaks the rhythmic word. (RV 9.113.6.)

423. Soma is imbued with Spiritual Bliss (*ma/dhumaaM*). (RV 9.63.13.)

424. Soma grants happiness (*she/va*) to the worshiper. (RV 9.82.4.)

425. Soma is rapturous (*ma/do*). (RV 9.69.3.)

426. Soma is Delightful. (RV 9.5.9.)

427. Soma is the Elixir of Divine Love (*ma/diSThayaa*). (RV 1.1.1.)

428. Soma is the Divine Elixir (*amitraha*). (RV 9.11.7.)

KNOWLEDGE

Knowledge occurs early in the worshiper's spiritual journey. Let's recap. The worshiper's spiritual journey begins when the worshiper is awakened.

- From the Awakening, or Enlightenment, the worshiper acquires Knowledge.
- From Knowledge, he worshiper gains Consciousness.
- From Consciousness, the worshiper has the capacity to be engaged in Contemplation or Deliberation.
- From the act of Contemplation or Deliberation the worshiper gains Insightful Knowledge.
- From Insightful Knowledge, the worshiper obtains Discernment.
- From Discernment, the worshiper obtains Divine Vision.

It is often said that knowledge is power. The same can be said about Soma. Soma is the Knower of all things (Epithet No. 429), All-Knowing (Epithet No. 433), and is guided by knowledge. (Epithet No. 438.)

In a simile used throughout the Vedas, Soma is the milk of knowledge. (Epithet No. 437.) This is one of the reasons why the Cows are said to be symbols for knowledge. (See, Epithet No. 452.)

It was explained earlier that the inner essence of Soma is the Knower of the two levels of existence of Heaven and Earth. "Knower" in this context was taken to mean that Soma is both the Subject, the Universal Atman, superimposing its nature on the perceiving Object of mortal consciousness.

This should be taken as the meaning of Epithet No. 429. As the "Knower of All Things," Soma is acting as the Universal Atman.

Power obtained is ineffectual if not acted upon. This is completely consistent with the Universal Atman, which essentially does not act, but simply "is." Thus, knowledge without the appropriate discernment or appreciation is sterile. Think of a computer supplied with all the knowledge in the world operating without an algorithm. With the proper algorithms, the capabilities are very powerful indeed. Just ask the folks at any internet website. Similarly, when knowledge and proper discernment are coupled, when applied to worshiper's spiritual journey, the quest is complete. It is under these conditions that Soma is capable of expiating sins. (Epithet No. 439.)

Having said this, it should be noted that Soma also nourishes. Soma accordingly imparts its knowledge to the worshiper in the spiritual journey. Thus, Soma discovers the brilliance of Knowledge for the worshiper. (Epithet No. 445.)

Soma acts in several capacities to aid and foster the worshiper's spiritual development. Knowledge is an essential part of that journey.

429. Soma is the knower of All Things. (RV 9.8.9.)

430. Soma Seeks inspired knowledge. (RV 9.10.1.)

431. When Soma is released he has many forms (*vi*), inspired knowledge (*shra/vaaMsi*), happiness (sau/bhagaa), the fullness of plenty (*vaa/jaan*), or the brilliance of knowledge (*go/mataH*). (RV 9.67.5.)

432. Soma is the Messenger for Advance Knowledge. (RV 9.99.5.)

433. Soma is All-Knowing (*ja/naanaam*). (RV 9.87.3.)

434. Soma is Wise (*dhii/ra*). (RV 9.87.3.)

435. Soma Discovers (*apiicya\M*) the Secret Meaning (*gu/hyaM naa/ma*) of the Vedas (*viveda*). (RV 9.87.3.)

436. Soma Gives Knowledge of devotional discipline (*Vrata*) to Worshiper. (RV 9.35.4.)

437. Soma is the milk of knowledge. (RV 9.96.24.)

438. Soma is guided by knowledge (*re/tum*). (RV 9.69.3.)

439. With his Knowledge (*cittii/*) and Discernment (*da/kSair*) Soma Wipes Away Sin (*agha/*) from the Worshiper. (RV 8.79.4.)

440. Soma takes the form of inspired knowledge from the internal force of Agni (*yu/vaa*). (RV 9.14.5.)

441. Soma takes the form of inspired knowledge. (RV 9.14.5.)

442. Soma flows to the Indra knowledge (*tirashca/taa*, i.e., the force of Vayra to combat Evil) with the application of subtle forces (*a/Nvyaa*). (RV 9.14.6.)

443. Soma creates the Inspired Knowledge (*ketu/M*). (RV 9.64.8.)

444. Soma nourishes with knowledge (*pi/nvamaana*). (RV 9.97.14.)

445. Soma discovers the brilliance of Knowledge for the worshiper. (RV 9.86.39.)

446. Soma awakens the knowledge (*ce/tasaa*) of his own consciousness (*cetayate*). (RV 9.86.42.)

447. Soma is united (*saMya/tam*) with the chants at the sacrifice and the knowledge obtained therefrom to produce the word of revelation (*i/Laam*). (RV 8.62.3.)

448. Soma is born from inspired knowledge (*shruSTii/*). (RV 9.106.1.)

449. Soma upholds the knowledge of the mortal mind (*babhra/vaH*). (RV 9.33.2.)

450. When pressed, Soma brings spiritual treasures (*va/suunaaM*) and brilliant knowledge (*raayaa/m*). (RV 9.108.13.)

451. The horses yoked to the chariot (*hari/taH*) make Soma's sweet (*ma/dhumad*) and bright (*ghRta/m*) milk of knowledge (*pa/yas*) flow (*kSarantu*). (RV 9.67.37.)

452. Indra has extracted mature milk from an immature cow (*aamaa/ sv*) through Soma, with Pusan. (RV 2.40.2.)

453. Soma is the knower of All Things (*svarvi/dam*). (RV 9.8.9.)

LIBERATION

Yes, this is the purpose of material life and the spiritual journey. Just as the main purpose of a parent is to allow the child to leave when the time comes, so is the purpose of living in the material world to be liberated therefrom.

The Vedic dharma has formulated precise methods to achieve liberation. Soma has its own role to play in this framework. A principal part of Soma's role in the Vedic dharma is to enable the worshiper to achieve liberation and salvation. There are three stages to the accomplishment of liberation and salvation. In the first stage the worshiper achieves an elevation of consciousness. This is accomplished in seven stages:

- The Awakening is the first step in the journey towards salvation and liberation.
- From the Awakening, or Enlightenment, the worshiper acquires Knowledge.
- From Knowledge, he worshiper gains Consciousness.
- From Consciousness, the worshiper has the capacity to be engaged in Contemplation or Deliberation.
- From the act of Contemplation or Deliberation the worshiper gains Insightful Knowledge.
- From this Insightful Knowledge, the worshiper obtains Discernment.
- From Discernment, the worshiper obtains Divine Vision.

In the second stage, the worshiper experiences rapture and bliss.

- From Divine Vision, the worshiper experiences Joy.

- From Joy, the worshiper is completely overcome by Rapture.
- From there, Rapture, the worshiper gets a taste of Liberation.

In the final third stage, the worshiper is saved through Soma's ability to expiate sins. These stages taken together are roughly equivalent to the path of liberation formulated millennia later with Vedanta. This formulation itself consists of three elements: Reality, "Sat" + Understanding, Consciousness, "Cit" + Ananda, or "Bliss." The last two elements are the first two methods to liberation as far as Soma is concerned. This is a recognition that the final liberation of the worshiper's soul is ultimately an act of Grace.

Most of the Epithets in this Element refer to the worshiper's "Immortality." This word, "Immortality," is found literally everywhere in Vedic scripture. The use of the "Immortality," is often used with its functional equivalent, "conquering death." This does not mean that an aspirant will, for example, "conquer death," in the sense that the worshiper will live forever as a result of various Hatha Yoga practices. The meaning of "Immortality," or, for that matter, "conquering death," should be properly understood. Immortality," or "conquering death" are codewords for "liberation and salvation" itself. Besides, the worshiper's soul is itself immortal. So if anything lives forever, it is the worshiper's soul. The worshiper's spiritual journey is a quest to re-acquaint that soul which is immortal with the immortal.

454. Soma creates the desire for transcendence, the Seven-Dimensional Universe (*Trita*). (RV 8.52.1.)

455. Soma is the finder of the Way to Liberation (*gaatuvi/ttamaH*). (RV 9.44.6.)

456. Soma makes the worshiper immortal in a place where Visavat (All the Divine Vedic forces) reign (*raa/jaa vaivasvato/*). (RV 9.113.8.)

457. Soma makes the worshiper immortal in the Sun's secret place (*ya/ traavaro/dhanaM diva/H*). (RV 9.113.8.)

458. Soma makes the worshiper immortal in the Cosmic Waters (*aa/ pas*). (RV 9.113.8.)

459. Soma makes the worshiper immortal in the third region (*diva/H lokaa/*). (RV 9.113.9.)

460. Soma makes the worshiper immortal in the third heaven of heavens (*tridive/ diva/H*). (RV 9.113.9.)

461. Soma is immortal, undying (*a/martyaaH*). (RV 9.22.4.)

462. Soma Makes the Worshiper Immortal. (RV 9.113.10, 11.)

463. Soma produces Immortality (*amrta ma/rtyasya*). (RV 8.48.3.)

464. When Soma is consumed the immortal enters the worshiper's heart. (RV 8.48.12.)

465. Soma reveals the two-fold world of Immortality (*dvitaa/ vyuurNva/nn amR/tasya*). (RV 8.94.2.)

466. Soma makes the worshiper immortal in that place where bliss resides (*ya/traanandaa/sh*). (RV 9.113.11.)

467. Soma makes the worshiper immortal in that place where joy resides (*mo/daash*). (RV 9.113.11.)

468. Soma makes the worshiper immortal in that place where delight resides (*mu/daH*). (RV 9.113.11.)

469. Soma makes the worshiper immortal in that place where intense delight resides (*pramu/daH*). (RV 9.113.11.)

470. Soma makes the worshiper immortal in that place where the innermost desires reside. (RV 9.113.11.)

471. Soma makes the worshiper immortal in the abode of the Sun, the source of Light (*bradhna/sya viSTa/pam*). (RV 9.113.10.)

472. Soma makes the worshiper immortal in that place where the inherent characteristics of the Vedic divine forces reside (*svadhaa/*). (RV 9.113.10.)

473. Soma makes the worshiper immortal in that place where all desires (*kaa/maa*) go. (RV 9.113.10.)

474. Soma makes the worshiper immortal in that place where all longing (*nikaamaa/sh*) goes. (RV 9.113.10.)

475. Soma Pavamana (*pa/vamaana*) provides the basis of Immortality (*amRtatvaa/ya*) to all Vedic divibe forces (*dai/vyaa*). (RV 9.108.3.)

476. Soma is the basis of Immortality in the Vedic divine forces. (RV 9.106.8.)

477. Soma proclaims Immortality (*amRtatvaa/ya*) to all things divine (*dai/vyaa*). (RV 9.108.3.)

478. The immortal (*amR/to*) Soma is made bright and pure by humans. (RV 9.91.2.)

479. The worshiper becomes immortal when Soma desires for the worshiper the ambrosia of life (*jiivaa/tuM*). (RV 1.91.6.)

480. Soma Throws Open the Doors of Cosmic Sacrifice (*a/pa dvaa/ raa matiinaa/m*). (RV 9.10.6.)

481. Soma is the Divine Door (*devir-dvarah*). (RV 9.5.5.)

LIGHT, ILLUMINATION, GRACE

Light is the very essence, not only of Soma, but of the Rg Veda, and the Vedas generally. The Vedas, the Rg Veda especially, is a doctrine, a religion, a belief system based on Light. There are literally hundreds of synonyms and derivations for Light in the Vedas, and that world was very much divided between light and darkness, good and evil. The Vedas are literally a panegyric to the Kingdom of Light.

These characteristics are emphasized in these Epithets. The variations for "light" --- *jyotir*, ksi/tisaa, gaurii, *ghRta*, and others --- all have their own specific meaning to the region of light and its application to the worshiper's spiritual development. But while those nuances exist, they are of secondary importance to the subject at hand: The worshiper's liberation and salvation.

There is no doubt from where Soma resides.

- Soma is Pure Light. (Epithet No. 484.)
- Soma resides in that space above the light (Epithet No. 489), that space in the Vedic dharma wherein dwells the Great Light. (Epithet No. 492.)

In order to accomplish this task, the spiritual powers of Soma are released during the Soma Sacrifice. An integral part of the Soma Sacrifice is where the Soma plant stalks are rubbed and prepared for distillation. The rubbing of Soma is important, because it is when rubbed that the properties of light are released. As these Epithets indicate, Soma is rubbed bright. (Epithet No. 510.) when pressed out Soma desires light. (Epithet

No. 491.) It thereupon takes residences in the navel of Light. (Epithet No. 490.) The rubbing is not simply a procedural sacrificial step. It is a process pregnant in symbolism,

- The luminous Soma Is Rubbed Bright and Pure in the Purifier. (Epithet No. 485.)
- Soma is rubbed bright (shubhro/) and clean by the internal force of Agni. (Epithet No. 515.) This is symbolic speech signifying that when rubbed the internal powers of Fire --- see the Epithet presented earlier --- are infused in the liquid drink.
- Soma is rubbed clean as the Sun (viva/svataH) purifies the daughters of Aditi. (Epithet No. 516.) This is symbolic speech working on different levels. The Sun is not only the source of all life but representative of Agni, again infusing the powers of Fire, which are the divine forces of Change and Transformation. These powers are essential to the worshiper, because this is what the worshiper is seeking in the spiritual journey --- Change and Transformation.
- Soma is rubbed bright by the Seven Rivers. (Epithet No. 517.) Here, the Seven Rivers are symbolic of the seven levels of existence.

Darkness is the functional equivalent to Evil (Epithet No. 487) and is to be overcome in order for the worshiper to achieve final liberation and salvation. What concerns the worshiper is that universe of light, how it is contrasted from darkness, how the forces of light overcome the cloak of darkness, and how Soma is able to convey the ability to conquer darkness for the worshiper's spiritual edification. In the accomplishment of this goal, Soma's role is specifically identified. Soma establishes the indestructible light in the worshiper. (Epithet No. 486.) Infused by the light of intuition (re/tum), Soma enables the worshiper, through its powers of Change, to transform the worshiper into the new charioteer. (Epithet No. 493.) This is because Soma itself is the Car of Light (Epithet No. 501) and creates Light (Epithet No. 496.)

482. Soma is Resplendent. (RV 9.5.9.)

483. Soma Causes Illuminations. (RV 9.3.2.)

484. Soma is Pure Light (*jyotir*). (RV 9.66.24.)

485. Luminous (*rashmayo*) Soma Is Rubbed Bright and Pure in the Purifier. (RV 9.86.6.)

486. Soma establishes the indestructible light in the worshiper. (RV 9.113.7.)

487. The light of Soma (*jyo/tiSaa*) dispels the darkness (*ta/mo vavartha*). (RV 1.91.22.)

488. The ten throwers of light (*kSi/paH*) milk (*duhate*) the Soma. (RV 9.80.4.)

489. Soma resides in that space above the light (*gaurii/*). (RV 9.12.3)

490. The pressed-out Soma (*so/mo*) resides in the navel of Light (*yo/niM ghRta/vantam*). (RV 9.82.1.)

491. The pressed-out Soma (*so/maH pavi/tre*) desires light (*gavya/nn*). (RV 9.87.7.)

492. Soma dwells in the Great Light (*dyukSa/tamo*). (RV 9.108.1.)

493. Infused by the light of intuition (*re/tum*), Soma becomes the new charioteer (*ra/thyaM*). (RV 9.21.6.)

494. The light (*jyo/tiH*) of Soma is eternal (*sa/naa*). (RV 9.4.2.)

495. Soma is a Ray of Light Emitting from the Golden Sun (*ha/riH*). (RV 9.76.1.)

496. Soma Creates Light (*jyotisa*). (RV 9.108.12.)

497. Soma destroys the Darkness with his Light. (RV 9.108.12.)

498. Soma Emits a Vaishvanara Light (*jyo/tir vaishvaanara/m*). (RV 9.61.16.)

499. Soma is Light (*jyotir*). (RV 9.35.1.)

500. Soma is like light (*ghRta*). (TB 1.4.2.3.)

501. Soma is the Car of Light (*ghRta/snuH*). (RV 9.86.45.)

502. Soma Puts on the Robe of Rays (*gavyani*). (RV 9.8.6.)

503. Soma shines with radiances (*dyumne/bhir dyumny*). (RV 1.91.2.)

504. Soma is radiant (*shukra/H*). (RV 9.109.6.)

505. Soma shines with a radiance (*rocaya*). (RV 9.9.8; 9.49.5.)

506. Soma's Rays are Resplendent (*rakmir*) (RV 9.15.5.)

507. Soma's Rays fill Heaven and Earth (*rodasi*). (RV 9.41.5.)

508. Soma is the Ruler of the World of Light (*svar*). (RV 9.59.4.)

509. Soma Upholds the Flow by Which the Sun (*suu/ryam*) Shines (*a/ rocay-aH*). (RV 9.63.7.)

510. Soma is rubbed bright (*ga/bhastyoH*). (RV 9.20.6.)

511. Soma is bright (*shubhraa/*). (RV 9.63.26.)

512. Soma is bright (*shukraa/sa*). (RV 9.63.25.)

513. Soma is Bright and Pure. (RV 9.64.17.)

514. Soma bestows terrestrial riches (*paa/rthivaa*). (RV 9.63.30.)

515. Soma is rubbed bright (*shubhro/*) and clean (*gaa/H*) by the internal force of Agni (*yu/vaa*). (RV 9.14.5.)

516. Soma is rubbed clean as the Sun (*viva/svataH*) purifies the daughters of Aditi (i.e., the Zodiacal Houses). (RV 9.14.5.)

517. Soma is rubbed bright by the Seven Rivers (*nadya\H sapta/*). (RV 9.92.4.)

518. Soma is Illuminated in Consciousness (*vipah chitam*). (RV 9.86.36.)

519. Soma is the illumination of the mind (*citto/ vipaa/na/yaa*). (RV 9.65.12.)

520. Soma is luminous (*ha/rim*). (RV 9.98.7.)

LORDSHIP

Lordship in the Vedic dharma is an equal opportunity entity. Lordship of course connotes a primacy of one over the other. While such distinctions are a relatively salient feature of Abrahamic religions, the basis to determine Lordship in the Vedic dharma is entirely different.

A frequent observation or complaint about the Hindu faith is the presence of so many gods. In the Vedic dharma, there is but one God, the Lord and Master. The Rg Veda specifically names this deity as The One, *ekam*. (RV 1.31.2; 1.93.4; 1.95.3; 1.96.5; 1.110.3, 5; 1.117.18; 1.161.2; 1.164.46; 1.164.48; 1.165; 3.1.6; 3.31.1; 3.54.8; 4.16.3; 4.19.1; 4.35.2; 4.36.4; 4.58.4; 5.32.11; 5.62.2; 5.85.6; 6.9.5; 6.17.8; 7.18.11; 7.18.17; 8.20.13; 8.58.2; 8.100.5; 8.101.6; 9.9.4; 9.21.3; 9.97.55; 10.14.16; 10.27.16; 10.48.7; 10.56.1; 10.80.2, 6; 10.92.15; 10.101.5; 10.109.5; 10.114.5; 10.129.5; 10.138.6; 10.142.6.) Subordinate to The One are the many divine Vedic forces and energies, such as Agni, Indra, or, the subject of this book, Soma. All these divine Vedic forces are manifestations of the One God. Lordship, therefore, is equally divided among the Vedic forces and energies to different responsibilities and duties, but all are subject to The One.

And even to those objects over which Soma or the other Vedic forces and energies exercise their lordship, that presiding exercise is many times shared with other Vedic forces and energies. It is not lordship as much as an exercise in influence.

It is one thing to say, as many of the Epithets do, that Soma is the Lord of discreet physical phenomena, such as growing plants (Epithet No. 536), nations (Epithet No. 541), all creatures in general (Epithet No.

548), rivers (Epithet No. 554), essentially all things material (Epithet No. 531.) Soma is also Lord of intangibles, Strength (Epithet No. 524), Thoughts (Epithet No. 527), Nourishment (Epithet No. 528.) And of course the Lord of Rapture (Epithet No. 543.) These intangibles signify their every-day meaning, but in the Vedic dharma these words have an esoteric meaning corresponding to their divine Vedic force. These Vedic forces are subject to their own laws, and Soma is the Lord to these laws. (Epithet No. 529.)

Soma is the Lord of tangible, physical phenomena possessing an esoteric meaning. For example, Soma is Lord of the Cows (Epithet No. 522), which can mean the physical animal or the specialized type of Knowledge explained in some detail in the introduction. Further, Soma is Lord of the Steeds (Epithet No. 532), which also refers to the animal and another type of specialized knowledge discussed in the introduction.

Soma's Lordship is over existence itself. It is the Lord of the Svar, an intermediate level of Heaven. (Epithet No. 521.) It is the Lord of the Upper Level of Heaven. (Epithet No. 547.) Soma is Lord of all levels of existence. (Epithet No. 529.)

The Lordship of Soma is vast and comprehensive.

521. Soma is Lord of the Svar (*Svarpatii*). (RV 9.19.2.)

522. Soma is Lord of the Cows (*Gopati*). (RV 9.19.2.)

523. Soma is the leader (*patim*) of all humans (*ja/nasya*). (RV 9.35.5.)

524. Soma is Lord of Strength. (RV 9.36.6.)

525. Soma is the Lord of Impulsion (*ishaspatim*). (RV 9.14.7.)

526. Soma is Lord of Enlightenment (*brahmana*). (RV 9.83.1.)

527. Soma is the Lord of Thoughts (*ma/nasas pa/tiH*). (RV 9.28.1.)

528. Soma is Lord of Nourishment (*uurjaa/m*). (RV 5.41.12.)

529. Soma is the Lord of the Laws Controlling All Existence (*saatya*). (RV 1.91.5.)

530. Soma is the Lord of the Brahmins. (T.S. 1.8.10; SPB 5.3.3.12.)

531. Soma is the Sovereign Lord of All (*vishva/tas pa/tiH*). (RV 9.5.1.)

532. Soma is the Lord of the Steeds (*hariiNaam pata*). (RV 9.105.5.)

533. Soma is the Lord of Riches (*rayipa/tir*). (RV 2.40.6.)

534. Soma is the Lord of All Worlds (*pa/tir vi/shvasya*). (RV 9.86.5.)

535. Soma is the Lord of the Plentitude, Fullness (*vaa/jeSu vaaji/nam*). (RV 9.65.11.)

536. Soma is Lord of the Growing Plants (*viiru/dhaam pa/tir*). (RV 9.114.2.)

537. Soma is the Lord of Directions (*dishaam*). (RV 9.113.2.)

538. Soma is Lord of the Impelling Forces (*i/sas pate*). (RV 9.108.9.)

539. Soma is the lord of Strength (*vRja/nasya raa/jaa*). (RV 9.97.10)

540. Soma is lord of all beings (*sata/H*). (RV 9.86.5.)

541. Soma is the Ruler of Nations. (RV 9.86.37.)

542. Soma is the Leader of Thousands. (RV 9.85.4.)

543. Soma is the Lord of Rapture (*madaanaam pate*). (RV 8.93.1.)

544. The King (raajann) is the essence (*ra/so*) of the rapture (*ma/do*) of the flowing Soma (*pa/vamaanasya*). (RV 9.61.17.)

545. Soma is the Master of Brave Progeny (*viirayu/H shavasas pate*). (RV 9.36.6.)

546. Soma is the King of the Sacrificial Paths (*patho/ ra/jaH*). (RV 9.22.4.)

547. Soma is the King of Upper Level of Heaven (*uttama/M ra/jaH*). (RV 9.22.5.)

548. Soma is the King of All Creatures (*vish/vam*). (RV 9.68.9.)

549. Soma is the Master of the Soul (*Brahmanaspati*). (RV 9.83.1.)

550. King Soma won the world of the Moon by chanting the sakamedha sacrifice. (T.B., 1.4.10.7.)

551. The actions of Soma are like that of King Varuna. (RV 1.91.3.)

552. Soma is King (*raa/jaa*). (RV 9.108.8.)

553. Soma is the King of Auspicious Deeds (*raa/jaanaM sukrato*). (RV 9.48.3.)

554. Soma is the King of the Rivers (*raa/jaa si/ndhuunaam*). (RV 9.86.33.)

555. Soma is the Leader (*puroyaa/*). (RV 9.5.9.)

LUMINOSITY

Luminosity lies both at the essential core of Light and is the product of Light. This Element is all about color. In many ways it is the essence of Soma. The Mahabharata states the word, "Soma," derives from it being "ever bright:" The letter "ma" means "bright" and the letter "u" means "always."

First and foremost, Soma is golden-colored. Gold in the Vedic dharma carries a special significance. This is another use of highly symbolic language; gold carries far more meaning than the metal itself. In the process of creation, the Veda provides the philosophical or spiritual basis, if not the inspiration, for the subsequent craft of alchemy. It is significant that Soma Pavamana, the distilled, purified form of Soma, has the ability to change anything into gold. (Epithet no. 858.) What can this possibly mean? The transmutation of gold is seen as not so much the acquisition of wealth, but the ability of the alchemist to harness, manipulate and ultimately transcend the limitations of the material world. The alchemist accomplished this feat through the purity of mind and focus of meditation. This is closely related to an advanced siddhi, or mental power, that is achieved in Patanjali Yoga when the worshiper accomplishes a higher stage of Samadhi, or spiritual awareness. The transmutation to gold informed the process to produce and represented the Philosopher's Stone, that concentration of the essence (rasa) of matter. Gold, the Philosopher's Stone, assisted the worship during the Vedic path to liberation and salvation. Gold furnished that which was the goal of the worshiper: Strength, Vigor, Immortality. This process was summarized in the Khila Suktas, a collection of ninety-eight "apocryphal" hymns of the Rigveda. From these Suktas, the worshiper may learn all that may be learnt about what gold offers:

- Gold possesses longevity (ayus), vital energy (prana), and wealth (rayim). (RV-K, 4.6.1.)
- Gold is highly powerful, overcomes difficulties, and is victorious against enemies. (RV-K, 4.6.2.) By understanding the essence and occult meaning (nama) of gold, the worshiper becomes lustrous and gains the effulgence of the sun. (RV-K, 4.6.3.) The worshiper also is united with the power of Indra. (RV-K, 4.6.4.)
- The gold produced by Transformation (Agni) confers Immortality among humans. (RV-K, 4.6.5.)
- Neither Evil nor evil spirits overcome the luster of gold, the first ray of light from the gods. (RV-K, 4.6.7.)
- Gold is derived from ghee (mental awareness and acuity) and madhu (divine ecstasy). (RV-K, 4.6.9.)
- Gold makes me the favorite to the gods, and walk in their footsteps, that I may shine like gold does. (RV-K, 4.6.10.)

Soma is associated with the Sun. (Epithet No. 558.) Savitr is also associated with the Sun, but more importantly associated with GOLD:

- Savitr is golden-eyed. (RV 1.35.8.)
- Savitr is golden-handed. (RV 1.35.9, 10.)
- Savitr is golden-tongued. (RV 6.71.3.)
- Savitr has golden arms. (RV 6.71.1, 5; 7.71.1; 7.48.2.)
- Savitr is golden haired. (RV 10.139.1.)
- Savitr wears a tawny, golden-hued garment. (RV 4.53.2.)
- Savitr drives a golden car with a golden pole. (RV 1.35.2, 5.)
- With his strong golden arms he blesses all creatures. (RV 2.38.2; 4.14.2; 6.71.1; 7.45.3.)

This characteristic of Savitr is crucial. Gold and all things golden represent Immortality and the eternal. Gold is also highly symbolic of the attributes of Immortality, aptly summarized in the Pacavimsa Brahmana:

- Mahas, the personification of strength.
- Prakasa, the light of consciousness.

- The light infused to the worshiper's soul.
- The world of heaven.

The rays of Soma and Savitr are luminous. (Epithet No. 559.) This is symbolic speech to represent the dispensing of the riches of Immortality --- read here, liberation and salvation --- to the worshiper. Gold is the metallic, material, representation of the immutable and eternal. (SPB 5.4.1.14.) These benefits are dispensed by Soma and Savitr. As the Principle of Immortality Savitr dispenses the benefit of Immortality to the other dynamic Vedic forces. Savitr also bestows Immortality to Agni. The essential nature of Agni is in the Principle of Change and Transformation. That aspect of the Principle of Change called Agni Vaisvanara is associated in the Vedas with lightning. Agni is associated with this material world. In his dominion over this world, Agni rules as the Principle of Change, encompassing the constant change and flux of the sensible world and is articulated in the mental and spiritual transformation of the mind and soul of the worshiper. In saying that it is golden-colored, Soma is not simply equated with Immortality, but facilitating Immortality --- read here, liberation and salvation --- to the worshiper.

Part of this luminosity is Soma being "green-hued." (Epithet No. 562.) Epithet No. 562 is a good illustration of word-play in the Vedas. This epithet is a good example of the Veda's use of double entendre to convey the full meaning of the word. The epithet itself has many references in Mandala Nine. The greenness refers to the color of the plant juice, which is thought of as being green in color. The metaphorical meaning of brilliance refers to the exhilaration experienced when the Soma juice is consumed during the Soma Sacrifice. Over time, long after the Soma plant was thought to have been eradicated through over-use, this meaning took hold. Thus, "hari" came to mean a salutation of reverence, as in "Hare Krishna. Hare, Hare."

That Soma has the property of being "hari," or "green-hued," is itself significant. The introduction spoke of Horses and their significance to Soma and the Vedas in general. The principal Vedic divine forces each had their own Horse. Symbolically, this represents different levels of consciousness of the worshiper. The Brhad-Devata describes the Bay Horses (Hari), the horses of Indra. (BD, 4.140, 141.) Hari represents an aspect of the mind-body relation as regards to conscious perception to each dynamic Vedic force wherewith it relates. In Hari, for instance, the horses of Indra, it is seen as the instrument of achieving divine inspiration, ecstasy and union. In reaching that goal, constant mention is made to "harness the horses" so that they may be "yoked." This is but another way of saying that the mind must be restrained, controlled, and focused to achieve liberation and salvation. In this aspect Indra acts as the Lord of the sense perceptions. Indra acts as a true Lord, one which exercises mastery to restrain and calm the mind which perceives the sense data. The dynamic force of knowledge and discernment (Indra), appropriately, plays a central role in the riding (restraint) of the horses (sense perceptions). Indra's horses, the world as perceived by the Subject, the Universal Self (Buddhi) are "golden." (RV 10.96.2.) Having "golden manes," (RV 8.32.29), and Indra himself, (the Universal Self, Buddhi), rides on a golden chariot. (RV 8.1.25.)

- The dynamic force of Knowledge (Indra), appropriately, is called the "Lord of the Bay (Horses), consistent with the need of knowledge to restrain the fluctuations of sense perceptions.
- The dynamic force of the Buddhi (Indra) is the "yoker" of the Bay Horses.
- The dynamic force of knowledge and discernment (Indra) yokes, or restrains, the fluctuations of the senses.
- The movement of the dynamic force of knowledge and discernment (Indra) in the chariot (body) thus becomes the seat of discernment. (RV 3.53.6.)

Other themes emerge:

- Indra (Buddhi) yokes (restrains) the horses (senses/vrttis). (RV 1.5.4; 1.6.4; 1.84.6; 1.161.6, 21; 5.33.2; 7.19.6; 10.23.1, 3; 10.44.2; 10.105.5.)
- The horses (senses/vrttis) yoked (restrained) by prayer. (RV 1.28.7; 1.82.6; 1.84.3; 2.18.7; 3.35.4; 4.32.15; 8.2.27; 8.17.2; 8.45.39.)
- Hari (the organs of sense perceptions) bring Indra (Buddhi) to the sacrifice. (RV 1.82.1; 3.35.2; 3.43.4; 8.12.15; 10.23.2.)

- The sacrifice is a journey, the journey of the worshiper's soul. (RV 2.18.2.) Hence, the harnessed horses (restrained senses/vrttis) transport the worshiper on that journey.
- Indra (Buddhi) yokes (restrains) Hari (the sense organs/vrttis) to battle the enemies, metaphorical for confronting evil, ignorance, or anything else which might retard progress in the Vedic path to liberation and salvation. (RV 1.81.3; 6.57.3.)
- Principal among the enemies is Vrtra, and the horses (senses/vrttis) must be yoked (restrained) to fight against Vrtra (ignorance). (RV 8.3.17; 8.12.25, 26, 27; 8.12.25.)
- Hari (the organs of sense perceptions/vrttis) bring Indra (Buddhi) to the sacrifice to drink Soma (divine ecstasy). (RV 1.10.3; 1.16.21; 1.55.7; 1.82.5; 1.177.4; 3.35.1; 5.43.5; 6.40.1; 8.3.17; 8.6.45; 8.13.31; 8.14.12; 8.32.30; 10.96.6; 10.160.1.) Symbolically, this signifies that the restrained mind is one of the means to achieve self-realization.
- Hari (the organs of sense perceptions/vrttis) bring Indra (Buddhi) to the sacrifice to eat food. (RV 1.82.2, 3, 4.)
- The horses (senses/vrttis) must be yoked (restrained) to receive the benefits of the sacrifice. (RV 1.82.1, 3.)

Related to this is the "unyoking" of the horses/vrttis. Soma, the divine dynamic energy and the elixir, is a significant participant in this aspect. Consider:

- The dynamic Vedic energy of divine union (Soma) acts to "unyoke" the horses. (RV 3.32.1.) This is the nature of the ecstasy of divine union. After the experience — any experience — of divine union, the worshiper's perception of the world is different. Instead of viewing the world in black and white, the world is suddenly, as in the Wizard of Oz, in living color. The worshiper experiences what Alan Watts states any seeker must do — get "out of your mind." In the language of the Veda, the horses are unyoked.
- Thus, when the experience of divine union is experienced after consumption of the Soma juice at the sacrifice, the senses

flow, like Soma, like a rapid horse. (RV 9.16.1; 9.23.2; 9.26.1; 9.36.1; 9.59.1; 9.62.6; 9.72.1; 9.74.1; 9.93.1; 9.96.20; 9.97.18; 9.101.2.)

Gold and luminosity unites Soma with the benefits the worshiper obtains during the spiritual journey.

556. Soma Glitters Across the Firmament (*anta/rikSeNa*). (RV 9.5.2.)

557. Soma is the Golden-Colored. (RV 9.5.9.)

558. Soma is the Sun (*suu/raM*). (RV 9.65.1.)

559. The rays (*bhaanu/naa*) of Soma are luminous (*dyuma/ntaM*). (RV 9.65.4.)

560. Purified Soma Appears Luminous and Golden-hued During the Day (*di/vaa ha/rir da/dRshe*). (RV 9.97.9.)

561. Luminous (*ha/ri*) it is mixed in many forms (*ruupai/r*). (RV 9.34.4.)

562. Soma is Luminous, Green-Tinted (*hari*). (RV 9.64.14.)

563. Soma is luminous (*raajati*) and illumines (*dyumaa/n*) everything. (RV 9.61.18.)

564. Soma Illuminates the Constellations. (RV 9.36.3.)

565. Soma is luminous (*dyumaa/M*). (RV 9.64.1.)

566. The Divine Golden Doors (*dvaa/ro devii/r hiraNya/yiiH*). (RV 9.5.5.)

MOTION

Motion has its own role to play in the worshiper's spiritual journey. This is an important spiritual Element in the Vedic dharma. This Element recognizes that nothing can exist without movement. Where there is movement there is life. Specifically, where there is movement there is spiritual development, for without movement there is no vehicle available to the worshiper to further advance the spiritual journey.

We saw earlier that Consciousness was in Soma's nature of flowing and symbolically this concept was represented by the flowing river. In motion, this notion is refined. Instead of rivers, however, the symbol employed by the Rg Veda is the Flood. The Flood is simply the amplified river (Consciousness), representing the intense surge in spiritual ecstasy. It is Consciousness in motion. It is a simile much more attuned the precise nature of Soma. References to "the Floods" are many: (RV 9.21.6; 9.97.21; 9.107.12.)

As Soma pervades the individual subject as it pervades the heavenly divine. The characteristic of individual conscious is its relation to the world, where the subject perceives the objects of its perception. The divine Consciousness of Soma, however, is self-referential and has nothing to reflect upon but itself. Soma is said many times as being "bright," the principal characteristic of Consciousness. (RV 9.9.3; 9.12.9; 9.13.2; 9.36.3; 9.38.3; 9.40.1; 9.52.5; 9.54.1, 28; 9.55.19, 26; 9.66.5, 30; 9.69.4, 5; 9.70.8, 9; 9.71.2; 9.72.4; 9.72.4; 9.73.5, 7; 9.75.3; 9.78.1; 9.80.2; 9.86.13; 9.89.4; 9.92.4; 9.97.3, 23, 31, 32, 46, 50; 9.99.1; 9.107.17, 22; 9.109.3, 6.) Soma shines. (RV 9.2.6; 9.5.3; 9.9.8; 9.15.3; 9.17.5; 9.23.2; 9.25.3; 9.28.3; 9.36.3; 9.37.4; 9.44.8; 9.59.3; 9.71.7; 9.75.3; 9.78.3; 9.85.9; 9.91.6; 9.97.9; 9.108.9; 9.111.1; 9.113.7.) For the purposes of the flow of Consciousness, Soma flows both to and outside itself. It is for this reason it is called the "thousand-streamed ocean," (RV 9.101.6) signifying both the pervasion of Soma and consciousness flowing to its vessel. Soma is flowing into itself but the "ocean" is the wooden vessel into which the purified Soma is deposited. Sayana explains it is a vessel which is meant when it is said that Soma itself flows to the ocean. (RV 9.66.12; 9.64.27; 9.85.10; 9.86.29; 9.88.6; 9.107.9.) Here the transformation bears to its essential core and is complete.

The Vedic dharma signifies the flow of Consciousness is keyed to some relation to rivers. One such attribute of this Eternal Law is "The Floods." The Rg Veda agrees with other ancient systems which tells about a great flood which destroyed the entire world as it then existed and from which Manu, the First Man, (Adam) arose. "The Floods" are representative of the Eternal Law of the intense flow of Consciousness. This is the intensity that is experienced in higher states of Consciousness and is the pathway to the divine. Consciousness is characteristic of intensity, for by its nature it is not inert but active, in motion. This mobility is perfectly adapted to the Floods, which like a Tsunami sweeps everything in its path. The Floods, on the other hand, is a much more intense Eternal Law of the flow of Consciousness. It is not unfair to compare the Floods to the kundalini sakti.

Having established the distinguishing characteristics of the generic purposes of the waters, the purification powers of the waters, and the Floods, it is apparent from the Rg Veda which roles Agni, Soma and Indra assume in this vast scheme. Agni represents the Waters' Eternal Law of pervasion and the Eternal Law of the Rivers; Soma represents the purification powers of the Waters; and Indra represents the kundalini sakti aspect of the Floods. This category provides the constituent parts to this movement. The Epithets are clothed in symbolic speech.

- That the movement is one of power (Epithet No. 567) speaks to the intense experience of spiritual awakening.
- The Epithet that "Soma is carried by a car" (Epithet No. 568) contains a double meaning. There is a sacrificial aspect referring to the Soma stalks carried on carts to the sacrificial grounds to be further processed to liquid. There is a deeper meaning of the "car" referring to the worshiper. In this meaning the worshiper literally "carries" Soma in the material

body after consumption of the liquid. The worshiper further carries Soma during the spiritual journey. Soma in this sense is literally the gasoline that fuels the worshiper's car, i.e., body.

- The same can be said in the Epithet No. 571 where "Soma sits on the vessels." The "Vessels," however, as akin to the rivers of consciousness where the meandering thoughts of the worshiper flow.

This category clarifies from where Consciousness originates. Soma moves in the "Land of Pure Being," (Epithet No. 572), wherein *Satya*, Truth and Existence, resides. From there Soma moves Speech, creating the subtle form of physical phenomena. Once passing through the filter during the Soma Sacrifice --- another level of discrimination --- Soma communicates its spiritual lesson to the worshiper. Like Tommy from the Rock Opera, Soma gives eyesight to the blind. (Epithet No. 570.)

These themes of movement will be explored and expounded centuries later in the doctrine of Spanda by the Rishiis of Khashiri Shaivism.

567. Soma is a Movement of Power (*angushah*). (RV 9.97.8.)

568. Soma is carried by a car (*rathiralH*). (RV 9.97.46.)

569. Soma moves swiftly (*jiiraalv*). (RV 9.66.9.)

570. Soma Heals the Sick and Gives Eyesight to the Blind. (RV 8.79.2.)

571. Soma Sits in the Vessels (*chamusu*). (RV 9.20.6.)

572. Soma Moves in the Land of Pure Being (*Satyabhih*). (RV 9.3.4.)

573. By incorporating (*bhuulrNayas*) Soma, Soma moves (*alkramuH*) by removing the worshiper's enemies. (RV 9.41.1.)

574. Soma has a thousand movements to make any path for the worshiper. (RV 9.106.5.)

575. Soma is the Mover of Speech. (RV 9.35.5.)

576. Soma moves with the power of intelligence (*manaalv*). (RV 9.65.16.)

577. Soma moves in the plane of the woolen filter (*alvya elSi saalnavi*). (RV 9.50.2.)

578. Soma is wide-moving. (RV 9.62.13.)

579. Soma rushes to the pitchers where it resides (*drolNaani dhaavati*). (RV 9.37.6.)

In the next category, we learn more on how Soma informs and educates the worshiper in the spiritual journey.

NOURISHMENT

This category refers to the method by which Soma informs and furthers the spiritual journey of the worshiper. The first method is by consumption. (Epithet No. 580.) This is the primary method. For further information on Consumption, please see its separate category. Prior to consumption there must first be the conditions for continuation of life to enable the consumption of Soma, as well as every other type of human activity. For this form of nourishment Epithet No. 581 states that Soma nourishes the Sun. (Epithet No. 581.) This method is also of great importance. The Sun is the source of all life, and without the warmth of the Sun's rays all life would cease.

580. Soma is Fully Perfected (*altyaviH*) for Consumption. (RV 9.13.1.)

581. Soma Nourishes the Sun by its Illuminations (*arkaiIH*) When Born. (RV 9.97.31.)

OPPOSITION (JUXTAPOSITION OF OPPOSITES)

The material world is reflected in the Two-Dimensional Universe. The Two-Dimensional Universe is based on polar opposites. Soma upholds this Two-Dimensional Universe (Epithet No. 582), as well as the other dimensions of the Vedic dharma. These opposites abound:

- Big, Small / Little
- Cheap, Expensive
- Clean, Dirty
- Deep, Shallow
- Down, Up
- Early, Late
- Easy, Difficult / Hard
- Far, Near / Close
- High, Low
- Hot, Cold
- Left, Right

The list is endless.

There is a difference between Opposition and Complementation. Opposition is grounded in conflict. The oppositions contained in this list are dichotomies in conflict, not a completion of an organic whole.

The dichotomies in Vedic dharma are considered two halves of one whole. (Epithet No. 587.) The principal dichotomies, as opposed to Opposites --- in the Vedic dharma are Heaven and Earth and the Sun

163

and Moon. It is Soma's function to complement these dichotomies in the Vedic dharma by uniting the two juxtapositioned forces. Thus

- Soma Gives Birth to Heaven and Earth (Epithet No. 583), while placing both in a "perfect abode." (Epithet No. 584.)
- Soma creates the Sun and the Moon before Creation (Epithet No. 588), all while Soma is considered the two halves of both. (Epithet No. 586.)

Soma throws light on our material world:

582. Soma is the upholder of the Two, the Two-Dimensional Universe (*tvaa dhartaalram*). (RV 9.65.11.)

583. Soma Gives Birth to Heaven and Earth. (RV 9.96.5.)

584. When purified Soma renders heaven and earth perfect abodes. (RV 9.97.27.)

585. Soma unveils the two-fold realm of the Vedic dharma, the natural order (*Rtaayalntiir*). (RV 9.94.2.)

586. The Sun and Moon are the two halves of Soma. (RV 9.68.5.)

587. Soma Rules the Universe with its Two Halves (*dhaalmani*). (RV 9.66.2.)

588. Both Aspects of Soma, the Moon and the Sun, are recognized Before Creation. (RV 9.68.5.)

589. In its Aspect as the Moon, Soma is Born in a Secret Place. (RV 9.68.5.)

OVERCOMING ADVERSITY

It furthers the worshiper's spiritual journey to be persevering. These Epithets provide a template for not only the worshiper's spiritual journey but the worshiper's code of conduct. This is the most overtly spiritual category in the whole system of Elements.

This is the category which emphasizes the spiritual strength of Soma. Soma destroys (*ni/tire*) the virility of the enemies. (Epithet No. 605.) This is tantamount to taking the wind out of Evil's sail. Soma both overcomes the spiritual adversity the worshiper experiences and convey that power to the worshiper to avoid the trap of temptation. Soma overcomes any adversity to spiritual development so that the worshiper may reap the spiritual rewards:

- Soma is the Killer of Demons. (Epithet No. 598.)
- Soma destroys All Demons. (Epithet No. 608.)
- Soma is Victorious over all dividing forces. (Epithet No. 623.)
- Soma is the Subduer of Enmity. (Epithet No. 627.)
- Soma destroys Ahi. (Epithet No. 609.) Ahi is another name for Vrtra, which is subject to its own separate category.

As a result of this cosmic battle Soma gains spiritual benefits:

- Soma Conquers the Cows (Epithet No. 607), symbolic of Insightful Knowledge.
- He conquers the third plane. (Epithet No. 616.) This is the upper level of existence in Heaven.

- Soma conquers the waters. (Epithet No. 590.) The waters represent the Vedic dharma.
- Soma Wins Gold. (Epithet No. 628.) This is symbolic to liberation and salvation.

Heaven, the Vedic dharma, liberation and salvation, these and others are what Soma gains for the worshiper in overcoming the adversities. At its essence, however, the spiritual battle is a personal one to be waged by the worshiper.

The worshiper must act as a skilled worker. (Epithet No. 593.) The worshiper must not be deterred by unfavorable circumstances, nor permit steadfastness to be shaken. The worshiper can avoid this by incorporating the quality of Soma to maintain the inner light to drive away dark forces (Epithet No. 595) and driving off Evil (Epithet No. 595), while outwardly remaining yielding and tractable. The worshiper must drive away Evil. (Epithet No. 597.) With this attitude the worshiper can overcome even the greatest adversities. (Epithet No. 602.)

In some situations indeed the worshiper must hide the inner light, in order to make the worshiper's will prevail in spite of difficulties the immediate environment. Perseverance must dwell in the area of the innermost consciousness and should not be discernible from without. Only thus is the worshiper able to maintain the will in the face of difficulties.

590. Soma conquers the waters (*apalH si/saasann*). (RV 9.90.4.)

591. Soma is the winner of the Svar (*RSikR/t svarSaa/H*). (RV 9.89.18.)

592. Soma opens the door (*a/paavRNod*) which had been closed to the `worshiper. (RV 4.28.1.)

593. Soma is a Skilled Worker (*kRtnu/r*). (RV 8.79.1.)

594. Soma Seizes Food From the Enemies (*sravasyavah*). (RV 9.10.1.)

595. Soma Drives Off the Dark Evil. (RV 9.41.1.)

596. Soma is the destroyer of foes (*bha-Nga/m*). (RV 9.61.13.)

597. Soma Drives Away the Enemies. (RV 8.79.9.)

598. Soma is the Killer of Demons. (RV 9.1.2.)

599. Entering the filter for purification, Soma defeats all enemies (*spR/dhaH*). (RV 9.20.1.)

600. Soma is undefeated in Battles (*a\rSaa/napacyuto*). (RV 9.4.8.)

601. Soma overcomes (*sama/tsu*) the foe (*saasahi/H*). (RV 9.4.8.)

602. After being purified Soma drives away the enemies (*sri/dhaH*). (RV. 9.27.1)

603. Soma swiftly flows to overcome obstacles. (RV 9.58.1.)

604. Soma destroys (*ni/tire*) the growth and pervasion (*va/yas*) of the enemies (*sha/troH*). (RV 9.19.7.)

605. Soma destroys (*ni/tire*) the virility (*vR/SNyaM*) of the enemies. (*sha/troH*). (RV 9.19.7.)

606. Soma destroys (*ni/tire*) the strength (*shu/SmaM*) of the enemies (*sha/troH*). (RV 9.19.7.)

607. Soma Conquers the Cows. (RV 9.78.4.)

608. Soma destroys All Demons. (RV 9.88.4.)

609. Soma destroys Ahi. (RV 9.88.4.)

610. Soma Accomplishes every task. (RV 9.11.7.)

611. Soma is invincible (*duSTa/ro*). (RV 9.20.6.)

612. Soma is Invincible (*ugra/M*). (RV 8.70.4.)

613. Soma conquers (*si/saasanto*) all for human beings (*vanaamahe*). (RV 9.61.11.)

614. While being flows (*pa/ri Sicyate*) into the purifier (*pavi/tre*), Soma conquers the svar (*svarji/t*). (RV 9.27.2.)

615. Soma is the Conqueror of riches (*sa/nitaa dha/naani*). (RV 9.90.3.)

616. He conquers the third plane. (*tRtii/yaM*). (RV 9.89.18.)

617. Soma conquers Dawn, the beginning of understanding (*si/saasann uSa/saH*). (RV 9.90.4.)

618. Soma conquers the Rays of the Sun (*si/saasann sva\r gaa/H*), the brilliance of enlightenment. (RV 9.90.4.)

619. Soma is the Conqueror of All (*vishvaji/d*). (RV 8.79.1.)

620. He conquers the third plane (*tRtii/yaM*). (RV 9.89.18.)

621. Soma conquers Dawn, the beginning of understanding (*si/saasann uSa/saH*). (RV 9.90.4.)

622. Soma conquers the Rays of the Sun (*si/saasann sva\r gaa/H*), the brilliance of enlightenment. (RV 9.90.4.)

623. Soma is Victorious over all dividing forces (*udbhi/d i/t*). (RV 8.79.1.)

624. By making a sound (*ka/nikradat*) while purified Soma overcomes all enemies. (RV 9.13.8.)

625. Soma slayed the enemies for Manu, the earliest man, and later bringing these riches to the worshiper. (RV 9.96.12.)

626. Soma overcomes all dividing forces (*udbhi/d*). (RV 8.79.1.)

627. Soma is the Subduer of Enmity. (RV 9.11.7.)

628. Soma Wins Gold. (RV 9.78.4.)

THE PATH

The Path is an integral part of the Vedic dharma. The notion of a path to liberation and salvation are not unknown to the Vedic dharma. RV 5.46.1 beseeches that enlightened person to show others the "straight path." The Path has taken many meanings, but as regards Soma that meaning is clear. In the worshiper's spiritual journey, it is the roadmap to liberation and salvation.

The Path of the Vedic dharma is one of personal liberation and salvation. Implied in the Epithets which follow are the means by which the worshiper travels while on this journey. The worshiper accordingly employs the following tools to achieve this goal:

- The laws of the Vedic dharma. (Epithet No. 629.)
- The insights of the Seers and Rishiis. (Epithet No. 630.)
- The insights gained at and as a result of the sacrifice. (Epithet No. 632.)
- Discovering the right path. (Epithet No. 638.)

Soma is the spiritual guide for the directions taken while on this spiritual journey. (Epithet No. 643.) Soma provides specific assistance during this spiritual undertaking. Soma provides the worshiper:

- The understanding of the Path obtained through Soma. (Epithet No. 633.)
- Subtle powers. (Epithet No. 636.)

- Soma gives the worshiper directions on where to travel on the path. (Epithet No. 639.)
- Soma finds the way for the worshiper. (Epithet No. 642.

This is because Soma flows along the Paths of Truth like a river. (Epithet No. 635.) This is symbolic speech for the flow of consciousness. The implication is that this consciousness inures to the worshiper prior to and during the spiritual journey

629. Soma Creates the paths (*pathaa/*) to the laws of the Vedic dharma, the natural order (*dha/rmann Rta/sya*). (RV 9.7.1.)

630. Soma provides the path to the Seers and Rishiis (*padavii/H kaviinaa/m*). (RV 9.89.18.)

631. Soma is the Guide to the Sages (*padavii/H kaviinaa/m*). (RV 9.96.6.)

632. Soma Creates the Path (*pathani*) During the Sacrifice. (RV 9.86.26.)

633. Soma leads the worshiper (*maniiSaa/*) to understand the path (*pa/nthaam*). (RV 1.91.1.)

634. Soma Follows the Path of the Vedic dharma, the Natural Order (*Rta*). (RV 9.97.32.)

635. Soma, the Lord of Heaven, flows (*pavate*), moving on the paths of truth (*Rta/sya pathi/bhiH*) and surrounds the rivers. (RV 9.86.33.)

636. Soma Attains Subtle Powers (*a/NvaM*) Directly Through a Path Unobstructed (*pathi/bhir adhvasma/bhiH*). (RV 9.91.3.)

637. The worshiper with Soma's help medicates (*manaamahe/*) on the happy path (*suvita/sya*). (RV 9.41.2.)

638. Soma discovers the right path. (RV 9.106.6.)

639. Only Soma can answer questions on the directions (*di/sha*). (RV 9.70.9.)

640. Soma finds the expansive growth (*va/yo dhaa*) in the worshiper. (RV 9.90.6.)

641. Soma discovers the golden riches for the worshiper. (RV 9.86.39.)

642. Soma finds the way (*gaatuvi/t*) of the Great Path (*raa/dhaso maha/H*). (RV 9.46.5.)

643. Soma is the guide to yamanas or worshipers (*nRca/kSaaH*). (RV 1.91.2.)

644. Soma is the Sacrificial Guide (*nRca/kSaaH*) for the Worshiper. (RV 9.78.2.)

645. Soma is the Divine (*deva/*). (RV 9.108.8.)

PERFECTION

There's no great mystery or surprise here. Soma is perfect, and it is perfection itself. By "perfect" this is to say Soma is completed in thought (Epithet No. 649) and multi-functional. (Epithet No. 652.) It is faultless (Epithet No. 647) and of perfect form. (Epithet No. 648.) Soma was perfect when it was born (Epithet No. 646), because it has a never-decaying body. (Epithet No. 654.) After its birth sits in a perfect place. (Epithet No. 651.) There, the divine Vedic forces prepare Soma. (Epithet No. 653.) When they --- and the worshiper --- consumes the Soma juice, Soma's qualities of perfection are acquired.

646. Soma is of the perfect birth (*pa/riSkRtam*). (RV 9.61.13.)

647. Soma is the faultless (*anavadyo/*). (RV 9.69.10.)

648. Soma is of perfect form (*suma~Nga/laH*). (RV 9.80.3.)

649. Soma is perfected, completed in thoughts (*da/kSaaya*). (RV 9.105.2.)

650. The powers of the consumed Soma take a perfect form. (RV 4.50.10.)

651. Soma sits in the perfect place (niSk*Rta/m*) of the gods (*devaa/naam*). (RV 3.62.13.)

652. Soma is Multi-Functional (*puruvratah*). (RV 9.3.10.)

653. Divine Powers Prepare Soma. (RV 9.78.2.)

654. Soma has a Never-decaying Body (*tanunpat*). (RV 9.5.2.)

PERVASION

The salient feature of this category is that Soma pervades the entire expanse of existence. The levels of existence were touched upon in the introduction with the discussion of the Vedic multi-universes. Soma Pavamana, the purified Soma juice, is all pervading. (Epithet No. 656.)

The cardinal numbers in the Vedic universe are two, three, five and seven. The cardinal numbers pertain to ever-greater, ever expanding, levels of subtly: As the numbers progress to higher levels, so does physical matter become ever more subtle and so intensify the worshiper's journey to liberation. These numbers are coordinates which are incorporated into the structure of the universe. The microcosm and macrocosm are interpreted with reference to these cardinal numbers, the microcosm and macrocosm, and the matter contained therein. The worshiper, during the Vedic path to liberation and salvation, traverses these stages of creation, these manifestations of the possible universes. The spiritual progression is very much an upward climb through these universes, from the duality present in the Two-Dimensional world to the transcendent world of the Seven-Dimensional Universe. With reference to matter itself, that level of subtlety progresses ever inward, until the very stuff of matter reaches the level of subtlety found in rarified sub-atomic level. We are getting ahead of ourselves here, and this is more properly addressed by the Vedic alchemist. The point being is the many possible worlds are born from the single, unitary, One (Ekam).

The Vedic multiple universes consist of:

- The Two-Dimensional Universe which the material world itself. This is the world of Maya.

- The Three-Dimensional world is the gateway, inching towards the Five-Dimensional Universe.
- The Five-Dimensional Universe. is the subtle aspect of the material world. It is at this point that the spiritual journey the Agni, the principle of Change accomplishes the world yajna in five movements, three and seven threads.
  This level is the gateway to the transcendent world of the Seven-Dimensional Universe.
- The Seven-Dimensional Universe which that which transcends the material world.

This category makes clear that Soma pervades the material world of the Two-Dimensional Universe. Soma fills, pervades, the Earth. (Epithet No. 658.)

Soma pervades the Three-Dimensional Universe. Soma fulfills the essential function of the Three-Dimensional Universe by transcending the Earth. (Epithet No. 659.)

Soma pervades the Five-Dimensional Universe. Here, Soma pervades the Five Quarters. (Epithet No. 660.) The Five-Dimensional Universe is the subtle aspect of the material world. This area of pervasion relies heavily on Sacrifice. That Soma pervades "Five Quarters" is not another example of the Vedas' love of paradox. In the Dakshayana Sacrifice, there are five quarters. (SPB 2.4.4.24.) This includes the four directional regions and the upper region, heaven (SPB 5.2.2.17.) In other contexts it consists of the four directions and the land of the fathers. (SPB 2.6.1.10.) This area of pervasion implicates the Five-Dimensional Universe. It is that point of the spiritual journey the Agni, the principle of Change accomplishes the world yajna in five movements.

Soma pervades the transcendent Seven-Dimension universe. Not only does Soma pervades Heaven (Epithet No. 658), but Soma is omnipresent. (Epithet No. 657.) The Purified Soma pervades in all directions (Epithet No. 655) and transcends Heaven. (Epithet No. 659.)

655. Purified Soma Pervades (*pariiNasalM*) on all directions. (RV 9.97.9.)

656. Soma Pavamana is all pervading (*aa/shviniiH*). (RV 9.86.4.)

657. Soma Is Omniscent (*visvavit*). (RV 9.86.29.)

658. Soma Fills the Heaven and Earth. (RV 9.97.38.)

659. Soma Transcends Heaven and Earth (*dyaa/M ca pRthivii*). (RV 9.86.29.)

660. Soma controls the Five Quarters (*pa/~nca pradi/sho*). (RV 9.86.29.)

PHYSICAL INTEGRITY
AND IMPROVEMENT

This category describes the physical benefits obtained through the experience of Soma consumption. The rigors of a spiritual journey to liberation and salvation is physically taxing and requires a strong, healthy constitution. The focus on physical well-being for the spiritual journey is roughly similar to that in Hatha Yoga. Both require a healthy body to support a conscious, healthy, and aware mind. This is coupled with the intensity associated with the surge of religiosity obtained during the Soma Sacrifice. This group of Epithets list those health benefits obtained during the Soma Sacrifice.

661. Soma makes the body agile. (RV 7.91.4.)

662. Soma grants growth to the worshiper. (RV 7.51.2.)

663. Soma is the healer of diseases (*amiivahaa/*). (RV 1.91.12.)

664. Soma kills all things causing diseases and harm. (RV 9.97.43.)

665. Soma is the healer of diseases (*amiivahaa/*). (RV 1.91.12.)

666. Soma gives vigor (*suvii/raM*) to the Worshiper. (RV 9.62.30.)

POSSESSION IN GREAT MEASURE

This category refers to the possession of wealth. We need to be clear on what is meant by "wealth." The Veda speaks of "wealth," "benefits," and "riches." These references are not to be taken literally to mean material wealth. This wealth are those spiritual benefits and endowments that guides the worshiper's spiritual journey. Ostensibly, the Vedic force of Agni, with whom Soma is intimately connected, in his aspect as the Sacrificial Fire, provides these spiritual endowments and entitlements to the worshiper. (RV 7.10.3.) The worshiper receives these riches once the worshiper approaches the Sacrificial Fire. (RV 8. 44.15.) These riches are interpreted to mean the specific characteristics of the spiritual increase personally experienced by the worshiper. The Sacrificial Fire of Agni creates and instills in the worshiper to seek the same during the spiritual journey. (RV 6.1.3.) The Sacrificial Fire of Agni casts the light on the path the worshiper should tread, (RV 6.1.3), although not completely. In a manner of speech relatively common in the Rg Veda, these spiritual endowments are the "treasures" obtained by Agni in his manifestation of the Sacrificial Fire.

The Vedic forces of Agni is not alone in providing the worshiper with these endowments.

Soma is Full of Possessions. (Epithet No. 667.) Soma is the Prince of Wealth of Many Kinds. (Epithet No. 669.) Soma represents the totality of spiritual riches. (Epithet No. 669.) Soma wins (Epithet No. 670) and provides Wealth. (Epithet No. 672.) Once Soma is in possession of these spiritual riches, Soma dispenses this wealth to Manu, the First Man, and then to the worshiper. (Epithet No. 671.)

667. Soma is Full of Possessions. (RV 9.4.9.)

668. Soma represents the totality of spiritual riches. (*rayi/r*). (RV 9.5.3.)

669. Soma is the Prince of Wealth of Many Kinds (*vaya/m vas/so*). (RV 9.98.5.)

670. Soma is the winner of wealth (*dhanaMjaya*). (RV 9.46.5.)

671. Soma gained wealth for Manu, the earliest man, and later bringing these riches to the worshiper. (RV 9.96.12.)

672. Soma Provides Wealth. (RV 9. 80.2.)

PRESSING

But how are these spiritual endowments and entitlements provided to the worshiper?

The Pressing is an important stage of preparation of the Soma juice. Soma juice is pressed out by the press stones. (Epithet No. 675.) The Pressing could be left at that, simply a ritualistic stage of the Soma Sacrifice. Instead, as in all things in the Vedic dharma, even every-day phenomena possess several layers of meaning. So it is for the Pressing.

On a sacrificial level,

- Soma is pressed out by the stones. (Epithet No. 677.)
- Soma is purified by those who pass the plant through the press. (Epithet No. 678.)
- Soma is pressed out by the stones. (Epithet No. 690.)
- Purified Soma is pressed out of the purifier. (Epithet No. 688.)
- Soma needs to be purified because the crime of purchasing the Soma plant. (Epithet No. 686.) This is a curious epithet. The Soma plant must be obtained in some manner in order for the preparation of the Soma juice. It is beyond the scope of this treatment of the step-by-step process of obtaining the Soma plant Suffice it to say there have been other references of the "crime" of purchasing Soma. For example, Soma had to be purchased from the Panis, the merchant class identified with Evil incarnate. (RV 6.51.4; 6.44.22; 8.75.7; See, generally SPB, 3.2.4.1 -7.) Be that as it may, this served another reason

why Soma was required to be purified, to cure the defilement caused by its purchase from the Panis.

There is a deeper sacrificial interpretation. This a return of the give-and-take present in the sacrificial rite. This is illustrated by the following epithets.

- Epithet No. 691 states that "Soma is Pressed Out by *Tapas*." *Tapas* is intensity of many forms, here, interpreted as the intense rays emitted by the Sun.
- Once pressed out, Soma thereupon is offered back for the rays of Surya, the Vedic divine force of the Sun. (Epithet No. 689.)
- From there, the pressed-out Soma supports the world. (Epithet No. 687.)

The give-and-take is illustrated in Epithet No. 684. In this epithet, Soma is pressed out by Vayu, the Vedic force which breathes in the midworld. In a marvelous exercise of word-play, the original Sanskrit for mid-world, maatari, originates from "he who breathes."

From this ritualistic interpretation, these epithets speak of the psychological state induced as a result of the Pressing. Soma is Milked to Produce the Intense Essence. (Epithet No. 67\6.) From there, the epithets further explain:

- Upon being pressed, Soma make people glorious. (Epithet No. 674.)
- When pressed Soma supports the gods' blissful state. (Epithet No. 680.) While the epithet speaks of the gods, this thought applies equally to mere mortals.

There is a purely sacred meaning to the Pressing. Here,

- The out-pressed Soma is divine. (Epithet No. 681.)
- Soma is pressed by the divine Vedic powers. (Epithet No. 682.)

- Upon being pressed, Soma destroys all enemies. (Epithet No. 673.) Here, "enemies" in the black-and-white world of the Rg Veda is taken to mean "Evil-doers."
- The pressed-out Soma is luminous. (Epithet No. 680.)

Finally, there is this epithet: "The thrice-seven cows (tri/r asmai sapta/dhena/vo) milk (duduhre) Soma with infusions of Truth." (Epithet No. 692.) Mystically shrouded in symbolic language, this epithet touches to the heart of the Soma's place in the Vedic dharma.

"Thrice Seven" is a phrase which makes recurring appearances in the Vedas. "Thrice Seven" combines the essential qualities of the cardinal numbers three and seven. The Three-Dimensional Universe is the subtle aspect of the material world. The Seven-Dimensional Universe is the transcendent universe. "Thrice seven" is the metaphorical leap from the subtle aspect of the material world to the transcendent. In this respect "Thrice Seven" implicates the collective microcosm and macrocosm.

The concept of the "Thrice Seven," trih sapta, recurs throughout the Vedas, in the Rg Veda in several rcs (RV 1.72.6; 1.191.12, 14; 4.1.16; 7.87.4; 8.46.26; 8.96.2; 9.86.21; 10.64.8; 10.90.15) and in the Brahmanas. Its meaning is tantalizingly obscure and varied. The Brahmanas unanimously indicate that "Thrice Seven" refers to:

- 2 months;
- 5 seasons;
- 3 worlds;
- One Sun,

and further state that the Sun is the world. (TS 7.3.10; 5.4.12; AB 30.4; TB 3.8.10; KB 11.6; PB 6.2.2;SPB 1.3.5.11.) This interpretation from the Brahmanas implicates the macrocosm. It encompasses both a division of time and its assignment to the physical worlds. The occult meaning of "Thrice Seven" according to these passages could be said to include both the "spatial and temporal expanse of the physical universe" and that area beyond the spatial and temporal boundaries of the material world.

"Thrice Seven" is an extension of the "Rule of Three" referenced in the Lagadha Vedango Jyotisa. (RVJ, 24; YVJ, 42.) This "Rule of Three" must be viewed against the many references in the Veda of the number seven which were listed above. References of this number have been widely interpreted as representative of the seven levels of existence, both the macrocosm and microcosm, the Seven-Dimensional Universe.

There are seven levels to the macrocosm and microcosm, and three different fuels impelling each level. (AV 19.6.15.) "Thrice Seven" communicates a deeper aspect of the macrocosm and microcosm. On one level it provides a cosmological framework for the transcendent Seven-Dimensional Universe where each level contains three different subdivisions. On another level it provides a mechanism whereby the worshiper can jump start from the material world to the transcendent world. This process is symbolized in the construction of the Fire Altar. The Fire Altar represents the whole world and the bricks the regions (SPB 7.3.1.13) and the vedi sacrificial altar, the entire sacrificial enclosure, represents the earth. (SPB 7.3.1.15.)

Specifically, when constructing the fifth layer of the Fire Altar with Stamobhaga bricks, twenty-one bricks are used to symbolize the three worlds and the regions. (SPB 8.5.3.5, 6.) Each level of the fifth layer contains three layers and represents a different, progressively elevated, layer of the cosmic order:

- The first three layers, one through three, is symbolic of the world;
- The second three layers, four through six, is symbolic of the mid-earth;
- The third three layers, seven through nine, is symbolic of the heavens;
- The fourth three layers, ten through twelve, is symbolic of the eastern quarter;
- The fifth three layers, thirteen through fifteen, is symbolic of the southern quarter;
- The sixth three layers, sixteen through eighteen, is symbolic of the western quarter; and
- The seventh three layers, nineteen through twenty-one, is symbolic of the northern quarter

There is here another intricate give-and-take. Soma bounces back and forth between these different levels of existence, from the macrocosm to the microcosm, all through the context of the Sacrifice, through its different constituent parts. The altar, the sacrificial bricks, all represent these worlds. "Thrice Seven," does not simply indicate the Seven-Dimensional Universe but reveals different aspects of this Seven-Dimensional Universe after taking into consideration its triplicate nature with respect to an aspect in some level in the divine, dynamic cosmic order (*Rta*), in conjunction with the Three-Dimensional Universe of this material world. Soma infuses these worlds with Truth, *Satyam*, in this cosmic give-and-take.

673. Upon being pressed, Soma destroys all enemies (*dvi/So*). (RV 9.61.28.)

674. Upon being pressed, Soma make people glorious (*yasha/so*). (RV 9.61.28.)

675. Soma is Milked by the Press Stones. (RV 9.97.11.)

676. Soma is Milked to Produce the Intense Essence (*rasa*). (RV 9.65.15.)

677. Soma is pressed out by the stones. (RV 9.68.9.)

678. Soma is purified by those who pass the plant through the press. (RV 9.86.15.)

679. When pressed Soma supports the gods' blissful state (*nRmaa/dano*). (RV 9.67.2.)

680. The pressed-out Soma (*suto/*) is luminous (*ha/rir*). (RV 9.38.6.)

681. The out-pressed Soma is divine (*devaa/ya*). (RV 9.4.7.)

682. Soma is pressed by the divine Vedic powers. (RV 9.109.15.)

683. The Soma pressed for Agni is like brilliant light (*ghRta*). (T.B., 1.4.2.3.)

684. Soma is pressed out by Vayu, (*maatari/shvanii/ndra*) the Vedic force which breathes in the midworld. (RV 8.52.2.)

685. Soma is Pressed Out by Faith (*shraddha*). (RV 9.113.2.)

686. Soma needs to be purified because the crime of purchasing the Soma plant. (TB 1.4.7.5.)

687. Soma pressed out of the pressing stones (*sutaa/*) supports the world. (RV 9.63.6.)

688. Purified Soma is pressed out of the purifier (*pa/ri Sya/ suvaano/ akSaa i/ndur*). (RV 9.98.1.)

689. Soma is pressed for the rays of Surya. (RV 9.61.9.)

690. Soma is pressed out (*suta/H*) by the stones (*a/dribhiH*). (RV 9.68.9.)

691. Soma is Pressed Out by *Tapas*. (RV 9.113.2.)

692. The thrice-seven cows (*tri/r asmai sapta/ dhena/vo*) milk (*duduhre*) Soma with infusions of Truth (*Satyam*). (RV 9.70.1.)

The Pressing Stones, Soma Pavamana, Thrice-Seven, these epithets together hold a deep meaning. The pressing stones provide the raw material for the spiritual endowments and entitlements provided to the worshiper. Soma juice is pressed out by the press stones. The Pressing Stones could be left at that, simply a ritualistic stage of the Soma Sacrifice. Instead, as in all things in the Vedic dharma, even every-day phenomena possess several layers of meaning. So it is for the Pressing Stones. On a sacrificial level,

- Soma is pressed out by the stones.
- Soma is purified by those who pass the plant through the press.

- Soma is pressed out by the stones.
- Purified Soma is pressed out of the purifier.
- Soma needs to be purified because the initial purchase of the soma plant is a crime. This is a curious epithet. The Soma plant must be obtained in some manner in order for the preparation of the Soma juice. It is beyond the scope of this treatment of the step-by-step process of obtaining the Soma plant Suffice it to say there have been other references of the "crime" of purchasing Soma. For example, Soma had to be purchased from the Panis, the merchant class identified with Evil incarnate. (RV 6.51.4; 6.44.22; 8.75.7; See, generally SPB, 3.2.4.1 -7.) Be that as it may, this served another reason why Soma was required to be purified, to cure the defilement caused by its purchase from the Panis.

The press stones are premised on the fuel which rule the Vedic dharma. This a return of the give-and-take present in the sacrificial rite. This is illustrated by the following rcs (mantras).

- "Soma is Pressed Out by *Tapas*." (RV 9.113.2) *Tapas* is intensity of many forms, here, interpreted as the intense rays emitted by the Sun.
- Once pressed out, Soma thereupon is offered back for the rays of Surya, the Vedic divine force of the Sun. (RV 9.61.9.)
- From there, the pressed-out Soma supports the world. (RV 9.63.6.)

The Pressing Stones are instrumental in this give-and-take. Soma is pressed out by Vayu, the Vedic force which breathes in the midworld. In a marvelous exercise of word-play, the original Sanskrit for mid-world, maatari, originates from "he who breathes." From this ritualistic interpretation, these epithets speak of the psychological state induced as a result of the Pressing. Soma is Milked to Produce the Intense Essence. From there, the rcs (mantras) further explain:

- Upon being pressed, Soma make people glorious.
- When pressed Soma supports the gods' blissful state. While the rc (manta) speaks of the gods, this thought applies equally to mere mortals.

There is a purely sacred meaning to the Pressing. Here,

- The out-pressed Soma is divine.
- Soma is pressed by the divine Vedic powers.
- Upon being pressed, Soma destroys all enemies. Here, "enemies" in the black-and-white world of the Rg Veda is taken to mean "Evil-doers."
- The pressed-out Soma is luminous.

Finally, the pressing stones are associated with Soma: "The thrice-seven cows (*tri/r asmai sapta/ dhena/vo*) milk (*duduhre*) Soma with infusions of Truth." Mystically shrouded in symbolic language, this epithet touches to the heart of the Soma's place in the Vedic dharma.

The culmination of these epithets and descriptors is that the pressing stones represent Soma Pavamana, Soma in its purified and pristine form, and all the meanings contained therein. The pressing stones thus symbolize both the spiritual journey and provide the means to undertake that journey. (RV 10.92.15.)

You have probably noticed there are seven layers to the Fire Altar. Those seven layers are representations of the Seven-Dimension Universe. There is, in addition to all that, an intricate give-and-take going on. The Vedic sacrifice ritual is intended to demonstrate a fundamental truth of the universe: that there is a give-and-take between the Microcosm (humankind) and the Macrocosm (the universe), of every object therein, encompassing the process from creation to dissolution. (Sannyasi Gyanshruti, Sunnyasi Srividyananda, *Yajna, A Comprehensive Survey* (2006), pp. 84 – 85.) This give-and-take process is the essence of how the natural order (*Rta*) and how it operates. Here, Soma bounces back and forth between these different levels of existence, from the macrocosm to the microcosm, all through the context of the Sacrifice, through its different constituent parts. The altar, the sacrificial bricks, all represent these worlds. "Thrice Seven," does not simply indicate the Seven-Dimensional Universe but reveals different aspects of this Seven-Dimensional Universe after taking into consideration its triplicate nature with respect to an aspect in some level in the divine, dynamic cosmic order *(Rta)*, in conjunction with the Three-Dimensional Universe of this material world. Soma, the product of the Pressing Stones, infuses these worlds with Truth, *Satyam*, in this cosmic give-and-take.

PROTECTION

Soma is the Protector. (Epithet No. 705.) The need for protection implies the presence of danger. Danger may either be an existential threat, expression of nurturement, or a method of empowerment. The various epithets in this category reflect these actions. Protection may be needed for the existential threat, real or perceived. In this manner Soma is seen in the greater role as guardian, much like a soldier standing in formation. Thus, Soma Protects the Seven Directions. (Epithet No. 693.) "The directions" are taken from the original *disha*. In the Vedic dharma *disha* has a specialized meaning and does not simply mean terrestrial direction but the subtle substance which weaves the fabric of the material universe. As recently explained by Sindhu S. Dange (Vedic Beliefs and Practices (2005), pp 85, et seq.), the *disha* are not simply the spatial and directional distribution of matter but possess a mystical meaning and significance. The *disha* are of divine origin. (SPB 6.1.2.4.) The East is the direction of the Gods (SB 3.1.26.) and is associated with Agni (KB, 7.6; SPB 1.4.1.10 - 14; 6.3.3.2; 6.8.1.8; 1.7.12; 8.3.18; 9.3.1.3; 1.2.5.17; 3.6.4.12); the South is the direction of the fathers (SB 3.1.27; SPB 3.6.4.12; 2.6.1.8, 9; AB 1.7 - 2.1) the West is associated with Evil (KB 2.2; TS 5.2.5.3; SPB 3.1.1.7; but See SB 3.1.28, where the Westerly direction is associated with Mankind) and the North is associated with the asterisms (SB 3.1.29) or mankind. (SPB 1.8.3.18; 1.7.1.12; 1.2.5.17; 3.6.1.23.) The *disha* are the essence of Ethereal Space — the element of akasha — and spread in all directions from the radiating soul in lines of living energy like subtle strands of woven cloth. In this respect they are akin to electromagnetic waves, which surround us all the time, only more subtle. Once radiated from the worshiper's soul they recoil to return to the radiating soul. (*The Wisdom of the Vedas* (1992), pp. 62 -65, 131.) Soma is lord and master of the *disha*. In the Ninth Mandela Soma is Lord of the Quarters, dishaam pata. (RV 9.113.2.) Soma is the King of the North. (AB 1.18 - 22; BSS 5.5.6.12.) Soma abides in all four regions or quadrants of the heavens. (RV 9.22.51; 9.63.10; 9.48.1; 9.54.3; 9.63.9; 9.72.8; 9.86.29; 9.894.3; 9.113.2.) Soma is the Guardian of the Brahmins. (Epithet No. 694.)

There is the issue of Guardianship, the second aspect of this category. Guardianship is a two-way street. Soma serves as a guardian, after becoming and being guarded by another Vedic dynamic force. This is yet another example of the give-and-take process which forms the basis for the Sacrifice. After receiving the benefits of being protected, Soma protects others.

- Vayu is the Guardian of Soma. (Epithet No. 700.)
- Soma is Guarded by the Gandharvas. (Epithet No. 701.) The Gandharvas frequently appear in the Rg Veda. (RV 1.22.14; 3.38.4; 8.1.11; 8.77.5; 10.139.4.) They are celestial spirits whose duty it is, among other things, to guard Soma.

There is a third aspect of this category which is in the nature of empowerment. Empowerment is what Soma conveys to others as a result of the give-and-take process of guardianship. This aspect is related to dispensation. In this form of protection:

- Soma Protects the Seven Invokers. (Epithet No. 695.) Taken literally, this would mean Soma protects the seven Hotr priests at the Soma Sacrifice. Taken metaphorically, it means Soma protects the seven layers of existence.
- Soma Protects the Seven rtviks. (Epithet No. 696.) The word *rtvik* is the nominative case of the noun *rtvij* "seasonal sacrificer." (*https://en.wikipedia.org/wiki/Ritwik*) Taken literally, this would exactly be the meaning of this saman, that Soma protects the seven seasonal sacrificers. Metaphorically, this again means Soma protects the seven layers of existence.
- Soma Protects the Worshipers. (Epithet No. 698.) Considered with the epithet which follows, "In protecting the worshiper,

Soma grants happiness," Epithet No. 667, it is illustrative of the benefits which accrue from the give-and-take of the Sacrifice. The first stage is Vayu or the Gandharvas protecting Soma; Soma thereupon protects the worshiper; as a result of this protection, the worshiper obtains happiness.

- Soma protects Manu, the first human. (Epithet No. 703.) Manu is the Vedic equivalent for Adam in the Abrahamic religions.

According to these epithets Soma provides its protection to various elements in the Vedic dharma:

693. Soma Protects the Seven Directions (*disha*). (RV 9.114.3.)

694. Soma is the Guardian of the Brahmins (*brahmadvi/Se*). (RV 6.52.3.)

695. Soma Protects the Seven Invoking Priests (*Hotrs*). (RV 9.114.3.)

696. Soma Protects the Seven rtviks. (RV 9.114.3.)

697. Soma Protects the Seven Aditya gods. (RV 9.114.3.)

698. Soma Protects the Worshipers. (RV 9.114.3.)

699. In protecting the worshiper, Soma grants happiness. (RV 9.90.6.)

700. Vayu is the Guardian of Soma. (RV 10.8.4.)

701. Soma is Guarded by the Gandharvas. (RV 9.113.3.)

702. Soma is the protector of the worshiper body. (RV 8.48.9.)

703. Soma protects Manu, the first human. (RV 9.92.5.)

704. Soma is the Protector of All Creatures. (RV 9.5.9.)

705. Soma is the Protector. (RV 9.5.9.)

PURIFICATION

Purification is one of the most important steps in the worshiper's spiritual journey. This is the reason why the worshiper begins the journey. This is the name of the spiritual game. If the worshiper cannot be purified, there is no reason to proceed further. Yet, it is not how and by which manner the worshiper is purified.

Soma is purified by the Waters. (Epithet No. 706.) This is the principal function of the Waters. The Waters are purifying agents. (RV 2.14.9; 2.27.2; 3.6.10; 3.31.20; S.P.B. 1.2.5.23; 2.6.2.18; 1.7.4.17.) Water is pervasive. It provides the subtle basis of the Vedic dharma, and it is the material basis for the material world. The majority of this earth is water or covered by water. The majority of the worshiper's own bodily constitution is water.

The powers of purification in the Waters are made very clear in the Rg Veda:

- The Waters dispel all bodily (RV 1.23.21) and spiritual ills and ailments. (RV 1.23.22.)
- The purification is accomplished through the sprinkling of water. There are numerous references in the Vedas to the purification of the object of sacrifice through the sprinkling of water. (RV 1.34.1; 1.85.1; 2.34.3; 1.114.7; 1.85.2; 2.16.1; 2.21.3; 5.55.3; 9.72.7; YV 1.28; 1.13; 2.5; 2.1; 4.22; 7.11; 8.32; 13.32; 22.19; 25.39.) There are also numerous references of the sprinkling of water in the Brahmanas. (S.P.B. 1.3.3.2; 1.3.3.3; 1.3.10.11; 1.1.3.12; TS 2.6.5.11.) The pouring of water also accomplishes the purifying effect. (RV 1.64.2; 1.135.9;

1.129.10; 1.166.3; 2.2.4; 2.7.5; 2.34.3; 3.7.7; 4.42.4; 4.56.2; 5.27.5; 5.42.14; 5.57.8; 5.59.1; 6.66.4; 7.79.1; 8.55.1; 10.86.13; 10.91.14; 10.92.5; 10.122.4.)

- The waters contain all healing herbs. (RV 1.23.20.)
- The waters have the power to heal. (AV 1.5.4; 1.6.2; 1.6.3.) The curative powers of the waters are legion. The waters are able to cure dropsy, heart disease, (AV 6.24.1) worms (AV 2.31.5) and hereditary diseases. (AV 2.10.)
- Indeed, the waters are the universal cure of all diseases. (AV 6.91.3; 8.7.3; 3.7.5.) Water is medicine. (Y.V. 9.6; S.B.P. 5.1.4.6.)

A related power is the expiating properties of water. In this regard, Soma is the Purifier. (Epithet No. 706.)

- The waters expiate, literally wash away the sins, of the sacrificer. (SPB 1.2.2.11; 12.4.1.8, 5.) The Sadvimsa Brahmana, devotes an entire Kanda on the expiating powers of the waters and the expiating bath where the sacrificer's sins are atoned. To accomplish this atonement of sins the sacrificer enters the bath, facing the Eastern quarter. (SB, 3.1.1.) A sacrificer thus consecrated kills evil, conveying it to the water. (SB 3.1.3.)
- The waters are also associated with Bliss, madh/, spiritual rapture. It is the source of happiness. (AV 1.5.1; 1.6.1.) This association is made when they are coupled with Soma juice (RV 3.1.7; 3.31.16; 3.35.8; 3.55.22; 6.40.2 (the Waters releasing Soma); 7.35.11; 7.101.4; 8.14.10; 8.33.1; 9.30.5; 9.66.13; 9.67.32; 9.82.5; 9.94.15; 9.97.48; 9.107.1; 10.9.6; 10.63.15; 10.97.5, 6) obtained through the Soma Sacrifice.

Purification and Soma are by-products of the Sacrifice. Once purified, Soma purifies the worshiper. These epithets show the way:

- Soma is the Purifier. (Epithet No. 707.)

- Soma is Purified during the Sacrifice by the Strainers. (Epithet No. 708.) This is a reference to a step during the Soma Sacrifice.

- Soma is purified by the strainer. (Epithet No. 723.) Another reference to a step during the Soma Sacrifice.

- After he is purified, Soma swiftly enters the bowls. (Epithet No. 727.) This is another reference to the Soma Sacrifice.

- The Purified Soma flows from the purifier to the two bowls. (Epithet No. 714.) Yet another reference to the Soma Sacrifice.

- Once purified Soma is rushed out of the sieves to the worshiper. (Epithet No. 726.) Yes, another reference to the Soma Sacrifice.

- Soma is Purified by Agni Jataveda and the Vasus. (Epithet No. 711.) Jataveda is a manifestation of Agni, the Vedic divine force of Change and Transformation. Jatavedas is "all knowing." RV 3.39.2 recites that Jatavedas is the two sticks impregnating the embryo. The "embryo" is so named because by kindling the fire starts the sacrifice. RV 3.17.4 interprets Jatavedas as "The light of consciousness," but whose name literally means "All Knowing." Change (Agni) has elsewhere been described as the "embryo." (RV 1.70.3; 1.95.4.) The sticks thus act as the penetrating vehicle conveying the seed of Knowledge to the embryonic Change (Agni).

- The purified Soma creates the Mind. (Epithet No. 722.) The kindled sacrificial fire is representative as providing the spark to elevation of the worshiper's consciousness. (RV 1.36.7.) The worshiper's consciousness is so raised conferring inner perfection when the sacrificial fire is kindled. Upon the kindling of the sacrificial fire, Jatavedas, the Vital Force of Knowledge, is created and conferred upon the worshiper. (RV 3.1.2; 3.5.4; 3.23.1.) So while the kindling of the sticks refers to starting the sacrificial fire, it acts on another level to symbolize the birth of Agni in his manifestation of all-pervading knowledge and conveys a deeper meaning in transferring that knowledge to Soma (so that it may be further conveyed to the worshiper).

- Purified in the Vessel Soma Creates the Mind. (Epithet No. 713.) The worshiper's mind is sharpened by consuming Soma. When read in conjunction with other epithets, the divine inspiration for the worshiper's acuity and enhancement is explained. Epithet No. 711 recited how Soma was purified by Agni Vaisnavara and the Vasus. The Vasus are attendant Vedic forces at the beck and call of Indra, the Vedic force of Articulation. Once purified and consumed at the sacrifice, and once that knowledge is communicated during the sacrifice through Agni Vaisnavara, the worshiper looks at the world with new eyes, aided by the attendant Vedic forces (Vasus) who purified the Soma.
- Soma is purified in the three worlds of becoming. (Epithet No. 715.) The "Three Worlds of Becoming" is simile for the Three-Dimensional universal. This epithet recognizes that the Soma juice is purified at the sacrifice here on earth.
- Once purified, the Soma juice becomes Indu. (Epithet No. 716.) Indu is another, popular, name for the purified Soma. It bears a close relationship to Indra, sometimes called the Vedic divine force for the Divine Mind, but more accurately defined as the Vedic divine force of Articulation.

This is what the Vedas have to say about the purification of the worshiper:

706. Soma is Purified (*dhutah*) by the Waters. (RV 9.62.5.)

707. Soma is the Purifier. (RV 9.96.3.)

708. Soma is Purified during the Sacrifice by the Strainers. (RV 9.17.4.)

709. Soma is the Purified Soma Impels Speech. (RV 9.30.1.)

710. Soma is Pure-Flowing. (RV 9.81.5.)

711. Soma is Purified by Agni Jataveda and the Vasus. (RV 9.67.27.)

712. Soma is Purified by All Divine Beings. (RV 9.67.27.)

713. Purified in the Vessel Soma Creates the Mind (*matim*). (RV 9.107.8.)

714. The Purified Soma flows from the purifier (*pavi/tre*) to the two bowls (*camvo\H*). (RV 9.36.1.)

715. Soma is purified (for Indra) in the three worlds of becoming (*bhu/ vat trita/sya*). (RV 9.34.4.)

716. Once purified, the Soma juice becomes Indu. (RV 9.76.2.)

717. Purified Soma (*pa/vamaanaasa i/ndavas*) rushes across (*aasha/ vaH*) the purifier. (RV 9.67.7.)

718. Purified Soma brings inner riches (*shatagvi/naM rayi/M*). (RV 9.67.6.)

719. Soma is purified by thoughts (*so/mo mati/bhiH punaano/*). (RV 9.86.15.)

720. Soma rushes (*hiyaana/H*) to be purified. (RV 9.92.1.)

721. While Soma is food for the gods, Sura, unpurified Soma juice, is for human beings. (T.B., 1.3.3.4.)

722. The purified Soma creates the Mind (*mati/M*). (RV 9.107.18.)

723. Soma is purified (*punanti*) by the strainer (*vaa/reNa*). (RV 9.98.7.)

724. Before he is purified, Soma is brown (*babhru/m*). (RV 9.98.7.)

725. Purified Soma Moves with Swift Urgings (*urugaaya/sya*). (RV 9.97.9.)

726. Once purified Soma is rushed out of the sieves to the worshiper. (RV 9.60.2.)

727. After he is purified (*puuya/maanaH*), Soma swiftly enters the bowls (*camvo\H*). (RV 9.97.48.)

RAPTURE

If one knows anything about Soma, it is this, Rapture. Rapture and Bliss, Joy. *Madhu*, the exhilarating experience of the bliss of divine union, this is a central element to Vedic salvation and a necessary companion in the Vedic path to salvation. In the classical English translations it has been rendered variously as "bliss," "ecstasy," "rapture," "fervor," or even "madness." All these words indeed are synonymous with *madhu*, rapture. These synonyms can be reduced to "Theosis" or "divine union." Soma is the symbol of divine rapture, that level of existence, the *Satya/m pavamana*, is that level of existence and reality wherein divine rapture is found. Indeed, the highest of the seven planes of existence in Vedic cosmology.

Rapture is sweet. (Epithets 739.) The prepared Soma is sweet. (Epithet 740.) But we should understand the real meaning of this sweetness. The Vedic dharma has been compared to honey. The Brhanaranyaka Upanishad in 2.5 gives the deeper meaning of honey and sweetness. Sweetness and honey form the very basis of the Vedic dharma:

- Water --- the fundamental essence of the Vedic dharma --- is the honey of all sentient and non-sentient beings. Thus, Soma emanates rapture in water-like waves. (Epithet 738.)
- Honey thereupon forms the basis of the divine existential levels in the Seven-Dimension Universe and physical and sentient-based existential level in the Two-, Three-, and Five-Dimensional Universes.

The sweetness accordingly consists of both the divine and the physical. It therefore consists of

- This earth.
- All sentient and non-sentient beings.
- The First Cause of all sentient and non-sentient beings. Soma upholds Everything with its Ecstasy. (Epithet 733.)
- That Self, the Immortal, that Brahman, that All. Thus, Soma is the Great Rapture of the universe. (Epithet 735.)

F. Max Muller, one of the first translators of Hindu and Vedic scriptures in the West, recognized that honey is not simply sweetness. In these passages honey and sweetness is a metaphor for the dependent processes of cause and effect. Just as the bees both make and are supported by honey, both earth and all living beings therein are mutually dependent, and the material and the intangible, the divine, where the latter is the cause of the former.

As the Brhanaranyaka Upanishad recognizes, the processes of cause and effect are in reality one process carried out in two steps. This is indicated in these epithets by the consumption of Soma. Through the rapture of purified Soma, the worshiper does directly to the divine. (Epithet 734.) The worshiper consumes Soma, and the worshiper experiences the divine. This is the Divine Ecstacy spoken of in the Vedas. (Epithet 730.)

The great misconception is that the sweetness is associated with the state of being happy. The samans (mantras) in the Ninth Mandala give some credence to this belief by saying that Soma gives a happy mind. (Epithet 737.) Happiness, however, is not the same as Joy or Bliss, a related topic, nor is the equivalent to Rapture. Again, this happiness should be put in its proper context. As we saw in the beginning of this volume in the Introduction, Soma is modernly associated with pleasure and recreational altering of mental states. But Soma is not simply the joy experienced by ingestion of mind altering substances as is understood today. It is the joy encountered by the worshiper while experiencing the divine mental awareness found in the Seven-Dimensional Universe. In the language of the Ninth Mandala, the greatness of Soma opens up in the worshiper with its rapture. (Epithet 736.) The totality of the Vedic dharma is what is opened up to the worshiper.

728. Soma is Rapturous. (RV 9.1.1.)

729. Soma is utter ecstasy (*madintama*) shining with rays of light (*go/bhir*). (RV 9.50.5.)

730. Soma is Divine Ecstasy (*madah*). (RV 9.80.2.)

731. Soma is the Ecstasy Experienced by the Worshiper when Reborn. (RV 9.59.1.)

732. In His Ecstasy the Force of Soma Goes with Indra. (RV 9.7.7.)

733. Soma Upholds Everything with its Ecstasy. (RV 9.18.1.)

734. Through the rapture of purified Soma, the worshiper does directly to the divine. (RV 9.98.7.)

735. Soma is the Great Rapture of the Universe (*ma/daH ma/hi*). (RV 9.108.1.)

736. The greatness of Soma opens up in the worshiper with its rapture (*vi/vakSase*). (RV 10.25.5.)

737. Soma brings the happy mind (*ma/no*) to the worshiper in its rapture. (RV 10.25.1.)

738. Soma emanates rapture in water-like waves (*apasyaa/t*). (RV 9.86.40.)

739. The prepared Soma (*pappivaa/Msam*) is sweet (*ma/dhumaaM+*). (RV 6.47.1.)

740. The sweet Soma juice (*pappivaa/Msam*) is rapturous (*ma/diSTha*). (RV 6.47.2.)

RELEASE

Release is not a separate stage of the worshiper's spiritual journey. It is rather the mechanism by which the spiritual benefits of Soma are conveyed to the worshiper and to world. Through the process of Release the spiritual endowments of Soma are not only dispensed to the worshiper during the spiritual journey but to all of creation.

Release is related to the other categories. It is related to Dispensation. Dispensation, however, is concerned with the give-and-take of the sacrifice. Release is concerned with the emission of the strength of Soma. Thus, "Swiftly moving Soma is released." (Epithet No. 751.)

Release is related to Flow. Flow, however, is concerned with the stream of consciousness in the worshiper's mind. Release relates to Soma's stream of bliss and rapture arriving to the worshiper's consciousness. Thus,

- Soma Releases (*asRkSata*) Delight. (Epithet No. 741.)
- When it is released, Soma provides divine ecstasy. (Epithet No. 750.)
- Swiftly moving Soma is released like horses to a chariot. (Epithet No. 751.) Here, "Horses" are taken in their metaphorical meaning. The Horses refer to the worshiper's sense perception centers. Under this metaphorical meaning, because they are being held by the chariot, the streams of Soma juice, when released, restrains the worshiper's consciousness.

Release is related to the Pressing. The Pressing relates to the stream of Soma juice by its extraction from the squeezing and compression the stalks of the Soma plan by the Press Stones. Any relationship is superficial. The Pressing is a manual step performed during the Soma Sacrifice. Release is inspirational, spiritual, and subtle results of the stream of Soma juice. Thus

- The pressing stones release the cosmic powers which are impelled in Soma. (Epithet No. 745.)
- From the Fullness of plenty (*bRha/t*) Soma is impelled (*vaavRdhe*) and released (*suvaana/*) into the world. (Epithet No. 744.)

Release is, however, related to Establishment. The essence of the experience of consuming the Soma juice lays the subtle and material basis for the spiritual journey the worshiper embarks. Soma establishes the transcendent world in the worshiper. (Epithet No. 755.) In addition, Soma provides the following framework for the worshiper to engage in the spiritual journey:

- When Released Soma Supports Heaven. (Epithet No. 742.)
- Soma releases the seers of wisdom. (Epithet No. 746.)
- Soma Releases the Waters. (Epithet No. 743.) Here Soma releases the very subtle foundation of the Vedic dharma. The next epithet explains what happens after Soma releases the Waters and why.
- Soma releases the waters for the benefit of the worshiper. (Epithet No. 747.)
- Soma releases the life energy. (Epithet No. 752.)
- When it is released, Soma perfects the abodes. (Epithet No. 748.) The "abodes" can refer to many aspects in the Vedic dharma. the houses of the zodiac relate to stellar abodes, the dynamic cosmic order establish the asterisms as mansions of the moon. (SPB 9.4.1.9; 10.5.4.17; VS, 17.40; Sad. Br., 3.12.) The Svar, an intermediary level of Heaven, is the new abode for the worshiper after rebirth. The Vedi, the sacrificial altar, is the abode of the sacrifice, and its heart and soul. (TS 1.7.5.) It is that sacred place where the Soma juice is consecrated, when it is explained that King Soma is "Possessed of water, you go clothed in the liquid water, to the great celestial abode to (take) the sacrifice." (RV

9.83.5.) Significantly, it can mean the Vedic dharma itself, the subtle region wherein the essence of the dynamic cosmic order is subsumed in the sacrifice. (RV 1.148.1.)

Release is related to Strength, which will we discussed later. Here, the flow of Soma juice is a metaphor for the Strength of the Soma experience. Thus

- Swiftly moving Soma is released like horses to a chariot. (Epithet No. 751.) Here, "Horses" are taken in their literal meaning. The Horse, the animal, is symbolic speech and a metaphor Strength, representative of the intensity of the Soma experience.

The Release is not a simple presentation of the Soma juice. It is symbolic of the very birth of the Vedic dharma.

741. Soma Releases (*asRkSata*) Delight (chandra). (RV 9.66.25.)

742. When Released (*a/sarji*) Soma Supports Heaven. (RV 9.86.46.)

743. Soma Releases the Waters. (RV 9.109.22.)

744. From the Fullness of plenty (*bRha/t*) Soma is impelled (*vaavRdhe*) and released (*suvaana/*) into the world. (RV 9.67.40.)

745. The pressing stones (*graa/vabhiH*) release the cosmic powers which are impelled in Soma. (RV 9.80.4.)

746. Soma releases (*asRkSata*) the seers of wisdom (*kaa/vyaa*). (RV 9.63.25.)

747. Soma releases the waters for the benefit of the worshiper. (RV 9.110.5.)

748. When it is released, Soma perfects the abodes. (RV 9.104.2.)

749. When it is released, Soma establishes the divine elements. (RV 9.104.2.)

750. When it is released, Soma provides divine ecstasy. (RV 9.104.2.)

751. Swiftly moving (*aasha/vo/*) Soma is released (*.asRkSata*) like horses to a chariot (*ra/thyaaso*). (RV 9.86.2.)

752. Soma releases (*asRkSata*) the life energy (*vaayu/m*). (RV 9.67.18.)

753. Soma is generated by the stone (*graa/vNaa*). (RV 9.113.6.)

754. Soma flows to the mind. (RV 9.113.6.)

755. Soma establishes the transcendent world in the worshiper. (RV 9.113.7.)

756. Soma is the Wise One (*dhii/raaH*). (RV 8.48.4.)

757. Soma is swift (aasha/vaH) as thought (*dhiija/vo*). (RV 9.86.1.)

REPLENISHMENT, SOMA THE SHOWERER, THE BULL

Soma is the Bull, symbolic for the principle of Regeneration. (RV 2.40.3; 8.93.19; 9.5.6; 9.19.5; 9.64.2.) These terms, the Showerer and Bull, are attributes of the Element of Replenishment, the active principle of regeneration and rebirth. Used virtually interchangeably, these terms consist of the Elements responsible for the general continuation of living matter and the spiritual rebirth of the worshiper's soul. This is a vital function belonging to Soma.

As the sun replenishes the rain, and the rain establishes the exchange between the heaven and earth, the worshiper should channel this energy in the Vedic path to salvation and liberation.

- Soma Is like Parjanya. (Epithet No. 758.) Parjanya is the Vedic deity for the physical phenomenon of rain. This is a reference to the rain replenishing the earth. In enlivening the earth, Parjanya recycles the worshiper's soul as well as and in the manner of rain.

The act of replenishment is symbolized the rain showers. Through this event the Earth is replenished, renewed. Similarly, with Soma, the worshiper's soul is replenished and renewed. Soma is the Showerer, as demonstrated in these epithets:

- Soma is the Showerer. (Epithet No. 761.)

- When Soma becomes purified, going through the strainer, he becomes the Showerer. (Epithet No. 762.)
- From the purifier from above, Soma the Showerer flows from the purifier into the fullness of plenty. (Epithet No. 763.)
- As the Enjoyer, Soma Showers Enjoyment (va/na) on the Worshiper. (Epithet No. 764.) (This particular saman employs one of the most extraordinary exercises of word-play the Rg Veda; all the words of this saman is a variation of the root *vrs*, which itself means "Bull," "rain," and "Showerer." Roman transliteration of this rc (mantra) is: *vR/SNas te vR/SNyaM sha/ vo vR/Saa va/naM vR/Saama/daH Satya/m vRSan vR/Se/d asi.*
- Soma is the Great Showerer for All. (Epithet No. 770.)

This function of Soma is not simply to replenish and renew. These epithets indicate the results of the downpour:

- Soma (indo) Showers Cattle, Bovine Knowledge on the Worshiper. (Epithet No. 765.) Soma showers insightful knowledge on the worshiper.
- Soma (indo) Showers Horses, Equine Knowledge on the Worshiper. (Epithet No. 765.) Soma showers the restrained mind on the worshiper.

The Bull is the Rainmaker, not just because the Bull's seed, the rain, as rain, brings water to renew the earth, but because the Rainmaker replenishes the worshiper's soul, replenishing the soul with strength, vigor, and other benefits, while traveling on the spiritual journey to salvation and liberation.

758. Soma Is like Parjanya. (RV 9.22.2.)

759. Replenishes the Two Mothers with the Waters. (RV 9.68.4.)

760. Soma the Showerer (*vR/Saa*) cries out (*a/cikradad*). (RV 9.2.6.)

761. Soma is the Showerer (*vR/Saa*). (RV 9.5.9; 9.108.11.)

762. When Soma becomes purified, going through the strainer (*pavi/tre*), he becomes the Showerer (*vR/Saa*). (RV 9.86.3.)

763. From the purifier from above (*saa/no a/vye*), Soma the Showerer (*vR/Saa*) flows from the purifier (*pavi/tre*) into the fullness of plenty (*bRha/t*). (RV 9.67.40.)

764. As the Enjoyer, Soma Showers Enjoyment (*va/na*) on the Worshiper. (RV 9.64.2.)

765. Soma (*indo*) Showers Cattle, Bovine Knowledge (*gaa/*) on the Worshiper. (RV 9.64.3.)

766. Soma (*indo*) Showers Horses, Equine Knowledge (*gaa/*) on the Worshiper. (RV 9.64.3.)

767. The chariot over which Soma and Pusan shower the worshiper has seven wheels (*sapta/cakraM*). (RV 2.40.3.)

768. The Act of Showering is the essential nature of Soma. (RV 9.64.1.)

769. When purified Soma is released with the shower of essence (*miiLhe/*). (RV 9.106.12.)

770. Soma is the Great Showerer for All. (RV 9.64.2.)

SENSE PERCEPTIONS (HORSES)

This category discusses how Soma affects the senses.

A silent movie, The Devil Horse, concerns the story of a wild maverick horse saving a frontier family from outside threats. An actor in the movie, Yakima Canutt, an authentic cowboy turned actor, worked as the stunt man in the movie and tells an amusing story about training the very real maverick horse used in the movie, Rex the Wonder Horse. You see Rex was a maverick, a wild horse, and was injuring other crew members on the movie set and generally proving uncontrollable and disruptive. Canutt, bring a real cowboy, however, knew how to train mavericks. Canutt told the director, "Just give me a half hour and a pool stick, and after he won't be a problem." During their half hour session, whenever Rex tried to attack him, Canutt would whack Rex on the nose with the pool stick. And sure enough, after a half hour transpired, Rex proved to be a fine screen horse, acting in fifteen other movies, and the filming of The Devil Horse continued.

The worshiper's spiritual journey to liberation and salvation, if not so violent, is similar. The Horses are symbolic speech for the sense perceptions. There are, of course, five senses --- sight, taste, smell, hearing and touch. Because there are five, the sense perceptions are grounded in the Five-Dimensional Universe. The Five-Dimensional Universe is the gateway to the transcendent Seven-Dimensional Universe. What the worshiper does in this portal of existence, then, is important, because once successfully traversed, the worshiper enters upwards to liberation and salvation.

It is critically important then to successfully deal to control the senses. In the journey on the Vedic path to salvation and liberation the worshiper strives to have the senses under control, learn to restrain the mind and manage the mental impressions (vrttis). If that skill is mastered, the worshiper will not be not subject to rebirth. If not, if the worshiper's mind is unrestrained, a "monkey mind," if the senses are not in control, the worshiper will be subject to constant re-birth time after time.

Horses are frequently associated with the Vedic divine dynamic forces:

- The horse is associated with the processes of The Principle of Change (Agni) through metaphor and simile. (RV 3.27.14; 3.29.6; 6.3.4; 8.22; 4.2.8; 1.36.8; 1.27.1; 1.6.53; 1.66.2; 1.69.3; 1.73.9, 10; 1.74.7; 1.149.3; 1.58.2; 2.1.16;. 2.2.10; 3.2.3; 3.26.3; 4.1.3; 4.2.4.4.39.6; 4.2.11; 4.10.1; 4.15.1; 5.6.3; 5.18.5.)
- Usas, mental and spiritual awareness, is seen mounting the carriage as the charioteer (the Self). (RV 3.61.2.)
- Owing to their extremely concentrated focus, the Maruts move with swift horses (senses) which are easily controlled. (RV 5.55.1; 5.54.1.)

The Horses (sense perceptions) however are ruled and governed by other aspects. The senses (horses) are harnessed in accordance with the dynamic force of *Rta*. (RV 4.51.5.) The Horse is primarily used as a metaphor for the senses, consistent with the interpretation given in the Katha Upanishad:

- The Soma plant is ground with the pistol and mortar much like reins are used to tether a horse. (RV 1.28.4.)
- Varuna (Lord Protector of the Dynamic Cosmic Order)'s mind, and by extension our own, are soothed by the praises at the sacrifice like the horses (sense perceptions) are soothed by the reins (mind). (RV 1.25.3.)
- The worshiper accepts the offering as a charioteer (the Self) accepts the reins (mind) to a horse (senses). (RV 1.144.3.)

Related to this is the "unyoking" of the horses/vrttis. Soma, the divine dynamic energy and the elixir, is a significant participant in energizing the senses towards a divine purpose and goal. Consider:

- The dynamic Vedic energy of divine union (Soma) acts to "unyoke" the horses. (RV 3.32.1.) This is the nature of the ecstasy of divine union. After the experience — any experience — of divine union, the worshiper's perception of the world is different. Instead of viewing the world in black and white, the world is suddenly, as in the Wizard of Oz, in living color. The worshiper experiences what Alan Watts states any seeker must do — get "out of your mind." In the language of the Veda, the horses are unyoked.

- Thus, when the experience of divine union is experienced after consumption of the Soma juice at the sacrifice, the senses flow, like Soma, like a rapid horse. (RV 9.16.1; 9.23.2; 9.26.1; 9.36.1; 9.59.1; 9.62.6; 9.72.1; 9.74.1; 9.93.1; 9.96.20; 9.97.18; 9.101.2.)

771. When Pressed Soma Is the Horse Carrying the Chariot of the Universe (*vajinam*). (RV 9.89.4.)

772. Soma's Horses Are Unborn (*Aya*) Energies That Protect the Worshipers In All Their Journeys. (RV 9.67.10.)

773. Soma is the Efficient Cause (*i/saH*) of the Inner Energies of the Horse (a/shvam). (RV 9.61.3.)

774. By uttering the name of Indra, the purified Soma (*i/ndur*) yokes (*ayukta*) the horses of the Sun (*hari/to*) to move in ten directions. (RV 9.63.9.)

775. Soma Flows to Indra, as the Resplendent Self (*carSaNiisa/he*). (RV 9.24.4.)

776. Soma is the cosmic horses (*pratnaa/sa aaya/vaH*). (RV 9.23.2.)

777. Soma Is the Subtle, Cosmic Horse (*Pratnaa/sa Aaya/vah*) Which Generates the Sun (*suu/ryam*). (RV 9.23.2.)

778. Soma is A Charioteer Leading Seven Horses (*septayah*). (RV 9.65.26.)

779. Soma is Like a Horse (*a/tyo na/*). (RV 9.32.3.)

780. Soma is the Charioteer (*ra/thyaM*). (RV 9.21.6.)

781. Soma is Harnesses the Horses. (RV 9.21.4.)

782. Invoking the Power of Indra, Soma Harnesses the Horses and Travels Ten Directions. (RV 9.63.9.)

783. Soma is like a Horse driven by its rider. (RV 9.13.6.)
Look again in the Introduction where the Katha Upanishad is discussed. Using the metaphor in the Katha Upanishad, Soma is the Universal Atman.

784. Soma is the Skillful Charioteer. (RV 9.66.26.)
According to the metaphor in the Katha Upanishad, Soma is the mind, controlling the galloping horses (senses).

785. Soma is made with the same material as the chariot (*rathiro/*). (RV 9.97.48.)
Soma is the functional equivalent of the chariot, the Body.

786. Soma ascends upwards in a chariot (*ra/thaM*) of universal movement (*vi/Sva-ncam aruhad*). (RV 9.75.1.)

787. Soma Occupies the same chariot with Indra. (RV 9.87.9.)

788. Soma Longs for a Chariot. (RV 9.3.5.)

789. Soma Establishes the Senses (*indriyam*). (RV 9.23.5.)

790. Soma flows (arSati) to establish (*dharNasi/r*) rapture in the mind (*da/dhaana*) and senses (*indriya/M*). (RV 9.23.5.)

791. When Soma becomes purified, the worshiper acquires the powers of Indra (*indriyaalya*). (RV 9.86.3.)

792. The Indriyas (Sense Perception Organs) Only Become Active When the Soma Drink Is Consumed. (TB 1.3.10.4.)

793. The Indriyas Are Similar to the Soma Drink. (TB 1.3.10.4.)

SOMA PAVAMANA

Briefly, Soma Pavamana is purified Soma juice, the finished product of the Soma Sacrifice. Another word, treated as a synonym for Soma Pavamana, is Indu. (Epithet No. 849 and Epithet No. 850.) You may be thinking the same thing I am: the word Indu is very similar to Indra. Is there a connection? To answer this question other divine forces must be examined.

Agni is traditionally mentioned as the god of fire; "agne" in Sanskrit means "fire." Classical grammarians, however, have derived Agni's name from the root, "ang." From the root ang the word angara for "charcoal" is derived. The charcoal is the result of the Sacrificial Fire, which represents the fire of Knowledge and the give-and-take process of the Sacrifice.

Just as fire consumes wood, leaving its essential elements in the form of charcoal, that same process is in operation and reduces the form and substance of the universe to its essential elements. Embers are the heated coals after the fire has subsided, and after the embers have subsided, charcoal remains from the smoldering Sacrificial Fire. This aspect of Agni represents Transformation, the true, essential nature of Fire. Anything which comes into contact with fire could and will be reduced to its essential elements. Agni also represents Change, owing in part to the constantly changing appearance of the flames of fire. It is especially appropriate, therefore, that the embers represent Knowledge. If the Sacrificial Fire represents knowledge, the charcoal and embers that remain afterwards represent the final irreducible essence of that fire.

Indha (RV 7.1.16; 7.8.1) --- another word for "ember" ---- is the manifestation of the divine force of Indra which represents the embers which are the heated coals after the fire has subsided. These embers remain after the Sacrificial Fire has been ignited. Just as in Agni in his manifestation of ang, Indha accordingly represents the irreducible essence of that Sacrificial Fire, the very essence of the Sacrificial Fire as knowledge, which is incorporated in Indra which is thereupon conveyed to the Vedic dharma. The foregoing is understandable as Indra serves as the incarnation of the Vedic force of Agni in several of his critical actions. Indra is the incarnation of Agni Vasivanara when battling the "enemies." (RV 1.59.6.) Indra acts as the incarnation of Agni as he commits those actions. (Mikhailov, (2001) *RgVedic Studies*, p. 14.) Specifically, Indra acts in that aspect of Agni in the form of the Sacrificial Fire when Vrtra is slain (RV 2.12.4), and in every other instance in which Indra comes in contact with Vrtra and its aftermath."

Similarly, Indu is the irreducible essence of Soma Pavamana. What is that essence?

- Soma Pavamana is pure. (Epithet No. 805.)
- Soma Pavamana is swift like thought. (Epithet No. 799)
- Pure Soma go to Vayu and the Ashvins, who confer life-force to the worshiper. (Epithet No. 804.) This Life-Force is Prana.
- Soma Pavamana Has the Ability to Transform Anything into Golden Form. (Epithet No. 809.) The Golden Form represents Liberation and Salvation.
- The Soma Pavamana arrives to the conscious worshiper (manaa/v) through the mid-world. (Epithet No. 807.)

If Soma Pavamana is the physical, purified, Soma juice produced at the Soma Sacrifice, Indu is the irreducible essence of that purified Soma juice, Soma Pavamana. Reduced to their inner essences, Indu is Purity, Thought, Consciousness, Life-Force (Prana), and Liberation and Salvation themselves.

Lest we forget what purpose is served with Indu or Soma Pavamana. Soma Pavamana, Indu, is to serve the worshiper and the spiritual journey:

- Soma Pavamana Purifies the Worshiper with a Thousand Powers. (Epithet No. 808.)

- Indu grants happiness to the worshiper by showing the right path. (Epithet No. 802.)

But let's look to see what the samans (mantras) have to say about Soma Pavamana:

794. Soma Pavamana gave birth to the Sun (*suu/ryaM*). (RV 9.110.3.)

795. When Soma is pressed out, it flows and is like the Sun, who establishes Soma in the body. (RV 9.63.13.)

796. Soma reveals the godhead (*devavii/tamaH*). (RV 9.63.16.)

797. Soma Pavamana Purifies the Worshiper with a Thousand Powers. (TB 1.4.8.15.)

798. Soma Pavamana is yoked by the steeds of the Sun, the wide-eyed ones (*suu/ra*). (RV 9.63.8.)

799. Soma Pavamana is swift like thought (*dhiiju/vo*). (RV 9.86.4.)

800. Soma is Indu. (RV 9.5.9, et al.)

801. Indu is Soma Pavamana, purified Soma. (RV 9.64.25.)

802. Indu grants happiness to the worshiper by showing the right path. (RV 9.97.28.)

803. Pure Soma (*pa/vamaano*) rushes to the luminous heaven (*rocanaa/diva/H*). (RV 9.37.3.)

804. Pure Soma (*punaanaa/sash*) go to Vayu and the Ashvins, who confer life-force to the worshiper. (RV 9.8.2.)

805. Soma is pure (*pa/vamaanaa*). (RV 9.63.26.)

806. Soma Pavamana is pure (*Pavamana*). (RV 9.86.4.)

807. The Soma Pavamana arrives to the conscious worshiper (*manaa/v*) through the mid-world (*anta/rikSeNa*). (RV 9.63.8.)

808. Soma Pavamana Supports a Thousand Powers. (TB 1.4.8.16.)

809. Soma Pavamana Has the Ability to Transform Anything into Golden Form. (TB 1.4.8.16.)

STREAMING

Related to Flow, the Streaming of Soma is the preparatory stage in the Soma Sacrifice to union of the mystical powers into the liquid. In this stage the priest merely shakes the cup with the plants with the following passage, "In the flow of the streaming (waters) I waft thee! in the flow of the gurgling I waft thee! in the flow of the jubilant I waft thee! in the flow of the most delightsome I waft thee! in the flow of the most sweet I waft thee!" (SPB 11.5.9.8.) As this passage indicates, the Streaming is not only the flow of purified Soma during the distillation process. On a psychological level, it is also the Flow Experience, namely, the experience of any emotional or psychological state unimpeded by outside thoughts or doubt, pure enjoyment, pure experience. Here, that experience is the approach with the Divine, without distracting thoughts, without objections or doubts. It is the type of experience consumption of the Soma juice is intended to foster.

This is the Streaming. Soma flows in streams with waves. (Epithet No. 822.) Streaming is the step after the Flowing; it is not the Release but it is purified. Soma is cleansed by streams of energize water and the brilliance of knowledge. (Epithet No. 828.) The streaming begins with Soma channeling the energy of the universe into simple water.

- Soma is Replenishes the vigor in the streams of water. (Epithet No. 823.)

Soma replenishes because Soma itself consists of streams of energies. (Epithet No. 828.) The purification of Soma is precisely that which gives it energy. It is once the waters have been invigorated that the true magic occurs. Then the streaming begins:

- Soma is in a thousand streams. (Epithet No. 821.)
- Soma flows with a thousand streams to sheath covering the Resplendent Self. (Epithet No. 819.)
- Soma Arrives in a Thousand Streams. (Epithet No. 826.)

What was said in the Insightful Knowledge category about the number One Thousand applies here as well. Thousands, says the Satapatha Brahmana, are the number of cows taken from the gods. (SPB 3.3.1.13.) Since the gods have thousands of cows, so is the extent of their insightful knowledge. "Thousand" or "thousands" thus connote an enormity of a quality, personage, or a deity, imbued with cosmic, divine scope. This is what is happening in Epithet No. 810. The initial event of Soma's streaming is that it offers great abundance, reflected in this epithet:

- Upon being pressed, Soma streams the abundance. (Epithet No. 814.)

"Abundance" is a term of art discussed at the beginning of this book. Abundance is related to the Vastness of the Vedic dharma, another term of art, and has specific consequences.

- Soma flows with a thousand streams to sheath covering the Resplendent Self. (Epithet No. 819.)

The streams occur before the union with Soma's psychic, subtle powers. Soma flows in a steam of wisdom. (Epithet No. 804.) Once these powers are incorporated in the Soma juice, two events occur. One, the worshiper becomes the recipient of those powers. The "streams of wisdom" rain to the worshiper to use in the spiritual journey.

- Streams of Soma are released to the worshiper. (Epithet No. 818.)
- Purified Soma is released to the worshiper as pure streams. (Epithet No. 817.)

- Streams of rapture are released to the worshiper. (Epithet No. 816.)

Two, Soma streams its benefits for all:

- Soma supports the world with streams of *Rta*, the Vedic dharma. (Epithet No. 814.)
- Soma released the seven streams. (Epithet No. 811.) This is symbolic speech for the seven layers of existence.
- Purified Soma releases streams of delight. (Epithet No. 812.)

To what purpose do the Streams of Soma serve? These epithets answer this question:

- Soma's streams of *Rta* are released to fight evil. (Epithet No. s 813.)

The Streaming is an overt ritualistic reference to the preparation of Soma juice. The Streams also have a deeper esoteric meaning. Both the ritualistic and esoteric meanings help the worshiper in the spiritual journey.

810. Soma is in a thousand streams (*saha/sradhaaraM*). (RV 9.80.4.)

811. Soma released the seven streams (*sapta/ si/ndhuun*). (RV 4.28.1.)

812. Purified Soma releases streams of delight (*i/ndur a/vye ma/dacyutaH dhaa/raa ya/ uurdhvo/*). (RV 9.98.1.)

813. Soma's streams of *Rta* are released to fight evil (*hva/raaMsi*). (RV 9.63.4.)

814. Upon being pressed, Soma streams the abundance (*ja/ne*). (RV 9.61.28.)

815. Milked by the Press Stones, Soma Flows in Streams of Rapture. (RV 9.97.11.)

816. Streams (*dhaa/raa*) of rapture (ma/dhor) are released (*asRkSata*) to the worshiper. (RV 9.106.14.)

817. Purified Soma (*pa/vamaanaa*) is released (*asRkSata*) to the worshiper as pure streams (*dhaa/rayaa*). (RV 9.107.25)

818. Streams of Soma are released to the worshiper. (RV 9.22.1.)

819. Soma flows (*arSati*) with a thousand streams (*saha/sradhaaraH*) to sheath covering the Resplendent Self (*ko/sham*). (RV 9.86.7.)

820. Soma flows (*arSati*) in a steam of wisdom (*dhaa/rayaa kavi/H*). (RV 9.12.8.)

821. Soma flows (*arSati*) in a thousand streams (*saha/sradhaaro*). (RV 9.13.1.)

822. Soma flows in streams (*dhaa/rayaa*) with waves (*uurmi/Naa*). (RV 9.68.8.)

823. Soma is Replenishes the vigor in the streams of water (*nadii/*). (RV 9.76.1.)

824. The streams of the Vedic dharma, the natural order (*Rta*), is glorified by Soma. (RV 9.63.21.)

825. Soma (*i/ndavaH*) Consists of Streams of Supreme Honey. (RV 9.7.1.)

826. Soma Arrives in a Thousand Streams. (RV 9.13.1.)

827. Soma covers (*va/saano*) with the streams of the Waters (*dhaa/rayaapo/*). (RV 9.107.4.)

828. Soma consists of streams of energies (*vakSa/NaabhyaH*). (RV 8.1.17.)

829. Soma is cleansed by streams of energize water (*adbhi/r*) and the brilliance of knowledge (*go/bhir*). (RV 9.68.9.)

830. Soma supports the world with streams of *Rta*, the Vedic dharma (*Rta/sya* dhaa/rayaa). (RV 9.36.4.)

STRENGTH AND MIGHT

Here is where the similes become muddled. Strength and Might is usually associated with Indra, the Vedic divine force of Articulation, among other powers. Indra is Maghavan, the Victor, who overcomes all foes (read, Evil doers) due to his strength and might. (RV 1.23.3; 2.32.13; 11.55.5;1.73.5; 1.77.4; 1.98.3; 1.103.2, 4; 1.136.7; 1.141.13; 1.146.5; 1.157.3; 1.171.3, 5; 1.174.1, 7; 2.6.4; 3.30.3, 22; 3.31.22; 3.32.7; 3.34.11; 3.51.11; 3.36.11; 3.38.10; 3.39.9; 3.43.8; 3.48.5; 3.49.5; 3.50.5; 3.51.1; 3.53.8; 4.16.1; 4.17.8, 9, 11, 13; 4.20.2; 4.22.1; 4.24.2; 4.27.5; 4.31.7; 5.31.1; 5.34.2, 3, 8; 5.42.8; 5.61.11; 5.79.6; 6.24.1; 6.27.8; 6.47.11; 6.58.4; 7.16.7; 7.20.10; 7.21.10; 7.26.1, 2; 7.27.4; 7.28.5; 7.29.5; 7.30.3; 7.31.4; 7.32.12, 20; 7.60.11; 7.29.5; 7.30.3; 7.31.4; 8.1.12; 8.21.10; 8.26.7; 8.33.9; 8, 13; 8.46.13; 8.49.1; 8.52.5; 8.61.1, 18; 8.65.10;8.70.15; 8.95.20; 8.96.20; 8.97.13; 8.103.9; 9.81.3; 9.96.11; 9.97.55; 10.23.2, 3; 10.10.27.4; 10.33.8; 10.42.6, 8; 10.43.1, 3, 5, 6, 8; 10.49.11; 10.74.5; 10.81.6; 10.89.18; 10.104.11; 10.113.2; 10.160.4; 10.162.2.) In the true tradition of Vedic interchangeability of divine powers, Soma also exhibits strength and might.

Soma acquires its strength from Indra, because Soma ascends to Indra. (Epithet No. 832.)

- After so ascending, Soma becomes Indra's Vayra, the weapon used to fight wrong-doers. (Epithet No. 843.)
- Soma is placed between earth and heaven to uphold the strength of Indra. (Epithet No. 840.) Soma is placed in an unusual position at this point. The divine force of Soma is usually domineering, prominent, overpowering. When

223

empowered by Indra, however, the divine force of Soma is used as an intermediary, communicating the force and vitality of Indra's power to both the upper and lower levels of existence. Soma becomes enveloped in Power. (Epithet No. 836.) Viewed existentially, in this capacity Soma is the Five-Dimensional Universe, straddling the Seven-, and Three-Dimensional and Two-Dimensional Universes.

That Indra, however, derives his strength from Soma, is another, significant, example of the give-and-take process in the Vedic dharma. (RV 1.10.3; 1.16.21; 1.55.7; 1.82.5; 1.177.4; 3.35.1; 5.43.5; 6.40.1; 8.3.17; 8.6.45; 8.13.31; 8.14.12; 8.32.30; 10.96.6; 10.160.1.) As a result of this intricate, intimate, interaction, Soma acquires all the powers and capabilities of Indra, many of the epithets of which refer to Indra as well:

- Soma is A Bull among the Cows. (Epithet No. 834.)
- The Bull of Soma sharpens his Horns. (Epithet No. 835.)
- Soma is the Great One. (Epithet No. 842.)
- Soma is the mighty one. (Epithet No. 845.)
- Soma is potent. (Epithet No. 854.)
- Soma stands above all things like a celestial Sun. (Epithet No. 856.)
- Soma is great (mahaa/n) and vast. (Epithet No. 831.)

It's one thing to be strong, but that strength is ineffectual if there is no value to the worshiper or the spiritual journey. The strength of Soma is his great influence on the worshiper (Epithet No. 852.) These epithets provide aide to the worshiper in the spiritual journey.

831. Soma is great (*mahaa/n*) and vast (*mahii/*). (RV 9.9.3.)

832. Soma Ascends to Indra. (RV 9.40.2.)

833. Soma Performs Great Actions. (RV 9.88.4.)

834. Soma is A Bull among the Cows. (RV 9.16.6; 9.69.4.)

835. The Bull of Soma sharpens his Horns. (RV 9.15.4; 9.70.7.)

836. Soma is enveloped (*va/saanaH*) in Power (*uu/rjaM*). (RV 9.80.3.)

837. When it is released, Soma has two types of strength, physical and mental. (RV 9.104.2.)

838. Soma is the Leader among the seer-poets. (RV 9.95.3.)

839. Soma is the bull among the animals. (RV 9.95.3.)

840. Soma is placed between earth and heaven to uphold the strength of Indra. (RV 9.70.5.)

841. Soma is swift in strength (*jiiradaano*). (RV 9.87.9.)

842. Soma is the Great One. (RV 9.66.16.)

843. Soma is Indra's Vayra. (RV 9.72.7.)

844. Mighty (*vaajii/*) Soma rushes to the luminous heaven (*rocanaa/ diva/H*). (RV 9.37.3.)

845. Soma is the might one (*mahiSa/H*). (RV 9.89.18.)

846. Soma is Powerful (*da/kSo*). (RV 9.76.1.)

847. Soma supports the world (*babhra/ve*) with his internal strength (*sva/tavase*). (RV 9.11.4.)

848. Soma is the force of propulsion (*uu/rjaM*). (RV 9.63.2.)

849. Soma is enveloped in Strength (*uu/rjaM*). (RV 9.80.3.)

850. Soma Pavamana (pavamaanaabhy) is propelled (*a\rSasi*) to provide strength (*uu/rjam*). (RV 9.86.35.)

851. Soma is the supporter (*da/dhaana*) of all powers (*o/jasaa*). (RV 9.65.10.)

852. The Strength of Soma Is His Great Influence (*vr/snyam*) on the Worshiper. (RV 9.64.2.)

853. Soma is strong and effectual (*i/ndraaye*). (RV 9.62.30.)

854. Soma is potent (*Satya/shuSmaH*). (RV 9.97.46.)

855. Soma is the Champion of Men (*puraetaa/*). (RV 9.87.3.)

856. Soma stands above all things like a celestial Sun (*devo/ na/ suu/ ryaH*). (RV 9.54.3.)

857. Soma is Rich in Brilliance (*ma/hy*) Like the Sun. (RV 9.86.34.)

858. Soma is Supreme and Sacred (*yahvii/r*). (RV 9.33.5.)

SURRENDER

Surrender is another category emphasizing the give and take of the Sacrifice. The notion of Surrender is similar to the Vedic force closely aligned with Soma --- Agni. In Agni, one of his many fires is the Fire of Self-Surrender. In this aspect, Agni becomes *Agnau*, the Fire of Self-Surrender, found in RV 1.169.19. in the Fire of Self-Surrender, that the worshiper finds the spiritual basis from which spring all fires. The Fire Altar is the centerpiece of the Vedic sacrifice on an exoteric level; the Fire of Self-Sacrifice is the centerpiece on an esoteric, personal level. It is here that the worshiper sits before the Fire Altar and opens the mind and heart to allow the consecrating Vedic forces and energies take possession of the Soul and mold it to their liking. It is here that the worshiper surrenders mind, body and soul. It is here that spiritual renewal is situated, and it is under these circumstances that the worshiper is reborn. This is where the worshiper's spiritual journey begins. The worshiper places complete trust in the Vedic forces and energies. The worshiper's soul and body is like putty, the Vedic forces and energies are the artisan, and the finished product is the reborn Soul of the worshiper. Thereafter, as far as the worshiper is able, the worshiper lives consistent with the Vedic forces and energies and according to the Vedic dharma. This is the fire of self-surrender.

In the case of Soma, the worshiper surrenders to Soma. (Epithet No. 861.) When the worshiper surrenders to Soma, the offerings to the array of Vedic divine forces increase. (Epithet No. 862.) Soma thereupon surrenders to Indra, the Vedic force of Articulation and Form. (Epithet No. 860.) Soma is thereby born of the laws of devotional discipline. (Epithet No. 859.) The process thus begins again.

859. Soma Is born according to the Laws of Devotional Discipline (*vrata*). (RV 9.3.10.)

860. Soma surrenders (*na/mobhir*) to Indra, the Vedic force of Articulation of Form. (RV 9.16.4.)

861. The Worshiper Surrenders (*namasya*) Before King Soma (*raa/ jaanaM*). (RV 9.114.2.)

862. Worshiper Surrenders to Soma, which increases the offerings to the Vedic forces. (RV 9.67.29.)

URGING

Urging in the Vedas refers to how the divine Vedic forces communicate their essential natures to the worshiper. Soma, for example, is possessed of the quality of abundance, and this quality is communicated to the worshiper as a result of the Soma Sacrifice. (Epithet No. 863.) Abundance is *urged* on the worshiper. The Waters is urged both on and towards humans. (Epithet No. 864.) The Waters symbolize the fabric of the Vedic dharma. The Waters here should be understood as in the fluid nature of consciousness. These two fundamental functions are at work with the Waters. Not only are the Waters, the essential quality of consciousness, placed on and into the worshiper, but Soma puts forward these riches in abundance, essentially a gift given to the worshiper. Soma very much acts as a mediator, a conduit, of these qualities. Soma is the recipient and is urged as well. Soma is urged by tridhaatu, the existential planes of Earth, the Mid-World and Heaven. (Epithet No. 866.) Soma is also urged by the Seven Thoughts. (Epithet No. 868.) The "Seven Thoughts" is a code-word for the entire expanse of existence, a more comprehensive description of the seven levels of the Vedic dharma, the tridhaatu, which includes the transcendent levels of Heaven.

863. Soma urges (*a/rSann*) riches to the worshiper in abundance (*shri/ya*). (RV 9.62.19.)

864. Soma Urges the Waters on Humans. (RV 9.63.7.)

865. Soma Urges the Waters Towards Humans. (RV 9.63.7.)

866. The three worlds (*tridhaa/tu*) urges Soma to flow (*agru/vo*). (RV 9.1.8.)

867. Together the mighty powers (*mahiSaa/*) urge (*aheSata*) Soma on by fixing and stirring it (*samya/k samya/-nco*) in the waves of the river (*uurmaa/v i/ndhor*). (RV 9.73.2.)

868. Soma is urged by seven thoughts (*sapta/ dhiita/yaH*) while it is being rubbed. (RV 9.8.4.)

UNION

Remember what was said a little earlier when discussing the Streams? That streaming is the step after the Flowing of Soma during the Soma Sacrifice? The Streams do not consist of the Release of the Soma juice, but it is purified. This is not mere verbiage. It is once the waters have been invigorated and energized that the full psychic and subtle powers of Soma emerges and imbue into the watery product of the Soma Sacrifice. This is accomplished with Union.

This is not the union of polar opposites, a major concern in some disciplines. Union --- and the invigoration of the Waters --- results with the coupling of Soma with the vast array of Vedic divine forces. The union is very much like a marriage. In uniting with the other Vedic divine forces Soma seeks the bride. (Epithet No. 879.) These epithets describe the other Vedic forces with which this union occurs: Soma is generally united with the Divine. (Epithet No. 875.) The epithets then go into more detail:

- Soma becomes united (sa/m) with the Adityas. (Epithet No. 869.) Not fully mentioned here before, the Adityas are multi-faceted Vedic divine forces. A full treatise can be devoted to the Adityas, but briefly, at the time of the Vedas, the Rishis believed the asterisms held sway over human affairs, an influence which had waned somewhat by the time of the Brahmanas. Originally, the lunar mansions (Nakshatras or asterisms) had influence and many different powers over humans and over the sacrificial rituals. (SPB 2.1.2.17.) Over time and through divine intervention that power and influence

231

was then usurped by the Adityas, the astrological houses, who since continue to possess that energy, power and influence. (SBP 2.1.2.18, 19.) In astrological terms, Aditya is sometimes identified with the Sun. By uniting with the Adityas, Soma channels that energy, power and influence.

- Soma becomes united (sa/m) with Indra and Vayu.(Epithet No. 870.) Indra is the divine representative for Articulation and Form. Vayu is commonly believed to be the Vedic divine form for Breath, which is accurate, but limited. Breath is more accurately described as "Life-Force," that, as Breath, from which all life depends.

- Soma is united with Rudra as Soma-Rudra. (Epithet No. 871.) This epithet presents a union within a union. The divine energies of Soma and united with Rudra. Rudra represents the material universe, the created beings, and whatever there is manifestly and profusely created, in the past and in the present, in the form of the world—all that is indeed this Rudra. (TA 10.24.1.) Soma-Rudra, then, represents those divine energies grounded in the material universe.

Soma unites with these and other energies. These spiritual qualities are installed in Soma. The impulses effused from these qualities are mixed by and blended into Soma. They communicate with each other. (Epithet No. 877.) Soma itself experiences an increase. That increase takes a particular form. The finished product is Illuminated Knowledge:

- Soma is united with Illuminated Knowledge when pressed out. (Epithet No. 873.)

That increase experienced by Soma is thereupon communicated to and united with the worshiper. (Epithet No. 876.) The illuminated knowledge is used in the spiritual journey. The epithets even mention the manner with which the psychic energies of Illuminated Knowledge are communicated to the worshiper:

- Soma Unites the worshipers' prayers with the Cows (Epithet No. 872), symbolic speech for Insightful Knowledge.

This is a skill the worshiper will used during the spiritual journey.

869. Soma becomes united (sa/m) with the Adityas. (RV 9.61.7.)

Aditi and the Adityas are the representatives of zodiacal houses. In its union with the Adityas (zodiacal houses), Soma rains its spiritual endowments to those houses and all sentient beings born under them

870. Soma becomes united (sa/m) with Indra and Vayu. (RV 9.61.8.)

871. Soma is united with Rudra as Soma-Rudra. (AV 19.7.3.)

872. Soma Unites the worshipers' prayers with the Cows. (RV 9.62.3.)

873. Soma is united with Illuminated Knowledge (*go/bhir*) when pressed out. (RV 9.109.15.)

874. The Seven from Heaven Unite in Soma. (RV 9.54.2.)

875. Soma is united with the Divine (*devaavii/r*). (RV 9.105.2.)

876. Soma's increase (*aa/ pyaayasva*) is united (sa/metu) in the worshiper. (RV 1.91.16.)

877. The impulsions (*iSe/*) of Soma unite together (*saMya/tam*). (RV 9.65.3.)

878. The Sun's rays join, envelope (*aa/vRtam*) Soma. (RV 9.86.27.)

879. Soma seeks the bride (*vadhuuyu/H*). (RV 9.69.3.)

880. In the sacrifice Soma is mixed with curds and grain (*aashii/rvantaH*). (RV 1.23.1.)

THE VAST

The Vedic world loves similes, and the Vast is one such example. The Vedic dharma is so expansive, sometimes a simple word is used for description. The Vast is such a word. The Vast is a simile for the Vedic dharma. Thus the epithets indicate that

- Soma is the Vastness of the Universe. (Epithet No. 883.)
- Soma is Vastness itself. (Epithet No. 881.)
- Vast streams of Soma are let loose. (Epithet No. 884.)
- Soma is the Vast, the Vedic dharma. (Epithet No. 886.)

In these epithets the Vast all refer to a material expanse tantamount to the Vedic dharma. It is used as a noun, as a synonym for the cosmos. The Vast includes all three worlds of the Vedic dharma --- the Earth, Mid-World, and Heaven. Don't be thrown off by the number Three. There are levels within these worlds which result in seven levels of Existence. The Vast is not necessarily limited to the material cosmos. It also includes the subtle, intangible levels of Existence and states of mind.

- Soma is the Vast Mind. (Epithet No. 888.)

In Epithet No. 888 the Vast is used as an adjective, which sometimes occurs. Thus

- Soma's glory is vast. (Epithet No. 882.)

Soma is the inspiration for the Vast (Epithet No. 889), meaning that the psychic and subtle energies in Soma provide the foundation for the Vedic dharma. If Soma is the foundation of the vast Vedic dharma, it is the foundation of all which reside therein. Thus Soma grants the Vast to the worshiper. (Epithet No. 889.)

881. Soma is Vastness (*bRha/nn*) itself. (RV 9.75.1.)

882. Soma's glory (*dhaa/ma*) is vast (*bRha/d*). (RV 1.91.3.)

883. Soma is the Vastness of the Universe (*bRha/t*). (RV 9.108.8.)

884. Vast streams (*dhaa/raa bRhatii/r*) of Soma are let loose. (RV 9.96.22.)

885. The powerful realm of the Vedic Truth (*Satya/mugrasya*) and the vast fulness of plenty (*bRhata/H*) join together (*sa/M*) in united streams (sa*Msravaa/H*). (RV 9.113.5.)

886. Soma is the Vast (*Bha/d*), the Vedic dharma (*Rta/m*). (RV 9.56.1.)

887. Soma is the inspiration vast (*shra/vo bRha/t*). (RV 9.44.6.)

888. Soma is the Vast Mind (*bRhanmate*). (RV 9.39.1.)

889. Soma grants the Vast to the worshiper. (RV 9.52.1.)

THE VEDIC DHARMA
(RTA AND SATYA)

It is difficult to overstate the importance of the Vedic dharma to the message of the Vedas. Let us set aside for the moment the fact that the Vedic dharma represents everything under the sky, mental, spiritual, and physical, and the greater macrocosm and inner microcosm. *Rta* and *Satya* is the framework that houses the Vedic dharma. To use a rough analogy, not only is the Vedic dharma the contents of a soda can, it is also the soda can itself.

Conceptionally, the Vedic dharma is represented by *Rta*, which has been rendered in English as the eternal law, the inner sacrifice and others. *Rta* is the natural order; *Rta* comprises *Satya*, the law of existence, as well; together they, *Rta* and *Satya*, are the Vedic dharma.

The Vedic dharma also provides the basis for a spiritual code of conduct. RV 4.23.8 states a true understanding of the Vedic dharma (*Rta*) destroys all evils and sins. The Ninth Mandala at RV 9.73.6 provides that the wicked do not walk on the path of the natural order. The life of a worshiper in accordance with the Vedic dharma is one in avoidance of sin and evil conduct. The worshiper is liberated on the true understanding of *Rta*. It is a life liberated from sin and evil. The Vedic dharma thereby provides the mechanism for the worshiper's salvation and liberation.

Soma encompasses all these various aspects of *Rta* and *Satya*. It represents the sacrifice and the natural, universal order that regulates the sacrifice and the existential context where the Sacrifice and the natural, universal order is found.

This category provides yet another example of the give and take of the sacrifice. Initially, Soma gives birth to the Vedic dharma, the Natural Order. (Epithet No. 910.) Afterwards,

- Soma is Increased by the Sacrifice According to the Complete Dharma. (Epithet No. 892.)
- Soma is Increased by the Sacrifice According to the Complete Dharma. (Epithet No. 892.)
- Soma is the Increaser of the Vedic dharma, the Natural Order. (Epithet Nos. 891 and 906.)
- Soma Increases the Vedic dharma, the Natural Order. (Epithet No. 900.)

In other words, after being increased according to the laws of the Vedic dharma, Soma is increased and becomes the increaser of the Vedi dharma.

What does it mean for Soma to "increase" the Vedic dharma? Soma's contribution to the Vedic dharma is the increase of *Satya*. In the beginning stages of creation, described in RV 10.190, *Satyam* and *Rta* are found at the highest level of Being. (RV 10.190.1.) Of the two, *Rta* prevails over and pervades *Satyam*. As Hickman notes in his "Toward a Comprehensive Understanding of *Rta* in the Rg Veda," *Satya* is "being" manifested by the establishment of the universe, but *Rta* is the mode of that being which promotes and supports the freedom and mobility of *Satyam*. The former, *Rta*, furnishes the framework for the latter, sat, and allows it, as well as all other subjects in the cosmic order, to function. *Rta* is the internal mechanism of the proverbial watch which regulates the ticking of the universe, which is *Satyam*. So what is Soma's role in all this?

- Soma speaks the truth of the Vedic dharma, the natural order. (Epithet No. 918.)
- Soma is the King because he speaks the truth of Existence, of the Vedic dharma, the natural order, and of faith. (Epithet No. 898.)
- Soma is Pressed through the laws and processes of the Truth. (Epithet No. 915.)
- Soma rains down *Satyam* on the worshiper. (Epithet No. 946.)

- Soma, with Indra, leads the worshiper towards the truth, which is in the nature of light. (Epithet No. 932.)

In speaking the truth, Soma presides over Existence. Soma accordingly occupies the Seat of the Vedic dharma, the Natural Order (*Rta*). (Epithet No. 905.) In addition:

- Soma is Triple-Seated (trivandhure). (Epithet No. 947.) Sayana, the classical interpreter of the Vedas, interprets this phrase to signify Soma's reach to the three Vedas — the Rg Veda, Sama Veda and Yajur Veda. As there are actually four Vedas — Sayana fails to mention the Atharva Veda — it must mean something else. That Soma is "triple seated" must refer to the Three-Dimensional Universe.
- Soma is the guardian of the Vedic dharma, the natural order. (Epithet No. 899.)
- Soma is the leader of heaven because he is the knower of the original Vedic dharma, the natural order. (Epithet No. 901.)
- Soma protects true (*Satya/m*) words. (Epithet No. 931.)

Soma is responsible for the articulation of the Vedic dharma. Soma articulates the Vedic dharma, the Natural Order. (Epithet No. 909.) Articulation is not simply speaking; more is implicated. The articulation of an object involves imbuing the object's defining characteristics, giving it name, form and substance. Thus Soma becomes the maker of all Forms. (Epithet No. 896.)

Conceptually, the Vedic dharma is the combined existential levels of *Rta* and *Satya*. The Vedas speak of *Rta* but does not define it. The concepts are clothed in veiled, mystic language. Much like the Dao, it is a concept subsumed in the essence of everything, an elusive concept which defies definition. There are contours to *Rta*, which this chapter seeks to chart for the benefit of the general reader or the worshiper while traveling the Vedic path to liberation and salvation. In the Vedic Dharma the anchor of the natural order is *Rta* itself as reflected in the Vedic deities, themselves the dynamic forces of that natural order which are incorporated into the lives of worshipers. Together, *Satyam* and *Rta* create the second highest level of being, *Tapas.* (RV 10.190.1.) Arrival at this level is the reason the worshiper undertakes the spiritual journey.

Rta is the Vedic dharma. According to Soma, *Satya* is known as "Truth":

- Soma is Pressed through the laws and processes of the Truth. (Epithet No. 915.)
- Speaking the truth of Existence (*Satya*), Soma is truthful in action. (Epithet No. 919.)
- Soma protects true (*Satya/m*) words. (Epithet No. 931.)

The spiritual journey is well served by the Truth --- and those other aspects of the Vedic dharma.

890. Soma is the Lord of the Vedic dharma (*dha/rmaNas pa/t*). (RV 9.35.5.)

891. Soma is the Increaser of the Vedic dharma, the Natural Order (*Rta*). (RV 9.9.3.)

892. Soma is Increased (aviivRdhan) by the Sacrifice According to the Complete Dharma (*Vi/dharma*). (RV 9.4.9.)

893. Soma Moves toward the Vedic dharma, the Natural Order (*Rta*). (RV 9.74.3.)

894. Moving (a/kraan) in the ocean (*samudra/h*), Soma was born according to the world's laws (*vi/dharma-n*). (RV 9.67.40.)

895. Soma Goes to the Ocean (*samudra/m*), the Source (*yo/niM*) of the Vedic dharma, the Natural Order (*Rta*). (RV 9.64.17.)

896. Soma is the Maker of All Forms (*vi/dharmani*). (RV 9.86.29.)

897. Soma is the King of the All Forms (*vi/dharmani*). (RV 9.86.30.)

898. Soma is the King because he speaks the truth of Existence, of the Vedic dharma, the natural order, and of faith. (RV 9.113.4.)

899. Soma is the guardian of the Vedic dharma, the natural order (*Rta/sya gopaa/*). (RV 9.73.8.)

900. Soma Increases (vivaa*vRdhe/*) the Vedic dharma, the Natural Order (*Rta*). (RV 9.108.8.)

901. Soma is the leader of heaven because he is the knower of the original Vedic dharma, the natural order (*Rta*). (RV 9.70.6.)

902. Soma Knows the original Vedic dharma, the Natural Order (*Rta*). (RV 9.70.6.)

903. Soma Becomes Bright by the Thoughts of the Vedic dharma, the Natural Order (*Rta*). (RV 9.111.2.)

904. Soma climbs (*roha*) to Vayu to support the Vedic dharma (*dha/rmaNaa*). (RV 9.63.22.)

905. Soma Occupies the Seat of the Vedic dharma, the Natural Order (*Rta*). (RV 9.64.11.)

906. Soma is the increaser of the Vedic dharma, the natural order (*RtaavRdhaa*). (RV 8.87.5.)

907. Soma Lives in the Realm Beyond the Vedic dharma, the Natural Order (*amR/tasya*). (RV 9.97.32.)

908. The Five Cardinal Points (*pa/-nca pradi/sho vi/dharmaNi*) are within Soma's Realm. (RV 9.86.29.)

909. Soma Articulates the Vedic dharma, the Natural Order (*Rta*). (RV 9.113.4.)

910. Soma Gave birth to the Vedic dharma, the Natural Order (*Rta*). (RV 9.66.24.)

911. Soma is Born in Humans through the laws of the Vedic dharma, the Natural Order (*Rta*). (RV 9.110.4.)

912. Faithful to the law of the Vedic dharma, the Natural Order (*Rta*). (RV 9.74.2.)

913. Soma Shines by the Light of the Vedic dharma, the Natural Order (*Rta*). (RV 9.113.4.)

The Epithets then proceed with an interesting series of equivalences:

914. Soma is Pressed through the laws and processes of the Vedic dharma, the Natural Order (*Rta*). (RV 9.113.2.)

915. Soma is Pressed through the laws and processes of the Truth (*Satya*). (RV 9.113.2.)

916. Soma is Pressed through the laws and processes of *Tapas*. (RV 9.113.2.)

917. Soma is Pressed through the laws and processes of faith (*shraddha*). (RV 9.113.2.)

Clearly the Rishiis are identifying *Rta, Satya, Tapas* and *shraddha* as one and the same, or at least occupying the same conceptual space. The significant fact is that these conceptual spaces are created when Soma is "pressed out." There is a ritualistic interpretation and a metaphysical one. Ritualistically, the worshiper seeks to learn the secrets of these ideas at the Soma Sacrifice when the purified Soma is consumed. Metaphysically, each and every one is a spiritual endowment from Soma. The Epithets proceed:

918. Soma speaks the truth of the Vedic dharma, the natural order. (RV 9.113.4.)

919. Speaking the truth of Existence (*Satya*), Soma is truthful in action (*Satyakarman*). (RV 9.113.4.)

920. Soma is the Vedic dharma, the natural order (*Rta/H*), personified. (RV 9.62.30.)

921. The Place where Soma is milked is the supreme abode of the Vedic dharma, the Natural Order. (RV 9.34.5.)

922. Soma is the Guardian of the Vedic dharma, the Natural Order (*gopaa/m Rta/sya*). (RV 9.48.4.)

923. Soma is possessed ("covered") of the Vedic dharma, the natural order (*Rtaa/vaapo/ va/saano*). (RV 9.96.13.)

924. In its Aspect as the Sun, Soma is born from the processes of the Vedic dharma, the Natural Order (*Rta/sya ga/rbho*). (RV 9.68.5.)

925. Soma is the Vedic dharma, the Natural Order (*Rta*). (RV 9.108.8.)

926. Soma is born from the Vedic dharma, the Natural Order (*Rta*). (RV 9.108.8.)

927. Soma Helps the Seeker of the Laws of the Vedic dharma, the Natural Order (*Rtaayu/m*) find them. (RV 8.79.6.)

928. Soma basks in the light of the Vedic dharma, the natural order (*rtadyumna*). (RV 9.113.4.)

929. Soma is glorified by the Seekers of the Vedic dharma, the natural order (*Rtaayu/bhir*). (RV 9.36.4.)

930. Soma is born in mortals (*amRta*) in the law of truth, the Vedic dharma (*dha/rmann*). (RV 9.110.4.)

931. Soma protects true (*Satya/m*) words. (RV 7.104.12.)

932. Soma, with Indra, leads the worshiper towards the truth (*Satya*), which is in the nature of light (*go/H*). (RV 4.28.5.)

933. Soma, with Indra, uncovered the Vedic dharma, the natural order (*aa/dardRtam*). (RV 4.28.5.)

934. Soma flows (pavase) according to the laws of the Vedic dharma, the natural order (*dha/rmabhiH*). (RV 9.86.5.)

935. The worshiper understands the Vedic dharma, the natural order (*Rta*), with food (*psa/raH*) obtained from the sweet Soma juice (*su/kRtaM somya/m*) and the rays of Aditi (*ga/vyuutir a/diter*). (RV 9.74.3.)

936. Soma sits on the birthplace of the Vedic dharma, the natural order (*Rta/sya yo/niM*). (RV 3.62.13.)

937. Luminous (*ha/ri*) Soma moves to the Sacrifice, the personification of the Vedic dharma, the natural order (*Rta*). (RV 9.69.3.)

938. Soma is the source of the Vedic dharma, the natural order (*Rta*) to the worshiper. (RV 9.32.4.)

939. Indu is faithful (*Rtvi/yaH*) to the Vedic dharma, the natural order. (RV 9.72.4.)

940. Soma is the underlying truth (*rtam*) of the Vedic dharma, *Rta*, the natural order. (RV 9.97.23.)

941. Soma sits in glory (*ratnadhaa/*) at the womb of the Vedic dharma, *Rta*, the natural order (*yo/niM Rta/sya*). (RV 9.107.4.)

942. Soma sits at the source of the Vedic dharma, *Rta*, the natural order (*yo/naav Rta/sya*). (RV 9.13.9.)

943. To those desiring the Vedic dharma, the natural order (*Rtaayate*), Soma provides happiness (*bha/gaM*). (RV 1.91.7.)

944. Soma is Pressed Out by the Word Articulating the Vedic dharma (*Rtavaake/na*). (RV 9.113.2.)

945. The Vedic dharma (*dha/rmabhiH*) is part of the delight of Soma. (RV 9.7.7.)

946. Soma rains down (*vRSan*) *Satyam* on the worshiper. (RV 9.64.2.)

947. Soma is Triple-Seated (*trivandhure*). (RV 9.62.14.)

948. Soma is the leader of the original Vedic dharma, the natural order (*Rta*). (RV 9.70.6.)

VEGETATION

Vegetation is a complex, intricate category, which cuts through the very heart of an important aspect of the Vedic dharma. Here is where matters really become esoteric, and it is not just about plants. On the surface, this category is straightforward. Soma is Vanaspati. (Epithet No. 952.) Commentators, among them Kashyap and others, have noted that "vana" means both "plant" and "delight." They note that "vana" connotes "delight" in the Upanishads. The double meaning is an appropriate use of wordplay which is so often found in the Veda. This particular epithet emphasizes how Soma is spoken of a deity and of the plant from which the juice is extracted at the sacrifice. On the surface, then, this category speaks on a simple sacrificial level to represent the plant from which the Soma juice is extracted and to say that the Soma juice is lord of them all.

Here is where the discussion gets esoteric.

"Vegetation" was a concept used by that greatest modern alchemist, Sir Isaac Newton, in his alchemical writings. Yes, the same Isaac Newton. The same Newton who uncovered the physical laws of optics, motion and gravity, was a notorious alchemist. In fact, he was more preoccupied with discovering the link between the physical and subtle worlds through alchemy than he was with discovering the laws of mechanical physics. Newton's musings on the mechanical laws of nature was only half of his endeavors. His work sought to discover those physical laws as complements of God's influence. It was through the alchemical arts that he thought the link between the physical and subtle existed. His alchemical writings, in fact, far outnumber his scientific dissertations, and their page count number is literally in the hundreds of thousands. It was through his writings that he developed Vegetation. It is a broad concept, extensively employed, and he sometimes changed the parameters of this idea. But in Newton's alchemical writings, it was a major concept and preoccupation. According to Newton, there were three kingdoms of nature --- animal, mineral, and vegetable. These kingdoms operated under two sets of laws: The physical, mechanical laws of nature, and the "Chemical Laws" of God. It was Newton's job to find the link between these two worlds. Newton found this link in the Vegetative Principle, which had these characteristics:

- The vegetable spirit is identified with Light and Illumination, representing the power of God.
- The congealed aether that pervades everything, "interwoven with the grosser texture of sensible matter."
- The "subtle spirit," or "nature's universal agent, her secret fire" or "material soul of all matter." According to Newton the Earth and all matter was a breathing, living organism, "draw[ing] in aethereal breadth for its daily refreshment and transpires again with gross exhalations."
- The Vegetative spirit was the agent which activated inert, dead, matter into living, breathing material.

If all this sounds very familiar, you are right. This all sounds very close to the psychic, subtle powers of Vayu, the Vedic divine force of Prana, the Life-Force and the radiance and effulgence of Soma. Where at one point in his book about Newton and alchemy, The Janus Faces of Genius, B.J.T. Dobbs wondered where Newton's ideas about Vegetation originated, it is very tempting to believe that the inspiration came from Soma. While tempting, it is hardly likely. The first English translation of the Vedas did not occur until one hundred years after Newton engaged in his alchemical ruminations. Further, what Newton was attempting to achieve was very different than a spiritual journey of a worshiper to liberation and salvation. Newton tried to integrate alchemy and the mechanical philosophy with his concept of Vegetation, which operates under the premise that metals "vegetate" — that is, grow — in the earth, being changed over time from one substance into another.

Still, with Vegetation both Newton and the Vedas tap into a very basic truth. Both concern the very essence of the material world and its link with the divine, psychic, and subtle. Both affirm that there is a link and essential sameness between these two worlds.

The story becomes even more esoteric.

Two epithets refer to the color of Vanaspati, Soma, the Lord of Plants. Vanaspati is golden (Epithet No. 953); flaming (Epithet No. 951), conceivably, flaming red; and resplendent (Epithet No. 954), again, likely golden-colored. What do these epithets possibly mean? Was the Soma plant gold in color or flaming red?

Classical alchemical was concerned about color. Joseph Needham, the noted scholar of Chinese science, writes that the entire purpose of traditional alchemy was to loosen the bonds of temporal existence to achieve perfection. In terms of metals, that meant turning base matter into gold, which, as we have seen here, represents liberation and salvation, but in the area in which Needham studied and wrote, represented longevity, Immortality, and finally grace and redemption. While alchemists attempted to transmute base metals into gold, in their upward journey, the base metals traversed through the color chart. Each color represented a different stage of development, the final color was gold, into which indeed the base metal had been transmuted.

The different schools of Classical Alchemy differed widely. There was general agreement on the meaning in the change in color base metals underwent in the transmutation process. The base metals began the journey upwards on the color chart, beginning with the color

- Black, called Melansis or Nigreda, representing Death. A case can be made that this was the vast, indiscriminate, undefined mass of matter described in RV 10.129, wherein began the process of evolution of the Vedic dharma.
- White, called Leukosis or Albedo, representing Resurrection.
- Yellow, Gold, called Xanthosis, representing Immortality.
- Red, or Ruddy Brown, called Iosis, representing Rebirth. Other traditions include a further step. The color in this additional step is Green, or Green-tinted, called Verditas.

After these progressions the alchemist is supposed to reach the Philosopher's Stone, the irreducible essence of physical matter, carrying within it life-giving properties, including, but not limited to, Immortality.

After reading the epithets which follow, you can see where this is leading. The epithets are positively full of color:

- Vanaspati, Soma, is golden. (Epithet No. 953.)
- Vanaspati, Soma, is resplendent. (Epithet No. 954.)
- Soma is Green-tinted. (Epithet No. 958.)

All these colors are high in the color chart. Thus, they are high on the existential level. Vegetation is highly symbolic speech for and a useful tool to achieve the liberation and salvation of the worshiper.

949. Soma's glories (*dhamani*) are in the plants or herbs (*o/SadhiiSv*). (RV 1.91.4.)

950. Soma is the Axe in the Woods. (RV 9.95.3.)

951. Vanaspati, Soma, is flaming (*bhraa/jamaanaM*). (RV 9.5.10.)

952. Soma is Vanaspati. (RV 9.5.10.)

953. Vanaspati, Soma, is golden (*hiraNya/yam*). (RV 9.5.10.)

954. Vanaspati, Soma, is resplendent (*ha/ritam*). (RV 9.5.10.)

955. Soma manifests (*ajanayas*) all the herbs (*o/SadhiiH*). (RV 1.91.22.)

956. Vanaspati, Soma, has a thousand branches (*saha/sravalshaM*). (RV 9.5.10.)

957. Soma Is Adept in Herbal Knowledge. (YV 4.37.)

958. Soma is Green-tinted. (RV 10.116.3.)

959. Soma is Soft (*rdu-udana*) in the Inside. (RV 8.4.8.10.)

VRTRA

The world of the Vedas was Manichean and uncompromising. The world was a constant battle between Good and Evil, and while Evil was terrifying, and while we would all like to think the forces of Good ultimately triumphed, in reality life in the Vedic dharma was a constant struggle.

Vrtra is representative of ignorance, avidya. Vrtra's name is indeed derived from the combination of the Sanskrit root of "to cover or obscure" and *Rta*, the natural order (i.e., v + *Rta* = vrtra). Ignorance, through the agency of Vrtra, covers the truth. More importantly, Vrtra covers the Vedic dharma, the mystic significance of the natural law (*Rta*), the cosmic laws of the universe, and obscures that meaning to the Worshiper. Thus, Vrtra covers, obscures, hides and conceals the information by which the worshiper needs to make intelligible the universe or the cosmic laws from which the universe operates. Vrtra is the barrier to liberation.

It is only after Indra drinks the purified Soma that he has the power to fight and vanquish Vrtra with his sword Vayra. Indeed, one of the most frequent references in the RV is that without quaffing a draught of Soma, Indra would be powerless to conquer Vrtra. (See, RV 1.23.7 9; 1.32.3 - 10; 1.52.2, 10; 1.54.8 - 10; 1.55.5, 6; 1.80.2; 2.11.17 - 18; 2.14.1, 2, 5; 2.19.4; 3.12.3, 4; 3.36.8; 3.40.7, 8; 3.41.1 - 5; 3.47.2, 3; 3.49.1; 3.51.9; 3.52.7; 4.19.8; 4.21.10; 5.29.7; 5.32.8; 5.40.1 – 4; 7.32.1; 8.1.13, 14; 8.2.26; 8.4.1; 8.6.38, 39; 8.8.13.15; 8.17.7 - 9; 8.33.1, 14; 8.8.37.1; 8.33.1 - 3; 8.45.25; 8.49.12 -13; 8.50.14, 15; 8.53.8, 9; 8.67.7; 8.71.1; 9.79.1; 8.81.23, 24; 8.82.15 - 18; 8.84.8, 9; 9.37.5; 9.88.4; 9.89.7, 10; 9.106.3; 9.113.1; 10.114.1, 2; 10.138.1.)

As these passages indicate, only Soma *pavamana*, purified Soma, possesses this energizing property. These mantras recite that once the Soma plant has been crushed and fermented and passed through the filters as Soma *pavamana*, the purified juices are offered to Indra as a libation at the sacrificial alter. It is only at that time after Indra drinks the Soma *pavamana* that he slays Vrtra.

Vrtra obstructs and conceals the waters. (RV 1.32.1, 2; 1.33.11, 12; 1.51.11; 1.52.2, 6, 8, 10, 14; 1.54.4; 1.57.2, 6; 1.59.6; 1.61.10, 12; 1.80.2, 5, 10; 1.125.5; 1.130.3; 1.131.4; 1.169.8; 1.174.2, 4; 2.11.5; 2.20.7; 2.30.1; 3.30.9, 10; 3.31.20; 3.32.5, 6, 11; 3.33.6; 3.38.5; 3.45.2; 3.51.9; 5.30.5; 5.31.6; 5.33.6.) But what does can this epithet possibly mean? The name of Vrtra is derived from the Sanskrit root meaning a covering. Etymologically, Vrtra is a derivation of the divine dynamic cosmic order, *Rta*, the Vedic dharma. Vrtra, indeed, is the "enveloper," and conceals access to and the knowledge of the divine dynamic cosmic order (*Rta*), the other element of its name. Vrtra becomes, then, the concealer of the inner truth of the Vedic dharma, V + *Rta* = Vrtra.

Equally enduring is the image of the results of Vrtra's death.:

- Indra (goodness) smote Vrtra (ignorance) who retained the waters (purification). (RV 6.20.2.)
- Indra released the streams after slaying Vrtra. (RV 1.33.13; 1.51.11; 1.80.10; 2.28.4; 3.31.11, 16; 4.18.7; 4.19.8; 5.30.10.)
- Indra cleaved the mountain which released the waters. (RV 1.55.5; 1.57.6; 5.32.2; 5.33.1.)
- Indra released the seven rivers. (RV 1.32.12; 2.12.3; 10.67.12.)
- Set the waters free. (RV 1.32.4.) The waters, as we saw in earlier chapters, has many metaphorical, esoteric meanings.
- Converted asat, the unmanifested mass of indiscriminate matter, into sat, the Vedic dharma. (RV 6.24.5.)
- Scattered the darkness. (RV 5.31.3.)
- Cut a path through the darkness to the Sun. (RV 6.21.3.)

Soma has its own role in this cosmic battle. Soma's participation in this conflict presents another example of the cosmic give-and-take of Sacrifice:

- Soma, with Indra, slays Vrtra. (Epithets Nos. 963 and 966.) This is metaphorical for spiritual bliss conquering ignorance. Soma subdues, arrests, ignorance, Vrtra, with spiritual bliss (Epithet No. 964.)
- In the ultimate paradox, in a scripture loving paradoxes, Soma, through Son, Tvastr, the demi-god Form-Maker, fashioned and gave birth to Soma. (SPB 1.6.3.8, 13 – 15, 17, 22.)
- To confound this paradox further, once Vrtr was born, it became endowed with the qualities of Soma (spiritual bliss and happiness) and Agni (Fire, Change and Transformation).
- Once Vrtra, Soma's offspring, is slain, Soma reveals its god-head (Epithet No. 962), or, its full divine expression.

Soma and Vrtr is at once the most distinctive feature of the Vedic dharma and the most universe archetype in world religion. Abrahamic and other Eastern religions all have dragon myths, and all meet the same fate.

960. With the Ecstasy of Soma, Indra Kills Vrtra. (RV 9.1.10.)

961. Soma Was Vrtra. (SPB, 3.4.3.13.)

962. Soma Reveals his God-head (*Devavii/tamah*) When Vrtr Is Subdued. (RV 9.25.3.)

963. Soma is the killer of Vrtra. (RV 9.37.5; 9.61.20.)

964. Soma is the Subduer of Vrtra (*vRtraha/ntamaH*). (RV 9.1.3.)

965. This Soma (*pappivaa/Msam*) overcomes Vrtra. (RV 6.47.2.)

966. Soma Killed Vrtra. (RV 1.91.5.)

THE WATERS

The Waters are the very foundation of the Vedic dharma. It is not the essence because the Vedic dharma is liquid, but that the essence of the Vedic dharma is fluid, constantly changing and transforming. This is borne out in Epithet No. 974: "Soma has a boundless watery foundation." While this might refer sacrificially to the liquid constitution of the Soma juice, it speaks of the capacity of Soma to change and elevate the worshiper. Soma indeed increases the worshiper with the Waters. (Epithet No. 968.)

A recurring theme in this book is that there is a give-and-take process which permeates and informs the Sacrifice. That process is at work in this category as well in a very elaborate give-and-take, beginning from Soma's literal birth from the Waters and Soma's nurturing of the Waters:

- Soma emerges from the Ocean as speech. (Epithet No. 983.) Ocean is symbolic terms for the Absolute Self, that State which existed before the articulation of forms. In symbolic terms Speech, vac, is Articulation;
- Articulation is Form; Form is name; and name is all the members in the Vedic dharma, material to subtle. So to say that Soma emerges as Speech from the Ocean is highly refined language to say that Soma was born of the Absolute Self to give articulation to all physical and subtle objects in the Vedic dharma.
- Soma is infused with the Waters. (Epithet No. 998.)
- Soma nourishes the Ocean. (Epithet No. 982.)
- Soma is the Creator of the Rivers. (Epithet No. 979.)

- Soma Gives Birth to the Sun in the Waters. (Epithet No. 970.
- As the Bull, Soma fertilizes the Waters. (Epithet No. 978.)

There is doubtless a ritualistic element to these epithets. The Soma juice, after all, is a liquid and a product of the Soma Sacrifice. But behind every ritualistic gesture and practice is the reason behind the actions. The physical, material Soma juice, therefore, stands for the Waters which is the foundation of the Vedic dharma. Of all the Vedic divine forces then Soma is a perfect symbol for the Waters. Still, it is equally undeniable the exhilaration experienced by the worshiper is the perfect representation for the Vedic dharma. The worshiper is a member of and represents the material world. Once the Soma juice is consumed, the worshiper's conscious mind is elevated upwards the existential ladder until reaching the upper levels of heaven. These epithets then serve as a symbolic account of that journey.

Soma releases the Waters, along with Indra, for the benefit of human beings. (Epithet No. 967.) But what does this phrase mean actually? This phrase has been used from time memorial to describe the exploits of Indra, primarily after defeating Vrtra. We just saw that Vrtra's nature is to conceal the inner truth of the Vedic dharma from the worshiper. We additionally saw in the Introduction that the fundamental essence of the Vedic dharma is Water. When Soma and Indra releases the Waters, then, it is revealing, or giving the worshiper the opportunity to receive, the inner truth of the Vedic dharma, or at least lifting the veil of the true nature of the Vedic dharma. In this sense Vrtra can be viewed as an early version of Maya, a concept developed in much greater detail millennia later. Just as Maya conceals the true nature of the Atman, the Universal Self, so does Vrtra conceal the inner truths of the Vedic dhama from the worshiper.

Soma, however, is not an enabler. The exhilaration of Soma and the Soma juice is spiritual and not recreational. As with all things, the intent is not that the worshiper relies on the Soma juice to traverse the upper reaches of liberation and salvation. The worshiper must learn to rely on the worshiper's mind alone. For this reason, Epithet No. 971 says that Soma abides in its own discernment in the Waters.

967. Releases the waters (*apo/*), along with Indra, for human beings. (RV 4.28.1.)

968. Soma is Increases Us by the River Waters. (RV 9.72.7.)

969. Soma Enters the Waters. (RV 9.7.2.)

970. Soma Gives Birth to the Sun (*Suryam*) in the Waters. (RV 9.42.1.)

971. Soma Abides with Discernment in the Waters. (RV 9.62.4.)

972. Soma Comes with the Waters. (RV 9.65.20.)

973. Soma Is Increased Within the Worshiper by the River's Waters. (RV 9.72.7.)

974. Soma Has a Boundless Watery Foundation. (RV 9.71.27.)

975. Soma enters the ocean of our joy (*priya/H samudra/m*). (RV 9.63.23.)

976. Soma is the all-sustaining water of the sun. (RV 9.71.1.)

977. Soma is the Bull of the Waters. (RV 9.44.28.)

978. As the Bull, Soma fertilizes the Waters. (RV 10.36.8.)

979. Soma is the Creator of the Rivers. (RV 9.86.36.)

980. Soma is Purified in the Waters of the Ocean. (RV 9.2.5.)

981. Soma flows in waves (*vR/thaa*). (RV 9.14.1.)

982. Soma nourishes the Ocean (*samudra/h*). (RV 9.64.8.)

983. Soma emerges from the Ocean (*samudre/*) as speech (*vaa/cam*). (RV 9.107.21.)

984. Soma (*i/ndo*) flows and moves the ocean (*samudramii~Nkhaya*). (RV 9.35.2.)

985. Soma is clothed (*va/saano*) in the delight of rivers (*si/ndhuun*). (RV 9.35.2.)

986. Soma is established (aa/hitaH) in the ocean (*samudra/*) through the offerings at the sacrifice and the chants. (RV 9.64.19.)

987. The nature of Soma the King is of the ocean (*samudri/yaH*). (RV 9. 107.16.)

988. Soma proclaims sovereignty to the fourth plane (*turii/yaM*) where the waters of the Ocean are located. (RV 9.96.19.)

989. Soma flows into the rivers (*si/ndhor*). (RV 9.86.8.)

990. Soma clings to the waves of waters (*.apaa/m uurmi/M*). (RV 9.86.8.)

991. Soma Sends the Ocean (*samudra/m*) upwards (*u/d*). (RV 9.84.4.)

992. Soma excites the Ocean with the help of Vayu. (RV 9.84.4.)

993. Soma lives in the rivers (*mahe/*). (RV 9.9.5.)

994. Soma manifests (*ajanayas*) all the waters (*apo/*). (RV 1.91.22.)

995. Soma is the Carrier of the Waters (*va/hnir apsu/*). (RV 9.20.6.)

996. Soma makes the pure waters (*a/rNasaa*) flow. (RV 9.21.6.)

997. Soma is the protector of the Waters (*apaa/m pe/ruM*). (RV 10.36.8.)

998. Soma is infused with the Waters (*a/po*). (RV 9.107.18.)

999. With Soma the Worshiper Made Aware Crosses the Waters (*aptu/ raM*). (RV 9.63.21.)

1000. Soma flows like the rivers (*sravaa/paa/miivaa*) for Indra. (RV 9.85.1.)

Consciousness is by its nature in motion. It is transformative, which is why Agni presides over consciousness. The thoughts, feelings, experiences, memories, impressions and beliefs mentioned above ebb, flow and meander, one after another, one changed into another, yet originating from one thinking, conscious subject. This attribute for the Eternal Law is mentioned many times in the Rg Veda with the simile of a river flowing. There are generic references of the flow of rivers and waters symbolizing the Eternal Law of Consciousness. As a river which ebbs and flows along its course, this simile depicts the thoughts flowing one after another in the conscious mind much like water flowing through a waterway. This is the Eternal Law of individual Consciousness. The thoughts and sensations flow one after the other, seemingly and hopefully to and with a specific goal. The transformative nature of Consciousness then is its malleability, its constantly changing nature. This quality of transformation is captured in sindhavah, the Eternal Law of the flow of the rivers, Sindhava, representative of Consciousness. The principles inherent in the Vedic force of Indra causes this Flow of divine union. Soma makes it all possible.

ABBREVIATIONS

AA	Aitatreya Aranyaka
AV	Atharva Veda
BG	Bhavagad Gita
BU	Brhad Aranyaka Upanishad
GB	Gopatha Brahmana
CU	Chandogya Upanishad
JB	Jaiminiya Brahmana
JUB	Jaiminiya Upanishad Brahmana
Kath. Up.	Katha Upanishad
MU	Mandukya Upanishad
RV	Rg Veda
SPB	Satapatha Brahmana
TB	Tattiriya Brahmana
TS	Tattiriya Samhita
VS	Vaisesika Sutras
YV	Yajur Veda

Printed in the United States
By Bookmasters